Penelope's Web

Penelope's Web

Some Perceptions of Women in European and Canadian Society

N. E. S. GRIFFITHS

Toronto
OXFORD UNIVERSITY PRESS
1976

© Oxford University Press
(Canadian Branch) 1976

Cover illustration by JOAN SIRR

ISBN-0-19-5402685

1234-9876

Printed in Canada by
WEB OFFSET PUBLICATIONS LIMITED

Contents

Preface: Changing Perceptions   7

1 The Immediate Questioning   13

2 Looking for the Roots of our Discontent   31

3 The Swing Door Between the Ages   52

4 Stereotypes and Politics   80

5 European Attitudes   102

6 Canadian Experiences   124

7 European Conventions and Regulations   148

8 Canadian Identities   169

9 Women and the Webs of Society   192

10 The Royal Commission   209

11 Women Without Boundaries   227

Select Bibliography   239

Index   244

Preface:

Changing Perceptions

In 1971 I recorded five programs for the CTV series 'University of the Air'. This was the beginning of *Penelope's Web*, a piece of work that has at times come to resemble its namesake far too closely. That structure, you may remember, was spun in the day and torn apart at night. My aim in writing the original scripts, twenty-eight-minute illustrated lectures, was simple: I wanted to provide some historical framework for a discussion of contemporary Canadian feminism. A twenty-eight-minute script gives enough time to ask questions, to present a few ideas and one or two facts, and to close out with a cheerful countenance. As a woman I was and am convinced of the importance of the debate over the status of women, so it was not difficult to find questions to ask. As a historian I was and am equally convinced of the value of the historical approach for a clearer understanding of present discontents, so it was easy to talk about what had happened in the past as opposed to what many people said had happened. With the help of my producer, Nancy Fraser, the scripts were brought together in three months during the summer of 1971.

The metamorphosis of script into book, however, has been a much more difficult process. There was no thought at first of making the book very different, except in length, from the original programs. As a woman my main interest was still trying to discover what I considered to be the disparity between socially determined sex roles and measurable biological differences between the sexes. As a historian I still wanted to look at the gap between what people thought 'women in history' had achieved, and what had actually occurred. But what was envisaged as a simple task of expansion turned out to be a major labour of interpretation. Sentences that passed lightly by in the hurried pace of a twenty-eight-minute script demanded analysis, required substantiation.

Ideas that seemed simple commonsense became matters for major investigation. Within six weeks of beginning to write the book a perceptive friend was calling it *Penelope's Macramé* as I stumbled across issue after issue that demanded elaboration, and for its elaboration reading and thought beyond anything expected.

I was attracted to Penelope as an image because I had always believed her situation as the wife of Ulysses to be one of the most challenging in Greek mythology. Ulysses was, you remember, the man who took such an unconscionable while getting back home after the Trojan wars, and during those years Penelope had a difficult time. She was beautiful, intelligent, witty, the daughter of one king and the possible widow of another. She had a great deal of status, of a rather ambiguous kind, and the power she controlled was not particularly visible. She was besieged in her own palace by a concourse of armed suitors, all clamouring that Ulysses was dead and that her instant re-marriage to one of their number was a strict necessity and a moral duty. Militarily speaking her unwelcome guests had more strength than she; if brute force and power were synonymous, Penelope was already conquered. She was at the mercy of those advising her against her wishes for her own good. But she had what one of her suitors described as 'an evil talent for getting her own way.' Her strategy was worked on a basis of faith and cunning: faith that Ulysses was alive, and the cunning to make her first object delay rather than victory. She agreed with her counsellors, she could do no other, but she agreed on one condition: first she must weave a winding sheet and not until its elaborate design was finished would she marry. The loom was readied and, as I have mentioned, what she wove during the day was destroyed at night. Her stratagem was discovered only through the treachery of one of her maids. Penelope was a woman trying desperately to achieve a balance between what she wanted, what she could obtain, and what the immediate circumstances permitted her to obtain. Intelligent, if devious, confronting circumstances with imagination, this pragmatic human being seemed to me a very attractive person. As she wove for the postponement of personal catastrophe, so, I think, do women generally work for the conservation of their own ideals.

For the television scripts Penelope was a helpful light, but for the book she proved to be a most confusing guide. The essence of Penelope as a symbol was the acceptance of women as human, as people, as individuals. In a television script I could use words as evocative codes, almost as poetry, not paying particular attention to the analysis. In the book, in the expansion, the symbol had to be much more firmly established. What did it mean to be human? I found myself pursuing ethnology, anthropology, and biology via Penguin book, university text, and article until my eyes spun. What were people about? And here my philosophical beliefs came in for examination in a way neglected since those undergraduate days of wine and argument. And how did people acquire their own individual personalities? Books on psychology and sociology began to edge books about history from the shelves in my office.

Penelope's Web was never designed solely as a historical work on the experience of women in the past; it was intended to look at a wide spectrum of problems, to question the relationship between biological gender and sex roles in society, and to represent the beliefs, attitudes, and point of view of a twentieth-century woman. This wide-ranging examination, rather than the investigation of a strictly delimited problem, was an unaccustomed context in which to work. All the careful training of a historian, all the commands to limit imagination and concentrate on the known and discoverable had to be supplemented. There was no question that the problem itself should be stated as clearly as possible, nor that the evidence must be discussed in the greatest possible detail and its reliability constantly checked. But the work of other disciplines had to be pillaged, although it was obvious that the authority of the work would rest on the quality of the historical material, for the material from other disciplines could not be presented with equal judgement.

Everybody knows that 'lies, damm lies, and statistics' can arise from the inexpert handling of statistical material. But statistics are not the only trap for a historian who dares to use the work of other disciplines. The danger with pillaging material from neighbouring fields is that one can so easily pillage what is no longer of value. Even in one's own field it is difficult enough to keep up with the flood of new information and theory. In adjacent disciplines the amount read, as well as the degree of expertise, will be less. Further, the division of the study of humanity among various experts has led not only to theories of human action centred upon a selected aspect of humanity, but to special vocabularies evolved to describe these activities. 'Group', 'society', 'community' rarely carry the same meanings for a psychologist as for a sociologist or a political scientist. The seventeenth-century philosopher Locke pointed out this difficulty and regarded such words as bundles of assumptions. He counselled us to undo these bundles at the start of any discussion if we would have any expectation of understanding each other. For even if the word is apparently obvious in meaning it can usually be interpreted in more than one way. If we talk about 'nature', do we mean the Canadian winter blizzards or an English summer day? Wordsworth's 'impulse from a vernal wood' or Fred Cogswell's force that makes the Maritimer

> the stunted strong
> Toughened by suns and the bleak wintry weather
> To grow up slow and to endure for long.*

It is not surprising that few scholars attempt such a challenge. There is a distinct flavour of 'fools rush in' about single-handed interdisciplinary work. The critic is handed the knife and shown the precise spot beneath the rib for the blow.

In some ways, however, the historian is accustomed to such a situation. While a study of the past can be carried on along very narrow lines, such a study always implies an effort to comprehend the wide variety of human action and all that has happened to humanity. The test of a historian, according to Sir Lewis Namier, is the ability to look at an explanation of what happened and say 'it couldn't have been that way', not because of some structured rule but from a sense of what human beings are about. Historians are used to cutting and sewing the seamless robe of the past and then defending their tailoring as the logical and probably the only way to understand the multitude of people and events. The major part of their evidence is written, and the need to crack its linguistic code and to translate it to the code of their own era is a commonplace of the craft. Distance for people dependent upon a horse or upon sail power for transportation is not the same as distance for those who rely upon the internal combustion engine, and such matters must be a part of the continual re-assessment undertaken by the historian. These basic elements of a historian's training, together with the magpie characteristic of the craft—that of lifting

*The Stunted Strong, p. 16.

any good theory from any branch of the social sciences if it will aid in the comprehension of what went on—provide a probably unwarranted courage for writing about human sexuality.

In any case such is the equipment carried into this enquiry. Arthur Lower, the great Canadian historian, has compared the historian to the ostrich: a bird that, hoping one day to soar into the realms of idealism and prophecy, always finds its great feet firmly attached to the rocks and hills of earth. Over and over again when the politician or the social commentator remarks that 'history tells us' or that 'history has shown us', the reaction of the professional historian is 'it didn't happen that way'. I remember being informed by one student that the essence of the eighteenth century was contained in the fact that 'everywhere women were oppressed'! All I could do, at that moment, was to consider Catherine the Great of Russia, Madame de Pompadour, the impact on literature of people like Mary Wollstonecraft. So while trying to find out what I thought about the position and status of women in the twentieth century, I was also trying to unravel ideas about women in the immediate past, about the lives of women during the seventeenth, eighteenth, and nineteenth centuries, and I was caught up over and over again into sentences beginning 'on the one hand' followed by sentences beginning 'but one must consider'. At this stage *Penelope's Web* came to seem not just a net of infinite interstices but some kind of enveloping fog penetrating thoughts, feelings, ideas, and actions on all levels. The book was a tar-baby, impossible to finish, impossible to stop, a burden to me and an aggravation to my friends.

Three factors helped me persevere with writing this book. Firstly my editor at Oxford University Press, Canada kept a continuous stream of acerbic encouragement coming towards me. Ms Crawley was able over and over again to persuade me that I really did have something to say, and that revision and re-thinking were merely minor details, obstacles to be overcome. Feeding me pickled onions, cheese, and good advice, she provided a support for my basic aim: the statement of problems rather than their solution, the description of ideas rather than their creation, the organization of material rather than artistic interpretation. The second support was also a person, a man who never ever lost patience with listening to me talk about ideas that puzzled me, who helped enormously by considering *Penelope's Web* something important, something valuable, and something to be completed. Finally there was my own wish to think about this question in the context of Canada, the country to which I came as an immigrant in 1956, of which I became a citizen in 1969, and about which I am most passionate, considering it the land to live in during this century. Along with the forbearance of colleagues, the active interest of other friends in particular chapters of the book, and the general sufferance of this interest by students and acquaintances, *Penelope's Web* has been written.

It has taken me from a consideration of the present discontent in Canada, back to the seventeenth-century roots of our contemporary society. It has brought me through the political structures of the eighteenth century and into the experiences of Upper Canada during the nineteenth century. It has made me look at prostitution and industrial society, at Canadian literature and Canadian cities. It has left me with even more questions than I had at the start. But for me personally it has done more and will do so I hope for the reader: it has made me really think about being human, being a woman, and being a Canadian. However imprecise the ideas that emerge, however superficial the perceptions, I now know better than I did four years ago some of the elements bound up in all three.

One

The Immediate Questioning

The most important questions to be asked about the present feminist movement (as opposed to questions asked by the feminists) are: will it last? Is Women's Liberation more than a passing fad? Isn't it perhaps just one more wave of comment by some women, like those who were active in the 1920s, something to watch dwindle away on the shore of more permanent and more fundamental concerns? One answer to these questions is the political reply given by people such as Juliet Mitchell, a New Zealander now teaching university in Britain. She remarked in her work *Women's Estate* that by '1970 there was some form of Women's Liberation Movement active in all but three of the liberal democratic countries of the advanced capitalist world,' the exceptions being Iceland, Austria, and Switzerland. For her 'Women's Liberation is an international movement—not in organization but in its identification and shared goals.' In her eyes it is a basic alteration in what determines the political climate of communities, and it can best be understood by using the vocabulary of politics, economics, and sociology. Women's Liberation must be taken seriously, not only because it involves questions of human freedoms, but because it involves the structure of politics. The financing of International Women's Year provides additional proof for this argument, since the granting of resources for such an endeavour has to be a sign of the importance of feminism in present-day politics. At the very least one might conclude that the feminism of the late twentieth century, generally known as Women's Liberation, has managed to compete for a measureable amount of communal resources— money for meetings, for government reports, for social activities, and for international conferences—as well as for the time and energy of individuals of both sexes.

This is no mean achievement. Government activity in aid of

women's rights has, in many countries, gone far beyond mere lipservice to a worthy cause, or measures designed to pacify critics rather than remove basic disabilities. While few countries have reached the level of the central government of Mogadiscio of the Somali Republic, which had tribal chieftains shot on the charge that they spoke against equal rights for women, many have set about considerable programs of reform. The policy instituted by the United States Department of Health, Education and Welfare to ensure equal employment opportunities for women is vigorous and sensible. It asks, for example, that American universities receiving federal monies set about actively looking for qualified women as candidates for available positions. The policy of the Ontario Department of Education—having all texts used in the school system checked for sexism—is an equally valid and important work.

Yet to assess the importance of present feminism solely in political terms is to end blinded to the wider questions. This danger entraps Juliet Mitchell herself and her own summary of her theory reveals what happens. She writes: 'Women are an oppressed people, we can learn about this oppression by using the "politics of experience",* we can combat oppression by attacking the agents and institutions of power (men and/or male dominated society) to produce either "equality" or "the liberated self": "whole people".'

The vital issues of social organization and sexual equality have suddenly been replaced by discussions of political systems without much reference to the actual conditions in human communities. Suddenly the attempt to wrestle with the complexity of the feminist movement is abandoned for sentences that speak in terms of always all-powerful males and always enfeebled women. One feels that the women Prime Ministers of India and Ceylon are as neglected as the work hazards of the asbestos miners of Quebec, that Mrs Thatcher, Britain's leader of the Opposition, is tossed aside together with the boredom of assembly-line workers in the Ontario auto industry. And what about other complex social issues? What about disease? What about drought? The list is endless, and the feeling of exasperation as a clear analysis gurgles into

---

*Mitchell's own footnote: 'a term now loosely used to suggest an analysis of society from the perspective of one's self. The experience of personal alienation is the means of testing the total social alienation.'

jargon is enormous. People have disappeared and the pages are filled with cartoon figures, little line drawings with no depths and only the ability to obscure the importance of the issue. Many writings about women seem to dismiss vast areas of human experience as irrelevant to their studies. Again and again complex human situations are reduced to interaction between puppets. Procrustes, whose habit was to insist that his guests exactly fitted the bed he provided, would lop off heads and feet or stretch out neck and toes to achieve his wish. Far too many books about women seem to have had him as their patron saint. Humanity is tidied up and the possibility of variation between human beings cut away. The most brutal surgery has been performed on human emotions. Sex, never quite defined, is seen as always the most important characteristic of human beings and always the mainspring of all human actions.

Interestingly enough, this attitude is to be found in *Chatelaine*, a monthly publication produced specifically for a female readership. It is dedicated to the interests of women and is fully in favour of equality of civic status for both men and women. But it is most uneasy about Women's Liberation. Reading through the twelve issues from May 1973 to May 1974, one is driven to wonder whether there is an interest in providing its readers with even a basic analysis of the movement. For example, in an article entitled 'The Single Girl Rip-off' by Myrna Kostash, February 1974, the writer equates the movement with sexual freedom, sexual freedom with sexual licence, sexual licence with sexual promiscuity, and sexual promiscuity with female misery. There is no attempt to present either some account of the origins and present support for Women's Liberation, nor any attempt to distinguish between this movement and other groups concerned with questioning the lives of women. Not only does the article present a simplistic view of Women's Liberation; it also provides a cartoon-like view of humanity. The problems of working women in Canada's cities are reduced to the problems of their sexual lives. There is no suggestion that such problems might be more complex and might also be found in the lives of men. Loneliness, depression, the pressures of twentieth-century city life, the difficulties of finding congenial work, the problems of making lasting friendships are all seen as matters that bedevil women alone. Yet all Canada's large cities— Toronto, Winnipeg, Vancouver, or Montreal—present both men and women with a struggle for a human kind of life in circumstances that can easily brutalize.

The coverage by the journal of issues touching the political, legal, and economic status of women within the present Canadian situation is usually good. But *Chatelaine* makes no real attempt even to argue about the serious nature of choices that are beginning to confront women. The most glaring example of this failure is the publication of an article entitled 'Are men obsolete?' by June Callwood in April 1974. At first sight the title affronts, and the article does nothing to lessen this affront. The advances in biological knowledge and their impact upon so many aspects of human life is a major problem confronting humanity. It demands public discussion. Advances in sperm preservation and artificial insemination, the idea that the procreation of the human species might be left to laboratories and women, or even laboratories alone, was bound to be thought about. What is startling is the manner in which Callwood treats the question. There is no real analysis of the human condition, no real consideration of the nature of men and women. The conclusion that men may perhaps be allowed to continue to exist is reached without any perception that a man is a human being as well as a male. Serious questions are treated with flippancy, and the need to consider with any depth the meaning and ramification of human sexuality goes, once more, unfulfilled. Perhaps this approach is the result of editorial policy. The editors seem unable in general to decide not only whether Women's Liberation is merely a passing fad or a movement with a serious and justifiable aim, but even to judge what its real concerns are. At times their journal reads as if they believed it was a dangerous attempt by psychologically disturbed minds to disrupt a vital area of human experience—the natural and accepted pattern of relationships between men and women. At other times the possible political and economic results of different life-styles for the majority of Canadian women appear as a stimulating adventure.

Admittedly the present discontent is not easy to pigeonhole and to categorize. But the confusion does not diminish the serious nature of the issues raised. A perception of this led the *Globe and Mail* to employ the vocabulary usually associated with the most strident supporters of women's rights when considering the Lavelle case and when commenting on the Murdoch decision. The Lavelle case involved the rights of Indian women who married non-Indians, and the *Globe and Mail* headed the correspondence about the matter 'Male Chauvinism'.[1] The decision of the Supreme Court on the property rights of a prairie farmer's wife, Irene Murdoch, led to a *Globe and Mail* editorial headed 'End Sexual Nepotism'.[2] In fact a perusal of this newspaper over the past year shows an erratic but valuable leadership from its editors over the question of Women's Liberation. While quite happy to run the occasional joke that depends for its humour on a vision of women as bird-witted or as summed up by their sex appeal, the paper has consistently given serious consideration to arguments over women's rights.

The most impressive and coherent estimation to be found in the Canadian press of the present discontents, however, is in the pages of the *Homemaker's Digest*. Perhaps because its declared interest has, as was stated in a recent editorial, always been the family rather than what is paradoxically the narrower field of women, its editors have found it easier to analyse the question of Women's Liberation. The long period of childhood experienced by every human being means the connection of every single adult with some kind of group, either a kin family or people who took on the roles of such a family. The acceptance by the *Homemaker's Digest* of these characteristics of humanity has obviously helped it to consider questions raised about women's rights along a very broad front.

The journal has as its sub-title 'Canada's largest Women's Magazine'. Paid for by advertising revenues in the same way as is commercial television, it is circulated free to most of its readers, and at the cost of $8 for a two-year subscription to a small minority. With such a sponsorship one might fear the worst, but a three-year reading shows that the *Digest* is written consistently from a position of intelligent enquiry. Perhaps the key to its approach on Women's Liberation was set by one of its earliest articles on the subject, an interview with York University psychologist Esther Greenglass published in the May/June issue, 1972. The article was entitled' 'Scratch any woman deep enough and you'll find a feminist'. Two things immediately strike the reader: one, the attempt made to define the question being discussed; two, the sense of humour that it shows.

For Esther Greenglass the aim of the present agitation is to improve the lot of Canadian women, and Canadian men and children. She considers that 'the self-contained nuclear family just can't satisfy all the needs of its members. The wife is disappointed that her husband can't fulfill all her needs—she feels more pressured and resentful—they use each other as scapegoats and produce a great many neurotic kids as a result.'[3] She believes, too, that 'there just aren't enough jobs to provide full employment for everyone, and men in our society are under tremendous pressure to perform. Why should they have to work 10 to 16 hours a day, at sometimes boring jobs, when women could benefit by taking some of the financial load from them?' For her the way to find solutions to these problems is to find a new pattern of life for the men and women who make up society. If the force of the present action comes from women, then that is where new changes are being originated. She has no objection to being associated with Women's Liberation and commented: 'The media present women's liberation groups as being shrill, hysterical brassière-burners —a very effective way to discredit the movement. Actually there were never any brassière burnings—some women threatened to do it, but when they were refused a fire permit, they retreated. Women are very law-abiding.'

Questions, of course, come quickly to mind: are the majority of families in Canada today 'nuclear', centred upon two generations alone with little or no linking to sibling branches? How do the new Canadians of Italian or Portuguese or West Indian origin fit into this picture? How is society going to cope with more women going into the labour force, since the 1973 figures reported by Statistics Canada show that women make up 33.2 per cent of our workforce already? But with these questions comes the impression that Esther Greenglass would be willing to discuss them. The final lines of the article provide not only the key to what she considers needs thought but also a suggestion of the complexity of the problem: her aims, the article quotes her as saying, 'are that the fight will result in freedom to choose what one will do without the undue influence of the fact of sex...' She looks forward to the time when 'everyone will be a human being first and a man or woman second.' The attraction of this aim is its simplicity, its appeal to our political instincts as members of a democracy. The difficulty about it is that it can only work if societies are seen as clans or tribes where every interaction between individuals is always worked out on the basis of personal contact: no one is ever a customer or a student or a shoemaker but always a human being. The possibility of a community where all approach one another as total human beings in all circumstances is Utopian, and while some future date may see it established, perhaps when Christ's teachings are seriously tried, at present twentieth-century life demands the playing of roles.

All over the world communities present their members with the need to evolve a personality for public consumption. Individual capabilities and desires are shaped as much by community demands as by personal aims. Karl Menninger in his book *The Vital Balance* summed up the matter by saying each of us lives a life balanced between native talent (mental ability, physical power, sexual energy), private ambition (the desire to excel in a particular field), and the opportunities presented by the environment (schooling, employment, economic situation). These are the parameters of human lives.

Yet work after work appears that suggests that all emotion is brute sex rather than that all human beings find that their sexuality affects the nature of their emotions. The gulf between much writing, which claims parentage from Freud, and the mind of Freud himself, is immense. He had far too much sense and far too much humility to offer the world such a simplistic argument for its behaviour. Firstly, his idea of sexuality was extraordinarily complicated. Sex was less a physical urge translated into all human action than the opening item in a table of human characteristics, one of the basic elements of all human transactions. It was something that was present because all human relations are between people of the opposite sex or people of the same sex. He saw sexual personality as a human given. To a large extent he considered the sexual orientation of an individual to be the key to both personality and character. How it was shaped and formed and the extent to which it was moulded by other than the individual was the field of his research. He moved always from the concept of the individual to the structure of society, and postulated that 'the development of civilization has . . . a far-reaching similarity to the development of the individual'.[4] As far as he was concerned, human sexuality profoundly affected the nature of human beings, but he was prepared to admit the importance of other influences upon humanity. He would seek to translate these other influences into the terms of his own particular analysis, but he never overlooked their existence or the need to discuss their importance. When faced with a friend who talked of religious consolation, of what Freud was willing to describe as 'a feeling of indissoluable bond, of being one with the external world as a whole' he wrote: 'From my own experience I could not convince myself of the primary nature of such a feeling. But this gives me no right to deny that it does in fact occur in other people.'[5]

Part of the nature of women (and part of the nature of men) is that they are half of a bisexual species. Arguments about the definition of women that overlook this basic fact quickly tend to become sterile. Whatever the future may bring, present humanity is marked by the bisexuality of the species, and this has had an immense impact on all members of the human race, male and female.

Sex is first a major characteristic of the human species. But any investigation of human sexuality demands a most intricate and detailed analysis of the situation being discussed. As a noted biologist has remarked, 'it is not merely the method by which children happen to be reproduced: it is actually a process which has itself been evolved and which is so cunningly arranged to increase the rate of evolutionary change that the animals and plants in which it occurs have prospered so much they have almost replaced those who have persisted in a more primitive system.'[6] But it is not merely a handy evolutionary device for the species, it is a matter of moment to each individual human being and a matter of concern to every human community. This is not to say that all individuals have a uniform sexual appetite; nor is it to say that each person copes with sexual needs in the same manner, even among those people who share the same culture. It is a statement that an individual's sex is as much a part of a human being as is bone structure, skin colour, the ability to see or to hear. Sex is given, as is height or weight. In the same way as height and weight differ among humans, so does the sexual drive. Each being has a sexual identity, one that is imprinted upon the chromosome pattern of the cells.

Sex is also of moment to the individual not because human communities are summed up by their sexual behaviour but because all human communities reflect human sexuality. The biological urge to preserve the species has assured sex a position of importance at all times and in all places. The sexual identity of the human individual is seen as something to be upheld and reinforced by the community in which the person lives. Human society exerts a tremendous control over its members, and the particular cultural interpretations of masculine and feminine in any community will profoundly affect the humans who belong to it. Masculinity permits men in France and Russia to kiss each other on occasions when such an action between Canadians would be looked upon as effeminate. Concepts of male and female are part and parcel of the thinking of all humans, but what constitutes true masculinity and true femininity and what should be the political and social consequences of these determinants have always been questions of much debate. Twentieth-century knowledge of the wide variety of sexual customs and activities among peoples has led some to think that no social differentiation of biological sex is necessary.

A discussion of human sexuality is a highly emotional matter, since its very basis, the attitude of one sex to another, is highly emotional. It is a question that really demands that one consider humanity, since any undertaking to think about women is really an undertaking to consider men, women, and children. The study of women as a self-contained category tends to lead either to amorphous generalizations or to cartoon portrayals. It was Meredith who wrote at the end of the nineteenth century that 'the generic woman appears to have an extraordinary faculty for swallowing the individual'; it also seems to have an extraordinary capacity for obscuring the essential link between men and women—that both are human. Whatever ideas are proposed about women, all need as a framework ideas about humanity as a whole.

This is easier said than done. In the last decades knowledge seems to have become fragmented as never before. The physiology of sex belongs to biology and medicine and rarely comes to the notice of any social scientist who is not a clinical psychologist. Even in the latter discipline, few follow the humility of Freud who, in the last sentences of his *Three Essays on Sexuality*, admitted that there was little precise knowledge about the location of the border between the physical endowment and the psychological development of the individual. The interest of the sociologist has been in patterns of marriage, organizations of families, and the impact of kin systems, and the question of individual motives has been blanketed out by the consideration of community beliefs and social restrictions. Cultural ideas of sex have been seen as the preserve of the anthropologist, and the variations of human custom in this area have led, far too often, not to questions about why all societies translate male and female into specific social roles but to a belief that rational humanity needs no roles. Any examination of the sexuality of human beings reveals an unending stream of monographs: sex as mechanics, sex as procreation, sex as recreation, sex as social activity, sex as political dynamite, sex as ad-man's delight, sex as morality, but rarely is it examined simply as a human function.

Dr Alex Comfort, in his *Sex and Society*, the book that was roundly condemned when it first appeared in 1962 for supposedly advocating a 'new morality', remarked that 'any attempt to isolate sexual behaviour from other factors in a social pattern is bound to hinder our comprehension of it and to lead to a false emphasis.'[7] This distinguished physician and zoologist, at present on the faculty of University College, London, considers that 'the study of human sexual behaviour . . . is not the province of any single science, but overlaps into the fields of psychology, physiology, social anthropology and ethics.'[8] This does not mean that only those fully qualified in these fields should write about the matter. If war is too serious to be left to the generals, then sex is too fundamental to be left to the experts.

The very wealth of material available is, of course, the stumbling block. Yet if a new dispensation for women is required, it must not only reach into all areas of human activity but be based upon the most comprehensive view of humanity itself. The possibility of a new synthesis, a new philosophy of human beings, is perhaps greater now than at any time since the immediate post-war years. After the last decades of intensive research, when scholars were people who knew more and more about less and less, there has been in the last five years a considerable shift towards interdisciplinary work. Learned journals are being born with new titles that deliberately incorporate more than one field of research. Institutes are being established that attempt to merge the concerns of the old entrenched disciplines into new fields: 'international relations' means co-operation between economists, political scientists, sociologists, and historians; linguistics involves computer scientists, engineers, and language experts as well as psychologists; the new enthusiasm for ecology is bringing together engineers, biologists, geologists, and sociologists. It is in such an atmosphere of questioning that the problems posed by human sexuality are being considered. Women's Liberation is not the beginning and end of the debate over the role of women in the twentieth century; it is merely one symptom of a much wider investigation of the question, supported by both men and women and reaching into all fields of intellectual endeavour.

This movement towards a new synthesis could not be started without the painstaking work of those who restricted their enquiries in the past. It is no denigration of the labour of those who raised questions about the vision of women in literature or the importance of public opinion on the social status of women that an attempt should now be made to bring lines of work together. Germaine Greer's *The Female Eunuch* provides an analysis of women in literature that is an invaluable background to Elizabeth Janeway's *Man's World, Women's Place*, on the way in which social pressures mould individual desires. One's sympathy for the last-named work is due not only to the intelligence and scholarship of the book but to the author's very human confession about the difficulty of organizing her thesis. The dictum of the psychologist Eric Erikson—that one must begin everything twice—is particularly applicable for Janeway when writing about women. First comes the necessity of stating the problem, but first also comes the necessity of explaining the context in which the problem exists. The need to analyse simultaneously subjects that can only be thought and written about in sequence is the major difficulty to be found in writing about women. At every turn the question comes: what is more important, the fact that women are human or that they are women? At every turn the complex answer 'a bit of both, but sometimes a little more of the one than the other' hovers in a vague, muddled cloud at the mind's edge.

In Canada today women's rights and women's role are a major and important topic of consideration. Writers present new reflections on the argument about masculine and feminine and about the Canadian view of these qualities. Robertson Davies, perhaps Canada's most distinguished novelist and critic, spent much time in his recent work *The Manticore* on Jungian analysis, with its emphasis on the twin principles of anima and animum, male and female, to be found mixed within all humans. Margaret Atwood, whose critical overview of Canadian literature, *Survival*, has been an immediate success, in her first novel *The Edible Woman* wrote of an age-old dilemma, a girl's choice of whom to marry. The choice is presented, however, less in terms of romance than in terms of the realities of marriage. One young man offers financial success and social status, and demands in return love and adherence to what are thought to be the social norms. Communication must be through the patterned responses of traditional society. The other offers probable though not inevitable poverty, and demands response on a much more intricate level: love between responsible beings. He refuses to accept the submission of the woman, for which she will be paid with happiness. Instead, happiness is seen as something both may, but only may, find if they accept final responsibility for their own actions. Margaret Laurence, whose most recent novel sums up the life of a middle-aged writer and confronts what love and children demand, answered the criticism that she is parochial, a woman writing of women, by replying that she *was* a woman and she wrote of what she knew.[9] After all, she commented, men wrote about men.

In *Lives of Girls and Women* Alice Munro brings out the pressures on young people to accept what they think their societies wish for them. Here, as in her book *Dance of the Happy Shades*, a collection of short stories that won the Governor-General's Award for Fiction in 1968, is portrayed the tension between individual and community and society. Del Jordan, the young girl whose life is the centre of *Lives of Girls and Women*, looks at her dreams, her aspirations to be a writer, in the light of her mother's ambitions, her father's acceptances of life, the family struggling with poverty, bound by the half-perceived rules of a small Ontario community on the eve of the Second World War. In all her work Alice Munro brings out the frame that holds humanity: the effect on the person of the perceptions other people have of them. Each person is aware of existing as an individual personality but among people whose lives are similar and who as a group impose rules and regulations—the perception of society.

This theme, the confrontation of reality by those who are women, is by no means confined to writings in English Canada. French Canada has produced works as powerful, and perhaps *La Sagouine*, Antonine Maillet's monologue of an old Acadian woman telling the story of her life on the Atlantic coast, is the best to select. Here again the sense of the book is the tension between what is wanted, what is possible, and what is allowed. In the pages of this work, which has received accolades in France and in Britain in the *Times Literary Supplement*, there is the constant pressure of sea, wind, and snow as well as the impact of religious and secular authorities. The old woman must absorb the deaths of those drowned, the commands of the priest, and the demands of social workers. Her ability to sort out which are most important, to give in to one in order to frustrate another, knowing always that life is a small space, makes *La Sagouine* unforgettable. Gabrielle Roy, Marie Claire Blais, Anne Hébert: these pages could become a catalogue. But even this short selection is not misleading: it represents a powerful concern among Canadian writers. It is part of the recognition that a vital element of human experience has been neglected, has not been translated adequately into art. And this surge in literature is accompanied by an equally strong movement in painting, in journalism, and in work in the academic disciplines.

It is worth underlining that the present questioning about feminism is evidence not only of concern for the rights of women but of recognition that prejudice and discrimination against women does exist in Canada and ought to be eradicated. The work of the Women's Bureau of the Canadian Federal Department of Labour clearly establishes this. In 1973 this Department published a volume entitled *Women in the Labour Force* that demonstrates clearly the realities of discrimination against women on the grounds of sex alone, now and today in Canada. In 1973 women made up 33.2 per cent of the labour force, an increase of 64.3 per cent compared with the female labour force in 1962.[10] This means that 37.1 per cent of the female population of fourteen years and over is working; 85.8 per cent of all the single women in the population aged 25 to 35 are working. In other words, women in the work force are an essential part of the economic life of the society, accounting for not quite one third of Canada's labour force. Further, for most of these women work is not a matter of choice but a matter of necessity. Only a quarter of all working women are working part-time. The comparable statistic for men is 6 per cent. In general, the conditions of work for women are less favourable than for men, and a comparison of hourly wage rates reveals discrimination against women. As the work of the Labour Bureau states:

In the inspector (electrical) occupation within the communications equipment industry, women's average hourly wages were

$2.38, compared with $3.53 for men. In the inspector (finished goods) occupation within rubber industries other than footwear, tires and tubes, women's average hourly wages were $2.17 compared with $3.20 for men. In the sewing machine operator occupation within the woman's clothing industry, women's average hourly wages were $2.11 an hour, compared with $3.11 for men. In the machine operator occupation within the motor vehicle parts and accessories industry, average rates for women were $2.42 an hour, compared with $3.56 for men. In the veneer grader occupation within the veneer and plywood mills industry, women's average hourly wages were $2.31, compared with $3.30 for men.[11]

These statistics leave the matter in no doubt: quite apart from the problems of career choice and career advancement for women, the Canadian people still have to face the elementary problem of 'equal pay for equal work' in most sectors of the labour force. The question of social justice is fundamental to the question of rights for women. Juliet Mitchell is quite right. But this concept is one of the thorniest. In theory nobody is against the idea of 'from each according to his abilities, to each according to his needs.' In practice nobody agrees on how one measures either need or ability.

So Women's Liberation is more than just questions about politics and economics. The whole tangled issue of human rights and responsibilities has to be considered. The establishment of the Royal Commission on the Status of Women in Canada in 1967, which reported in 1970 that 'discrimination against women still flourishes and prejudice is still very much alive '[12] in Canada today, was as much the cause as the result of public realization that a problem existed. The work of Maxine Nunes and Deanna White in The Lace Ghetto[13] reached similar conclusions: Canadian society contains many accepted injustices against women.

The work of the Royal Commission is significant enough to need a complete chapter for its consideration later in this book, but the points made in The Lace Ghetto provide illustrations that prejudice against women is accepted in Canadian society. Nunes and White assembled advertisements that show women as weak-minded, weak-willed, and defined by their sexuality. They investigated the opinions of children—a six-year-old believed that 'Girls can't be doctors because they would look silly if they were doctors.'[14] They canvassed teenagers who believed that 'aggressiveness is when a girl has her own ideas, ideas which are not a pat, set feminine formula. . . . If she is an individual, not just one of a group but an individual that you can clearly identify as one, then I think that many guys would get turned off because they wouldn't know how to handle her . . . ' (this opinion advanced by Mark, aged 19).[15] In sum, their work showed that the most blatant pressures do exist within Canadian society for women to conform to a particular image, and the extent to which such pressures can cripple many people.

So far the discussion has been about the existence of discrimination in Canadian society. But at this point a distinction should be made between 'society' and 'community' as these words will be used throughout this book. The community is the human species, a particular community all the people who live within a designated territory except for the rare person who cuts all ties with other people. Within the community the relationships of human beings to each other is governed by individual personalities. If one thinks of the community in this way, problems of existence and procreation become visible, questions about human habits are more easy to formulate.

The society is the formal organization of the community to produce an ordered pattern of life desired by the group. It is the web of recognized institutions, laws, and accepted conventions, concerned with debate over political and social issues. Society is the mechanism used by human beings to transmit beliefs, to establish ways of solving common problems, and to promulgate particular patterns of relationships between defined categories of people. To look at society is to be concerned with problems of culture and of political power.

This use of 'community' and 'society' may be debatable, but it is necessary in order to make the distinction between people as a species and the organizations that put people into structured groups. Only in this way can a bridge be made between the work of the ethnologist, the anthropologist, and the biologist—those who study the human community; and the work of the sociologist and political scientist—those who study the human society. *Women in Canada,* a collection of essays, is concerned with discrimination in Canadian *society* against women—the treatment of women by the prison system, by the insurance companies, within the universities, throughout the labour force. *Mother Was Not a Person,* a collection of writings, deals with sexism in the community, with perceptions and feelings that led one of the contributors to say:

just
  because
    i wore pants
  they said
i was not a woman underneath my pants
  because
    they could not believe a woman was more
than a dress of the latest fashion; . . . [16]

Prejudice and discrimination against women exist in Canada, then, and are considered with seriousness, but of course they are neither looked at nor thought about in a vacuum. Canadians are also concerned about the quality of life, pollution, economic advancement, unemployment and inflation, national sovereignty and national unity. And sometimes all Canadians are concerned about none of these issues but only their own personal situations, their loves, their joys and sorrows, their enjoyments, and their difficulties. So while the question of feminism and of Women's Liberation in Canada in the mid-seventies seems very often to be important, it is only one among many important issues. Yet those who see it as a much more radical issue than any of the others at present demanding attention are closer to the truth. For there is no denying that one of the major images of women throughout western civilization has been woman as mother, as child-bearer, and thus as woman within the family—an image that reflects reality to a considerable extent. But at a time of dwindling primary resources, with the present population explosion and the present techniques for contraception, this image of woman is now being queried: Mother how often? Mother for how long? And perhaps, mother at all?

Behind all the rhetoric about social roles, political rights, human needs, and individual aspirations, lies the tremendous emotional investment of western civilization in the blood family and in woman as child-bearer. So great is this investment that many are unwilling to talk about it. It is much easier to pretend that the demands made by Women's Liberation either do not really involve a rearrangement of fundamental attitudes within society or are merely an evanescent cry, a fad, a passing fashion. The need to consider Women's Liberation in the context of fundamental beliefs about human beings often goes ignored. After all, surely questions about the meaning of life, the value of humanity are best left to the very young, the very old, the members of the counter-culture, or the ministers of religion? Surely action is what counts? Surely it is possible to admit that discrimination against women exists, ought not to exist, and can be eradicated, all without having to argue first principles?

Unfortunately, while some advance can be made without uncovering questions of fundamental principle, prejudice against women is not precisely the same as prejudice against any other group. Women are not a minority, and because social roles are stereotyped by sex, ideas of difference between men and women are easily accepted, so that sooner or later concepts of the rights of the majority, the fitness of certain behaviour patterns, and the innate characteristics of men and women are brought into question. The problem under discussion can be as simple-sounding as the provision of day-care centres, but it will entail beliefs about the proper care of young children, the duty of the mother to provide that care, and society's approval for the correct personal behaviour of the mother in providing that care. The question of university posts for women can become quickly embroiled in questions of lack of employment for men in universities, the need for men to support their wives, the place of women in the home. Even on purely quantitative grounds, prejudice and discrimination against women is different from prejudice and discrimination against other human groups. It is not merely that there are more women to suffer under such differentiation, but that prejudice on the grounds of sex is often added to some other bias—here is a white, or a black, a Jew, or a Christian who is also a woman. Plato's prayer has an echo down the centuries: Thank God I was born a man, in Athens, at the time of Socrates.'

So the debate over feminism or Women's Liberation or whatever label one wishes to attach to the present discontent is a debate that arouses people on many different levels and involves questions about a great number of disparate human activities. At first sight the argument appears so wide-ranging and so diffuse as to defy any attempt to organize it. But at least some structure can be applied to the matter if one starts with the notion of finding out the extent to which the immediate situation represents a norm or an aberration for western civilization. To what extent, in other words, is prejudice and discrimination against women a fundamental part of western civilization? To what extent is the present structure something that is a perversion of western traditions rather than their fulfilment?

NOTES

[1] Toronto *Globe and Mail*, 10 Sept. 1973.

[2] Toronto *Globe and Mail*, 8 Oct. 1973.

[3] Esther Greenglass, *Homemaker's Digest*, May/June 1972.

[4] S. Freud, *Civilization and its Discontents*, trans. and ed. by J. Strachey (Norton, 1962), p. 91.

[5] *Ibid.*, p. 12.

[6] C. H. Waddington, 'The Biology of Sex', quoted in K. Whaler and P. Fletcher, *Sex and Society* (Penguin, 1969), p. 22.

[7] A. Comfort, *Sex and Society* (Penguin, 1962), p. 48.

[8] *Ibid.*, p. 9.

[9] 'The Matriarch of Manawaka', *Saturday Night*, (May 1974), vol. 89, 17-20.

[10] Labour Canada, Women's Bureau, *Women in the Labour Force: Facts and Figures* (Information Canada, 1973), p. iii. All data refer to 1972 unless otherwise stated.

[11] *Ibid.*, p. 73.

[12] Royal Commission on the Status of Women, *Report* (Information Canada, 1970), p. xi.

[13] M. Nunes and D. White, *The Lace Ghetto* (New Press, 1972).

[14] *Ibid.*, p. 41.

[15] *Ibid.*, p. 19.

[16] M. Anderson, *Mother was not a Person* (Content Publishing, 1972), p. 122.

Two

Looking for
the Roots of our Discontent

To question whether a particular attitude or convention is characteristic of western civilization is to pull forward a great tangle of
enquiries. What is western civilization? Come to that, what is
civilization? How does one decide whether something is a dominant force or merely a temporary aberration in a sprawling, cen-
turies-old culture? The whole enterprise bristles with traps—of
definition, of evidence, of organization. But this present enquiry is
not an attempt to answer all possible questions about the status
and position of women in western civilization. The aim is much
more restricted. It is to provide some idea of a historian's attitude
towards the present turmoil about women's status. In looking for
the roots of present prejudice and discrimination against women,
an obvious beginning seemed to be to look at an earlier period
that had been studied in some depth and consider how women
were regarded at that time. And since the seventeenth century is
the writer's particular interest, it was chosen as the starting point
rather than an earlier or a later period.

Of course periodization in history—dividing time up into eras
and talking about centuries as if they had some type of intrinsic
coherent unity—is a dangerous business. Eras and ages are boxes
into which historians put the past in order to cope with it. Most
eras do have a fundamental texture that justifies their being considered as the 'Renaissance' or the 'Edwardian Age', but in the
main the names are applied to make the years easier to talk
about. There has to be a constant awareness that such labels are
much more often imposed than discovered. They are to the historian what a theory is to the physicist—a way of looking at a
problem. As such they are very practical tools, but it should be
constantly borne in mind that people live according to more
subtle distinctions. Most divisions say much more about what

those who propose them have as priorities than about the development and thrust of human life that took place within the times outlined. Yet some manner of organizing the period a historian selects for study is necessary. Not every steam engine can be traced back to the steam kettle, and the purely mathematical divisions of centuries are rarely the best guide to the divisions in culture and civilization brought about by changing life styles and emerging ideas. It is 1789, the French Revolution, and the Fall of the Bastille that really mark the political opening of the nineteenth century, as 3 August 1914, the outbreak of the First World War, brings it to its bitter close. Similarly 1600-1700 are not the best dates to mark the period known as the seventeenth century. The beginning could be set in 1610 when Henri IV of France was assassinated, and the end in 1714 when the English Queen Anne died, the change of country saying much about the changing balance of power in Europe during the century. Whatever single years are chosen to open and close this era, however, its interest remains. Here is the period when Europe really went out to encounter the rest of the world. It is the age of the European settlement of North America. At the same time it is an era of major changes within Europe itself, some produced by the very fact of European expansion overseas, others the result of internal phenomena. It is the century that sees the final flowering of many European medieval traditions as well as the first new leaves of the modern era. Every happening seems charged with a Janus-face, looking both ways, so that the France of Louis XIV, whose reign began in 1643 and ended in 1715, can be seen both as the last of the great medieval kingdoms and the first of the modern states.

The seventeenth century is an age when witchcraft still flourished, but when enough scientific discoveries were made to earn it the name of the Enlightenment. Its problems were a mixture of ancient difficulties and modern crises. Interpretations of Christianity were of central importance, but half the villages of France saw neither minister nor priest from one year's end to the next. Famine caused by poor agricultural techniques struck the lands, but there was unemployment due to technological advances in some of the cities. Questions of civil liberties and the rights of the individual were the stuff of the political commentaries of the age, yet lynch mobs, such as that of Loudun in 1634, sought to burn those known to consort with the Devil. It is an age that could be opened, instead of with Henri IV of France, with Elizabeth of England dying and leaving a wardrobe of two hundred dresses and only one change of underlinen. It is an age that could close, instead of with Anne of England, with Louis XIV of France, a stickler for etiquette who never used a fork in his life. It was also the age that saw Europeans establish themselves not only along the banks of the St Lawrence but also on the shores of the Bay of Fundy.

Almost any brief survey of such an age is bound to mislead. But there is one aspect of it that provides the inescapable framework for everything else that happened during these years, that had an effect upon young and old, rich and poor, men, women, and children. This is the population density and the demographic pattern of birth and death. England and Wales had a population of less than seven million then; today more than fifty million inhabit the same space. France numbered approximately twenty million; today more than forty million live within its boundaries. From first to last death confronts the seventeenth century, dominating Europe and ceding ground only slightly in North America. Goubert, one of the great French historians who has studied population developments during this period, writes:

> In 1969, the average expectation of life is something over seventy years. In 1661 it was probably under twenty-five. These brutal figures show how, in those days, death was at the centre of life, just as the grave yard was at the centre of the village. Out of every hundred children born, twenty-five died before they were one year old, another twenty-five never reached twenty and a further twenty-five perished between the ages of twenty and forty-five. Only about ten ever made their sixties.[1]

Goubert goes on to point out that, because it was so unusual to live to old age, the death of the old was a major event. Any other death was unremarkable. In fact 'cut-price' funerals for children who died at the end of the summer were common in France.

People died from starvation. The amount of foodstuffs available in seventeenth-century Europe was nowhere near comparable to that of today, either in quantity or in type. Fish from the North Atlantic was of growing importance but was not yet a standard, fail-proof source of protein. Other foods, which would come to Europe from the Americas, were only just being introduced. The most obvious item not yet used was the potato, barely known in Europe in 1600 and looked upon with such suspicion that it was generally believed to cause leprosy. But the list of products that would be a common part of the European diet in later ages but that were almost unused at this time is a long one: it includes turkey, tomatoes, maize, avocado pears, pineapples, lima beans, scarlet-runner beans, chocolate, peanuts, vanilla, red and green peppers, not to mention the products of the sugar cane. Further, even the crops and herds native to Europe gave poor yields. This was partly owing to poor agricultural techniques. Farming methods had more in common with those used a thousand years earlier, at the time of the Roman Empire, than with those used even two hundred years later. Grains were sown broadcast and, except in Holland, little was known about crop rotation. Almost nothing was known about the use of turnips and other root crops to keep cattle fed during the winter. As a result, herds were small, trimmed by autumn killing to a bare minimum.

Farming was also complicated during this century by the appalling weather. Braudel, another eminent French historian, has attempted to sum up the debate about 'yesterday's weather' by pointing out the recent work done by historians and meteorologists, which reveals that temperature, pressure systems, and rainfall vary continuously and considerably through the centuries. In his *Capitalism and Material Life, 1400-1800* Braudel comments that one could call the reign of Louis XIV the 'little Ice Age', and he goes on to say: 'Everything moved to its rhythm: cereal growing Europe and the rice fields and steppes of Asia; the olive groves of Provence and the Scandinavian countries where snow and ice, slow to disappear in normal circumstances, no longer left the corn sufficient time to ripen: this was the case in the terrible year of 1690.'[2] Local scarcity leading to general famine was common in France, and, in fact, throughout Europe during these years. England was to a certain extent excepted from this rule.

But England could not escape the impact of disease and of inadequate medical knowledge even if its sheep and fish hedged it against the worst food shortages. It, like the rest of the world, suffered deaths from the diseases that killed then but that we now have under control, such as infantile paralysis, smallpox, diptheria, and typhoid. It also suffered from diseases that have since become less virulent in their effects. Since its appearance in

Marseilles in 1720, plague has not been a major scourge in the western world. In the seventeenth century, however, its effects were devastating. Accurate calculations for Bavaria, according to Braudel, show that when plague struck between 1621 and 1635 deaths rose phenomenally: 'for every hundred deaths in a normal year Munich counted 155 in an abnormal year; Augsburg 195; Bayreuth 487. . . . Children under a year old were primarily affected on each occasion and women tended to be more susceptible than men.'[3] Plague, Braudel goes on to write, 'was in Amsterdam throughout every year from 1622 to 1628 (the toll: 35,000 dead). It was in Paris in 1612, 1619, 1631, 1638, 1662, 1668 (the last). . . . Plague was in London five times between 1593 and 1664-5, claiming, it is said, a total of 156,463 victims.'[4] Statistics for towns are often more reliable than statistics for the countryside, but it is generally thought that when towns were struck, the surrounding countryside inevitably suffered the epidemic and that its effects in small villages and hamlets were even more severe.

If starvation and disease were death-dealers that have now been tamed for the western world, another killer common to both the seventeenth and the twentieth century is warfare. The Thirty Years War, 1618-48, was so ruinous in its effect upon the human and material resources of the countries it involved that, according to one of Canada's foremost military historians, S. F. Wise, it led to a moderating trend in European warfare.[5] C. V. Wedgewood, in her summary of its devastation at the end of her work *The Thirty Year's War*, considers that 'the German Empire, including Alsace but excluding the Netherlands and Bohemia, probably numbered about twenty-one million in 1618 and rather less than thirteen and a half million in 1648.'[6] A generation had seen a population loss of six and a half millions, a reduction in size of almost a third. Germany's loss in the five and a half years of the Second World War was two and a half millions, a loss of about three per cent of the population. Less important to remember than this particular comparison is the devastation caused by boiling oil, fire, and uncontrolled soldiery, which could produce results more than equivalent in their time and place to napalm, massed bombing raids, and scorched-earth policies.

This predominance of death meant that the emotional climate of the seventeenth century was much closer to that of its preceding centuries than to that of our own era. The reigns of Louis XIV and Charles II were indeed the time when Europe and North America moved from separate development to a path where events on one continent inevitably produced a reaction in the other, something previous centuries had not known. But this age, when the first building blocks of our own society were being cemented together, when state bureaucracies first emerged, had very different priorities than does contemporary Canadian life.

It is probable that Champlain's vision of life and death was much closer to that of the Inuit described by Coccola and King in *Ayorama* than with the generality of Canadians today. The author-priest tells us that after influenza had decimated the population of the Inuit at Burnside, the living departed for new grounds: 'They soon forgot the recent disaster. Like their ancestors, oppressed by countless centuries of privation and failure against the evil spirits of the land, they were too concerned with their daily fight for existence to worry about the past.'[7] Europe had more structure, more complexity in the seventeenth century than does the Canadian Arctic in mid-twentieth century, but its context was still that of a struggle for survival. The most vivid picture of society during this era is one that was actually written to open a book about Europe of the fourteenth and fifteenth centuries. Nevertheless Huizinga, a great Dutch historian, has spoken in these paragraphs for all the years before the eighteenth century.

> To the world when it was half a thousand years younger the outlines of all things seemed more clearly marked than to us. The contrast between suffering and joy, between adversity and happiness, appeared more striking. All experience had yet to the minds of men the directness and absoluteness of the pleasure and pain of child-life. Every event, every action was still embodied in expressive and solemn forms, which raised them to the dignity of a ritual. For it was not merely the great facts of birth, marriage and death which, by the sacredness of the sacrament, were raised to the rank of mysteries; incidents of less importance, like a journey, a task, a visit, were equally attended by a thousand formalities: benediction, ceremonies, formulas.
>
> Calamities and indigence were more afflicting than at present; it was more difficult to guard against them, and to find solace. Illness and health presented a more striking contrast; the cold and darkness of winter were more real evils. Honours and

riches were relished with greater avidity and contrasted more vividly with surrounding misery. We at the present day can hardly understand the keenness with which a fur coat, a good fire on the hearth, a soft bed, a glass of wine, were formerly enjoyed.[8]

This description was written in the 1920s, and Huizinga might have revised the last sentence in the light of events since 1933. Nevertheless the point stands clear that an effort of both learning and imagination is needed to appreciate human life in such a framework.

The status and power of women in the seventeenth century was controlled as much by the realization of the frailty of the human species as by any other factor. Marriage could be entered early or late, but when it came it usually meant pregnancy as a career. That eminent New Englander, John Winthrop, the man on whom, in the words of a contemporary, 'the welfare of the Plantation depends',[9] was married at seventeen and lost his first wife after ten years; during this decade she bore him six children. While the average peasant in France, male or female, rarely married before the early twenties, the upper class throughout Europe often married very young. Alice Boyle, one of the Earl of Cork's daughters, was married at thirteen; her sister Sarah was married and widowed at fourteen. The expectation of life made ideas of childhood and adolescence a very different matter from those of the twentieth century. Children were not set apart in special clothes, even when they were members of wealthy families. Schooling, even for the wealthy, was over at the age of sixteen or seventeen. The attainment of legal majority was fourteen. Louis XIII arranges a murder to make his personal rule possible when he is barely seventeen; Louis XIV holds a powerful position at the same age. We tend to think of the twentieth century as a youth-dominated century, but this only comes from our belief in an average long life. The real youth-dominated centuries were in the past because most people, 75 per cent of the population, died before the age of forty-five. Most people had nothing but youth; a quarter not even that, and another quarter only the years before twenty-one.

The importance of the family in this framework was such that the arranged marriage took place at all levels of society and constrained the freedom of choice of both sexes. The vast major-

ity of Europeans at this time lived on, with, and from the land.
The common experience was agriculture, the common society the
village. Variation was due to soil, climate, and crop conditions.
Was the terrain mountainous, as in Wales or in the Pyrrennees?
or lush green valleys, such as the Thames and the Loire? Was the
sun to be welcomed as in England and Scotland? or feared as it
dried the grasses on the shores of the Mediterranean? There were
also political differences between the villages. Was the land held
in common, as in some parts of Wales or in the Auvergne? Was it
held at the pleasure of a large landowner, as in much of England
and the Bordeaux country of France? Was it held by individuals,
as in Normandy and in Languedoc?

But however much these factors differed, and even when considerations of state and church are taken into account, there is a
foundation of similar experience that links much of Europe. For
the vast majority of people what was eaten was grown or raised,
what was worn was tanned or spun, woven or sewed, utensils
were usually locally made, and the general attitude to those not
born or raised in the area was expressed in the old Sussex saying:
'There goes a furriner! 'eave 'alf a brick at 'im!' The seasons of
the year established the pattern of work, and if many tasks were
sex-typed, many more were done by men, women, or children as
the need required. Minding flocks and herds was most often the
children's task, and milking usually fell to the women. But crop
gathering was a joint enterprise, and spinning, weaving, and sewing, tanning leather or dyeing cloth were tasks that, if done in the
family, would be taken up by either sex. Woman's status in
Europe at the opening of the seventeenth century depended on
the life of her village, one that had only minimal contact with the
larger society of the town and the far-away institutions of state
and church. The extent and impact of these contacts varied considerably, depending on whether the village was close to a trade
route, part of an important frontier area between warring jurisdic-
tions, or the centre of a supply district for a town. Essentially,
however, its life would be self-sustaining. The character and personalities of its humanity would mould the society. The community would wield enormous social pressure. The seventeenth century, with public executions, the use of the stocks, the tradition of
burning at the stake, was a century of overt social punishment for
those who broke its laws. But the pressure on the individual in its

opening decades was not, in the village society that was the life of the majority, a pressure linked to a clearly perceived and well-structured image of social convention.

The villages resembled clans, and it is possible for clans to be matriarchal. The status and power of both men and women were related more than anything else to the families to which they belonged. Character, personality, and talent were important, but as important, if not more so, was the position of one's parents. For the home could provide a trade to take into town, a skill to sell in a greater household, and the possibility of entering a family whose lives embraced wider horizons. The relationship between town-dweller and villager was a complex one at the opening of the seventeenth century, and it was in the development of this relationship that European life was to find its major revolutions during the next three hundred years. Although there are many variations, not only in the nature of towns themselves but in the nature of their connections to the surrounding countryside as well as in the nature of seventeenth-century villages, there are a number of common denominators that bring together Marseilles, the old seaport, with Rennes, a tiny inland provincial capital, and both with London, seaport and state capital.

Some of these links make common cause between town and countryside. Death was a commonplace in one as in the other. Food scarcities were almost as well known by both. For both, the family was of immense importance. Peter Laslett, in his stimulating book about the world before the Industrial Revolution, *The World We Have Lost*, points out that the family was the basic economic unit, no matter what commercial or even industrial undertaking is being considered. His chosen illustration is a bakery that employed thirteen or fourteen people: 'the baker and his wife, four paid employees, who were called journeymen, two apprentices, two maid-servants and the three or four children of the master baker himself.'[10] He goes on to analyse the situation.

The only word used at that time (1619) to describe such a group of people was 'family'. The man at the head of the group, the entrepreneur, the employer, or the manager, was then known as the master or head of the family. He was father to some of its members and in place of father to the rest. There was no sharp distinction between his domestic and his economic functions.[11]

Laslett goes on to point out that he is not describing 'a golden age of equality, tolerance or loving kindness' but a world where people could live, where there was in the general occupations of the individuals that 'extraordinarily cohesive influence which family relationships carry with them.'[12]

This is the world that W. H. Lewis catches in his book on life in the France of Louis XIV, *The Splendid Century*. The image of the family, the emotional force of the family, and the ever-present necessity of withstanding death united village and town, rich and poor, employer and employee. Not until this is fully grasped can ideas about the status and power of both men and women become understandable. It is worth quoting a passage from Lewis that illuminates the matter.

To those of us who can remember the glacial contact between employer and employed in too many English households of yesterday, it is difficult to visualize the situation of a domestic servant in seventeenth-century France. Scolded, kicked, beaten, with a liberty of speech which would not have been tolerated two hundred years later, the domestic's was a rougher but a more human life, in which it was never forgotten on either side that the servant was one of the family. To our ideas, startlingly so at times. There were few haughtier men in France than the Duc de la Rochefoucauld, but he thought nothing of sitting down to a game of chess with one of his footmen; and, more extraordinary still, his sister was married to one of the Rochefoucauld footmen, the celebrated Gourville; and the marriage, though never acknowledged openly, was an open secret both in the family and in society.

St. Simon, rather unexpectedly, speaks with approval of the Duchesse d'Orléans' chambermaid, who was 'familiar like all good old servants', and did not mince her words in reproving the duke himself when she thought he deserved it. Nor need we waste much indignation on the habit of beating servants, for it was a pleasure which it was safer to discuss than to practise; the Princesse d'Harcourt was much given to it until she engaged a new maid, a strong country girl unaccustomed to beatings, and not caring much for the novelty: 'without more ado the maid knocked her mistress down. . . . And society was so amused that the princess did not dare to seek her revenge.'[13]

One can repeat the warning of Peter Laslett: this was no golden age, but it was a period when people did not automatically slot each other into categories. It was a period when most methods of earning a living were those that involved close companionship with a small group, and in which the finished product was within sight of those engaged on every stage of its production.

But the towns were much more than merely somewhat crowded countryside. They had been built for defence, for government, for trade, for convenience. They were above all communication centres. Each town, small or large, reached into the countryside for food and reached out to other towns for trade, for politics, for religious institutions, for knowledge. It is in the towns that the lines of power, of politics, and of social conventions are most easy. to discern. It is from the towns that the political system of seventeenth-century Europe emerged. The political structures established in the sixteenth century reached out to bind the towns together. Louis XIII fought, on the advice of Richelieu, against La Rochelle not merely from Catholic piety but because it was an Atlantic port with a wide influence in the surrounding countryside. It was the independence of the Huguenot towns that exercised those trying to build a stronger centralized state in seventeenth-century France, an independence of political and judicial life rather than an independence of religious thought that made them dangerous to Louis XHI and Richelieu. The control of London was crucial to the course of the English Civil War. 'There is never a revolt but a town is the centre'—so sighed Louis XIV. Whether administrative centres, judicial centres, economic centres, artistic centres, or centres for universities, the seventeenth-century European towns were small, lived in by a miniscule percentage of the population. But they were the very arteries of the developing civilization. It was by their influence that Europe slowly turned to a more structured society. Social pressure at the opening of the seventeenth century was the powerful but diffuse pressure of the village. At the end it was the pressure of the town.

One way to look at the towns and what they reveal about seventeenth-century life is to recognize their position as centres of communication. The Canadian economist Harold Innis, whose *Bias of Communications*, first published in 1951, is the solid basis for much of the highly publicized work of Marshall McLuhan, wrote simply of an efficient way to analyse the political and cultural structure of human societies: 'Western civilization,' he wrote, 'has been profoundly influenced by communication and . . . marked changes in communications have had important implications.'[14] The way that information is moved across space and through time was, for Innis, an indication of how a society worked. For him a change from oral traditions, from a Europe of villages to a Europe of small towns, meant a change from unregulated life to one much more tightly organized. The seventeenth century, seen with this perception, is a civilization of analphabetic villages caught up by a net of literate towns. During its decades communications improved, not only because canals were built, roads were established, and brigands controlled, not only because horse-drawn streetcars appeared in Paris and the navvies of western Europe built faster, safer ships, but also because seventeenth-century Europe saw what James Cassedy has called the beginnings of the statistical mind. The political systems of France and England began enumerations of their territory on a scale that had been in abeyance since 1066, William the Conqueror, and the Doomsday survey of England. The opening of the seventeenth century was the period when Europe absorbed not only material discoveries that demanded new political ideas and machinery, overseas expansion and colonization that posed new problems of political authority, but also new ideas about humanity and the universe. What had evolved by the end of the century was a much clearer political structure capable of controlling the impact of these new forces, but in this very capability imposing upon European civilization a new rigidity.

Harold Innis considered that the alphabet and printing brought to Europe a flexibility that produced 'diverse vernacular literatures and . . . a basis for diversive nationalism.'[15] But these gifts and these developments also meant the existence of widespread discussion during the seventeenth century about the nature and the responsibilities of power, a discussion carried on throughout western Europe. In this discussion, set usually within the framework of either the Protestant or the Catholic interpretation of Christianity, argument turned on questions about the business of the state as well as upon the nature of the state and the foundation of authority in the state. It was a discussion in which the most diametrically opposed views were advanced. Louis XIV could see himself as the summation of all political power in France, whether or not he actually said 'L'état, c'est moi!' His answer to a general who questioned his orders on the grounds of Christian conscience, when these orders involved the destruction of the German-speaking towns of the Rhine in winter, was that the 'necessities of state will take the burden from you.' In other words, government orders excuse personal responsibility. One must hasten to add that this opinion of Louis XIV did not go unopposed. There is a constant tendency to tidy up the past, to forget that one is translating a multi-faceted waterfall into a frozen linear drawing. Seventeenth-century France did not end as a totalitarian state with centralized power evenly applied over a whole country and over a wide area of human action. Louis XIV did achieve an absolute monarchy, however, and made certain that standards of action and behaviour were argued in relation to the theoretically unlimited power of the Crown. In England, on the other hand, while social conventions and political institutions also increased in importance and force throughout the land, such questions were argued in relation to a Crown explicitly limited in authority. Though many of the concepts of democracy that we take for granted were more honoured in discussion than in action, the principle of human equality had been voiced, perhaps most impressively by Thomas Rainborowe during the debates of the Army at Putney, 29 October 1647: 'The poorest he that is in England hath a life to live as the greatest he.'

The seventeenth century saw the growth not only of political structures but also of theories about the power of these structures, the responsibilities of governor and governed, and the spheres of action in which government should be exercised. The question of women's status and power in these debates is as complex as the debates themselves. On the one hand status conferred by birth meant that the wives and daughters of the nobility in France attained levels of power and authority far beyond that reached by most men not so genealogically endowed. At the same time the legal rights of women were limited at the opening of the century and were to be further circumscribed at its end. In England women would petition Parliament to remind that body that 'Christ has purchased us at as deare a rate as he hath done Men. ... Women are sharers in the common calamities that accompany both Church and Commonwealth.'[16] Yet Laslett states that 'the only public appearance of women and children, almost their only expedition outside the circle of the family, was at the service in Church. Wives and maidservants might take and sell their poultry and their eggs to market, . . . but otherwise they stayed at home.'[17] In New England women had rights guaranteed in law. Puritans considered women as human, with certain inalienable rights to civil and religious liberty. Yet laws also spelt out a degree of subordination to the husband, as head of the household, that strictly limited the exercise of political rights for women.

In all this confusion several points emerge with prominence, like rocks above a water-line. The attitude of literate seventeenth-century Europeans to sex was one of curiosity, acceptance, and enjoyment. Catholic tradition had allowed the development of the idea of 'courtly love' during the Middle Ages, and this had flowered in the Renaissance to a positive valuation of body and sex. Puritan tradition considered, in the words of Winthrop's biographer, Edmund S. Morgan, that 'A man must love his wife, and she must love him. Love was a duty and hopefully a pleasure too, but it must be kept within bounds. It must never exceed or overpower or in any way diminish love for God.'[18] Such an ideal led to a consideration of marriage as a partnership dedicated to a heavenly goal. Winthrop's second wife, Margaret Tyndal, wrote him letters of tenderness and caring while bearing in mind that 'she is as much a Puritan as her husband and never forgets that he is only a man and that her biggest love must be reserved for God, who is pleased "to exercise us with one affliction after another in love, lest we should forget ourselves and love this world too much."'[19] It is necessary to emphasize this point because the vision of Eve put forward by Milton in *Paradise Lost* is far too often taken as a picture of everyday seventeenth-century life instead of merely a poet's vision. Humanity of both sexes was far too robust to be summed up by the lines:

> For contemplation he and valour formed;
> For softness she and sweet attractive grace,
> He for God only, she for God in him.[20]

If the seventeenth century was willing to consider human sexuality without too much introspection, it also tended to accord women their measure of status and power on the basis of the opportunities that their lives delivered to them. In the villages, circumstances might ensure that such opportunities were minimal, but the route of emigration was becoming more and more open to both sexes during the seventeenth century. In the life of the towns and in the circle of political power at the level of the whole country, women made their mark in both Catholic and Protestant countries. In the study she made for the Royal Commission on the Status of Women, M. W. Labarge chose as an example

> ... the royalist Ann Fanshawe, ... who lived through the Civil War. She managed the family affairs and finances, both in England and abroad, and procured her husband's deliverance from gaol after he was captured at Worcester. All of this she achieved while bearing twenty-one children—of whom only five survived during the twenty-three years of married life. ... [21]

Mrs Labarge commented on the impact of the regents in France, Marie de Medici and Anne of Austria, both of whom dominated French politics during the early life of their sons. Further she noted that 'middle-class women in France were able to exercise a certain professional activity, especially the widow who inherited the right to exercise her husband's mastership in his craft', and picked out Barbe Lequeux for special mention, the woman who had 'the title of "plumber of Paris" and was in charge of the city waterworks.'[22]

This was an era when many Europeans, both men and women, had the possibility of carving a life for themselves very different from the one into which they were born, providing only Death held his hand. The word that more than anything else summarizes the tenor of this era is 'arbitrary'. It was not a democratic age, as that word is usually understood in Canada today. Rank counted. Money counted. Birth counted. But society was not a vertical mosaic where any or all of these factors organized all citizens into an easily perceived hierarchy. Any or all of these factors might be the determinant of an individual's life, but none can be pointed out as the single barrier to influence, power, and status in society. The career of Madame de la Tour, one most important for Maritime Canada, illustrates the possibilities open to wit and good luck. Born the daughter of a barber in France in 1602, she would confront John Winthrop when he was Governor of the Commonwealth of Massachusetts, demanding justice in the courts of Boston against merchants attempting to impound her ships. She spent part of her early life as an actress, and became the second wife of the man who was one of the claimants for the governorship of what was then the French colony of Acadia, present-day Nova Scotia. She was considerably more than a decoration for his life, capable of defending his forts against his rival as well as seeing that his lodgings were comfortably furnished and bearing him at least one son.

There is a considerable difference between leading an exceptional life as Madame de la Tour did, and being an exception. The same type of energy was displayed by Celia Fiennes, granddaughter of the Viscount Saye and Sele, who came of a notable Hampshire Roundhead family. She voyaged the length and breadth of England, leaving when she died a magnificent journal of contemporary life. There was the energy of Mrs Anne Hutchinson, who challenged John Winthrop's concepts of colonial government and of religious orthodoxy. There was the energy of Marie de l'Incarnation, whose work with her religious order so benefited Quebec. There was the energy, too, of the numberless unrecorded women who helped run family farms, family businesses, and who brought up children at the same time. It is an energy that has gone largely uninvestigated by historians.

While the neglect is interesting and important, it is scarcely surprising. History is a creature of humanity, in its making and in its recording. Historians are themselves shaped and formed by the times in which they live. The lack of knowledge about the status and position of women in the seventeenth century, coupled with beliefs about their role; the willingness to believe that the lot of women has always been one of oppression, so that songs even are written talking of women's submission; the argument that present demands for women's rights are a new and vicious development, all these are not so much a comment on the past as on present-day attitudes and the need for further research. It is common knowledge that the way questions are framed affects the answers obtained. Research about the legal oppression of women in history will yield something very different from research about the legal rights of women. Richard Wright, author of *White Man Listen*, addressed himself to this problem when he wrote 'I state that emotion here precedes the idea, that attitudes select the kind of ideas in question. . . . We are human; we are slaves of our assumptions, of time and circumstance, we are victims of our passions, and...our critics can ask of us.... "Have you taken your passions, your illusions, your time and your circumstances into account?"'[23] As a university subject, an academic discipline, history evolved in the nineteenth century in Europe, when the life and influence of political élites seemed to many to be the essence of human drama. Histories dealt with kings, governments, wars, and the lives of the eminent. Only in the twentieth century, as psychology and sociology have posed new questions, both about what should be considered important for a human being and about what is important for human communities, have historians slowly begun to turn to the past with new questions about the pattern of life.

To disentangle what the words power and status meant to seventeenth-century Europe, both to men and women, means to set out questions about the economic basis of life at this time, what particular crises Europe faced, and what hierarchy of values people had in their minds and hearts when they set about solving the problems with which they were confronted. Above all it means grasping that a process was at work during this century of transforming a community into a dense culture. This is not to suggest a sudden New Age, cut off from past eras. But it is to point out that during these decades a particular tide can be seen as running with some strength. Europe in many ways was still a kaleidoscope of local customs, dominated by famine, plague, and the particular structure of local authority. But during the century states—France, Brandenburg, England—were organized, and localities coalesced into larger units in ways that meant visible government in tiny, scattered villages. At the same time these new organizations were themselves organized by observable élites. In France, for example, intendants appointed by the authority of the king and working from the centre of the country held power and status over areas on the borders, and a new tension grew between local and central government, local and central traditions, local and central rights.

· The pattern is, as always, the mingling of traditions and new ideas. The alteration that takes place is like new growth of leaves on a plant stem: the leaf is new but its life and structure comes from what already exists. Just as the new institutions were the development of old structures, linking the courts of Louis XIV with Charlemagne, tying together medieval saints with contemporary bishops, so the new conventions were built from ancient beliefs evolved from past habits. The world of Greece and Rome, the medieval world, the years of the Renaissance and the Reformation, all had rules of conduct, public manners for basic human relationships, those of parent and child, of ruler and ruled, as well as those turning specifically upon sexuality. After 1600 ruler and ruled become more and more often government and governed, with much more overt analysis of the processes of political life. At the same time there was a much greater articulation of the rules of social conduct; these were much more widely applied and much more rigorously interpreted than ever before. At the Court of Louis XIV etiquette was rigid and covered not only how you lifted your hat to a passerby but how you knocked on a door. While for the vast majority life was still the village, still the turning seasons, still landlord always and priest sometimes, still, and above all, fleeting, it was a life that was acquiring a new dimension as the century closed. The world outside the immediate community became better known, wider and of more importance for the people of the seventeenth century than it had been for their immediate ancestors.

Social pressure, from being merely the opinion of one's immediate neighbours, expanded to include, on a much greater scale than heretofore, ideas purveyed from a capital, styles developed elsewhere, fashions first born in a more crowded centre of humanity. The rural peoples of Europe were slowly being encircled by new communications, new bureaucracies, new economic demands. In 1643 peasants in Brittany and fishermen in Marseilles spoke dialects that were almost different languages. By the 1680s the idea of pure French, of a correct language to which all dialects were related, had been accepted. Louis XIV's government was a centralizing force that saw variations as a challenge and a danger. His wish for a state church, which is the essence of what is known as the Gallican controversy, is central to his concern for a state fully united that would have its citizens defined as French, visibly stamped by the mark of the country in which they lived. France would be Catholic, despite the Huguenot tradition, and Royalist Catholic, despite the long history of independence within the ranks of the French episcopacy.

Historians often call the seventeenth and eighteenth centuries the period of 'early modern Europe'. The rationale is that one can discover within these years the roots of so many ideas that become dominating beliefs in the nineteenth and twentieth centuries. Further, the actual life-style of Europe begins to undergo radical change, for these two early centuries see not only Europe's contacts with the rest of the world develop and multiply, but the occupations and living conditions of European peoples alter. The creation of modern Europe meant the development of a civilization that had little use for a splintered Christianity as a philosophy and much interest in nationalism as an ideology. It meant a culture that placed enormous emphasis upon economic status, at times equating economic worth with moral status. It also meant a civilization where definitions of masculine and feminine became enmeshed in this development of a highly structured society. New articulations about humanity turned from a common use of the words 'soul' or 'body' as neutral words to designate both men and women, to the use of words related to the male: the medieval world had talked about 'the soul's flight to God'; the eighteenth century talked about 'Man's search for the Divine'. The traditions that placed women, not so much subordinate to men as in a category that in some manner lessened their responsibility for their own lives, were developed. As Sheila Rowbotham has pointed out: 'The father reading the Bible, instructing his family, became responsible not only for their material but for their spiritual welfare. The worship of the Virgin, the reverence for female saints were replaced by stern assertions of God's fatherhood.'[24] At the end of the seventeenth century, however, the tyranny of social customs was mitigated by the uncertainties of life. It is during the eighteenth and nineteenth centuries that individual action becomes the business of public scrutiny and community judgement in a way that makes 'public opinion' a phrase that needs a new interpretation.

To use the distinction made in the first chapter, western civilization during the seventeenth century was more a matter of community than of society. The dominant factors in the lives of most people were the instant and the immediate, family and village, the passage of the seasons. Prejudice against women existed but its strength would vary from place to place. Further, the constant awareness of the brevity of life would make most other discriminations against a person of much less importance. The older one lived, the more one would have seen death—death by accident, because there was no antiseptics for wounds, death by illness because there was no cure for fevers, death by starvation because of a poor food supply, death by execution because of a harsh penal code. Life was the exception, and the organization of a society, of laws and institutions, took place slowly and gradually in this context. As the seventeenth century drew to a close, life expectancy began to alter, populations grew, and work patterns changed. As this happened western civilization began to build new forms of authority that webbed all individuals into a more general pattern. If one concedes that during the seventeenth century Europe knew a civilization that gave women considerable opportunity to govern their own lives, what is interesting is the development of discrimination against women as the new and tighter structure of life is built.

In other words, Europe in the seventeenth century contained both discrimination and prejudice against women, but it was not essentially a sexist society. It is undeniable that women were sometimes paid less than men for the same work. In Wiltshire in 1604, for example, men labourers in haymaking were given 4d a day, women 3d, and men reapers were paid 5d a day, women 3d.[25] One can find texts among Protestant divines arguing the need for complete submission of wives to their husbands, and the work by the Calvinist John Knox in the sixteenth century entitled *The First Blast of the Trumpet Against the Monstrous Regiment of Women* found considerable acceptance. But as has been shown, this is not the whole picture. Women were often both independent and valued. Fénélon in his work on the education of daughters, published in 1687, considered that women should know law in order to control their own affairs. In New France, as in France itself, women were frequently authorized to act as their husbands' representatives.[26]

For a civilization to be sexist, discrimination against men or women must be the norm within that civilization. Otherwise prejudice and discrimination against a particular sex is some part of the life of some of the people, a part that may infect the whole but is not universally accepted. By 1700 western civilization certainly included much sexist thought, and in some situations prejudice against women had become embedded in laws so that it was approaching discrimination, the institutional sanction of such prejudices. The question is less to what extent did such sexism dominate the diverse and diffuse civilization in Europe during the seventeenth century, than why such prejudices became so important during subsequent ages as to seem acceptable beliefs, normal attitudes, and the right way of organizing lives to so many people.

NOTES

[1] P. Goubert, *Louis XIV and Twenty-Million Frenchmen* (Allen Lane, 1972), p. 21.

[2] F. Braudel, *Capitalism and Material Life, 1400-1800*, Eng. trans. (Weidenfeld and Nicholson, 1973), p. 19.

[3] *Ibid.*, p. 48.

[4] *Ibid.*, p. 50.

[5] R. Preston and S. F. Wise, *Men in Arms* (Praeger, 1963), p. 129. (The book referred to by Field-Marshal Montgomery as the only sensible thing written about war.)

[6] C. V. Wedgewood, *The Thirty Years' War* (Penguin, 1957), p. 451.

[7] R. de Coccola and P. King, *Ayorama* (Oxford University Press, 1956), p. 312.

[8] J. Huizinga, *The Waning of the Middle Ages* (Penguin, 1955), p. 9.

[9] Quoted in E. S. Morgan, *The Puritan Dilemma—the Story of John Winthrop* (Little, Brown, 1958), p. 47.

[10] P. Laslett, *The World We Have Lost* (Methuen, 1965), p. 1.

[11] *Ibid.*, p. 2.

[12] *Ibid.*, p. 4.

[13] W. H. Lewis, *The Splendid Century* (Anchor Books, 1957), p. 199.

[14] H. A. Innis, *The Bias of Communications* (University of Toronto Press, 1951), p. 3.

[15] *Ibid.*, p. 55.

[16] Quoted in S. Rowbotham, *Women, Resistance, and Revolution* (Allen Lane, 1972), p. 15.

[17] Laslett, *op. cit.*, p. 77.

[18] Morgan, *op. cit.*, p. 12.

[19] *Ibid.*, p. 13.

[20] Milton, *Paradise Lost*, I, lines 293-6.

[21] M. W. Labarge, *Studies for the Royal Commission on the Status of Women* (Information Canada), no. 8, p. 15.

[22] *Ibid.*, p. 17.

[23] R. Wright, *White Man Listen*, quoted in G. Myrdal, *Asian Drama* (Twentieth-Century Fund, 1968), vol. 1, p. 7.

[24] Rowbotham, *op. cit.*, p. 26.

[25] Justice of Wiltshire, 1604. Historical Manuscripts Commission, *Report on Manuscripts in Various Collections*, vol. 1, p. 163.

[26] J. Boucher, *L'histoire de la condition juridique et sociale de la femme au Canada français* (Montreal, 1966), pp. 13-14.

Three

The Swing Door
Between the Ages

If the attempt to determine what are the important traditions in western civilization is difficult because it requires an analysis of a wide variety of beliefs, yet it is simple compared with the attempt to determine how certain ideas and attitudes became important, because the latter demands an examination of theories of cause and effect, of how change takes place, of whether events are the inevitable result of a chain of reactions or brought about by planning, or are even perhaps the child of both free action and predetermination. It is easy enough to draw a picture of change in the status and position of women in western civilization from the opening of the eighteenth century to its close. The organization of life, both at the level of the community and within the structures of society, was very different at the time that Acadia finally became Nova Scotia in 1713 from what it was when Lord Dorchester helped implement the constitution for Upper and Lower Canada in 1791. If the use of Canadian dates to define time periods is startling, perhaps it will serve as a reminder that periodization in history is artificial, for the history of peoples never really obeys datelines. While some major event—an assassination, an earthquake, the discovery of a new source of power—may make an observable change in some aspects of the life of people, revolutionary change, change that brings about a new dispensation for the majority, takes place more slowly. But change does happen. And the years bracketed by the dates 1713 and 1791 witnessed both the development of new ways of obtaining the essentials for survival—food, clothing, and shelter—and new ideas about the aim of living once these necessities had been provided.

But these decades, while a period of perceptible and measureable change, were not a period of abrupt alteration. They were really a swing door between the seventeenth century, dominated by patterns of life that had been in existence for a long while, and the coming centuries when the pace of change will so increase that it can be measured by variation between one generation and the next. The appropriate god for these years is Janus, two-faced, looking forward and back at the same time. Too much emphasis upon what is new in this period falsifies the tenor of the age quite as much as too great an emphasis on what had endured from the past. Accounts of such a period can easily mislead, particularly since the printed page describes sequentially events that in reality take place simultaneously. Historians usually solve the difficulty of dealing with the multifarious facets of the past by selecting certain aspects only. Harold Nicolson, having called his book about the years 1700 to 1789 *The Age of Reason*, wrote: 'The fact that this study deals mainly with the development of ideas should not blind the reader to the fact that the Age of Reason was also the Age of Violence.'[1] To a certain extent the title given the work guides the reader, as the title of this chapter signals the approach of the writer to this period. Max Beloff's work about the years 1648 to 1815 is called *The Age of Absolutism*, and the theme of political life is the theme of the book. Behrens' *The Ancien Régime*[2] treats the eighteenth century as a complex of traditions about social and political behaviour that ended with the collapse of France into the chaos of the Revolution in 1789. For some scholars these years are best approached as the years of music, opening with the glories of Handel and Bach, closing with the genius of Mozart. Philosophers have seen them as the Enlightenment, a development that is rooted in the works of John Locke, nurtured by Montesquieu and Voltaire, concluded with the impassioned cry of Rousseau: 'Man is born free, and everywhere he is in chains!' For many it is an age that can be summed up by an understanding of the fall of Quebec; for many more it is the century of the American Revolution.

All these approaches can be looked at with profit by those interested in the lives of women, for the study of women in history should not be isolated from the general enquiry into past human development. The study of women ought to be, as the study of men must be, in the context of what actually happened. Nevertheless, monographs and detailed studies are still needed, and in these studies areas of human experience that have been particularly, even predominently, and on occasion exclusively the lot of women should be taken as seriously as matters usually seen as male preserves—family relationships as well as the battlefields of war, private joy and grief as well as public events. Only by combining studies of both sexes will the whole span of human life eventually be understood, for it is impossible to sum up humanity on the evidence of one sex alone.

Women were involved in eighteenth-century diplomacy, whether as queens to whom envoys reported and with whom ministers consulted, or as advisers to male rulers. Those who write diplomatic history need to assess not only the plans of Louis XV but the influence of Madame de Pompadour on those plans, not merely the ambitions of Marie-Thérèse of Austria but the impact of her love for her children on those ambitions. Examination of Europe as a society called the 'ancien régime' needs to consider the status and power of women within their families. The work already done needs expansion, not destruction.

This is now generally admitted. The changes that result from the decision to acknowledge the importance of all human beings is quickly apparent when David Ogg's *Europe of the Ancien Régime, 1715-1783*, published in 1965, is compared with E. N. Williams' *The Ancien Régime in Europe, 1648-1789*, published five years later. Ogg's description of Louis XIV centres around the monarchy as machinery of government, and the characteristics of the human beings who produced and ran this machinery are barely sketched. For Williams the connection between daily life, private aims, and personal beliefs, and public decisions, political ambitions, and state concerns is so important that he spends as much time presenting the former as analysing the latter.

For example, he shows the importance of social status by describing a squabble about precedence between four women, members of the French aristocracy.[3] Two of the proponents are marquises who believe that they outrank two duchesses because the marquises think that they have a historical right for taking precedence. The marquises accuse the duchesses of wanting to go first 'in order to show off your fine clothes, which came from your father's shop', a taunt about the duchesses' origins. The duchesses, unable to defend themselves on grounds of their birth, reply: 'If we are not from such a good family as you, at least we are not whores like you', a direct reference to the well-known affaires of the two marquises. Why did Williams include this and other apparently trivial incidents in his book, particularly since the presentation of so much detail makes it difficult to comprehend the overall picture of the period he is writing about? It is because he wants to show that incidents like these, incidents that affect people in their daily lives, have an impact on them and the way they react, not only in their private lives but in their public lives too; or, to make the distinction used earlier in this book, the effect of events in the lives of people as members of the community will be carried over into their lives as members of the society—that the private attitudes of public persons are as important as their public acts. It is no wonder that many historians still cling to writing about some severely limited aspect of human activity.

Narrowly defined investigations of the past—the concentration upon the method of tax-collecting, for example, rather than upon the whole question of taxation and the relationship between government and people—are not to be scorned. They provide the bricks with which historians build. To the extent that history is a science, this is the work of the laboratory: the testing, the sifting of all available evidence to discover whether something was done or thought or said is the basic, inescapable chore of the historian. Interpretation must be founded on such work, whether carried out personally or by others. But it is this kind of basic research that is so often lacking when one seeks details of women's lives in the past, and without it conjecture becomes fantastical and argument opinionated. However the lack of specialized studies on the eighteenth century, for example on women and the law, the conditions of women as servants, the question of women as property and as property owners, does not mean that an examination of the status and power of women in the eighteenth century ought to be laid aside until such work is done. Much can be deduced from the work already completed about this century, because, since human existence requires the almost continuous connection of the two sexes, if one writes about one, the tale of the other is half-told. And unless the work of interpretation is continuously attempted, the work of research loses almost all its value—the bricks remain a pile of possibilities, evidence of knowledge waiting to be understood. If the final analysis of human experience in the eighteenth century has yet to be written, enough work has already been done to see what sorts of questions ought now to be asked, and what particular aspects of eighteenth-century life continue to exert an influence upon the twentieth-century world.*

The eighteenth century led, in the words of Williams, to 'the conception and birthpangs of the new order in which we now live.'[4] Prejudice and discrimination against women appeared only haphazardly in seventeenth-century Europe, but were more widespread and more consistently held in the eighteenth century. There are two aspects to this development. One is the alteration in daily life brought about by changes in agricultural practices and other techniques for obtaining the essentials of life. The second is the emergence of certain beliefs and ideas as the accepted mental currency of those with political and economic power. Again it makes sense to place all other human activity in the framework of the demographers' charts. For the new pattern of life and death that was slowly established in Europe during these decades gave the men and women of the eighteenth century a context for their lives that their ancestors did not have. Some say that the most dramatic change in Europe's population really developed only at the very end of the eighteenth century, that its major results were in the nineteenth century.

On purely quantitative grounds there is some justice in this argument. During the first half of the eighteenth century famine ceased to cull the villages with cyclical regularity and diseases stopped short of epidemic ravages. But the foundation for the population explosion in the early decades of the nineteenth century was laid nearly two generations earlier. In fact this growth in population, coupled with the developments in technology, has been seen by the Italian scholar, Carlo Cipolla, as paralleled by only one other event in the history of the human species. This, he considered, was discovery of agriculture somewhere between 7000 and 6000 B.C. 'The first Revolution', he said, 'transformed hunters and food-gatherers into farmers and shepherds. The second one transformed farmers and shepherds into operators of "mechanical slaves" fed with inanimate energy.'[5] We know little of the increase in population following humanity's discovery of how to grow and harvest food, but the population growth accompanying technological changes over the last two hundred years has been documented.

*In fact more work has been done in the field of women's experiences during the eighteenth century than one would suspect. In particular see Olwen Hufton, *The Poor in Eighteenth Century France*, (London, 1975).

Even at its beginnings during the eighteenth century, when the statistical mind was still in its infancy, approximate figures have been compiled. Carr-Saunders in his studies for the United National estimated Europe's population in 1750 as 140 million, and in 1800 as 187 million. In half a century the population jumped by 36 per cent. In this time Great Britain's population increased from eight million to nearly fifteen million; France's from twenty-three to twenty-eight million; Russia's from 1.7 million to 3.1 million. Or, as Bowden, Karpovich, and Usher wrote in their monumental *An Economic History of Europe since 1750*,[6] Europe moved from being fifth of the world's people to being a quarter.

It is not easy to grasp the real impact of this growth upon the people who lived through its early stages. It was a change that by its very nature took place almost imperceptibly. Infant mortality declined. Yet Dr Johnson, consoling Boswell on the loss of a child, did so with judgement shaped by the experience of the previous generation: 'to keep three out of four', he wrote, 'is more than your share.' Those who lived through the early years did not see it as it appeared to the twentieth-century historian, Ashton, who considered that the central problem of the eighteenth century 'was how to feed and clothe and employ generations of children, outnumbering by far those of any other time.'[7] But life expectancy was also very slowly increasing by a scattering of years per generation. There had always been some who had lived on, a marvel to all concerned. John Bales is reported to have died in 1706 aged 106.[8] At least one gentleman born in 1724 was able in 1815 to recount the changes in transportation he had seen: 'We used', he said, 'to bring the mine for the Dale on pack-horses . . . We used also, to take minerals on horseback all the way to Leighton, where there was plenty of wood and charcoal, and water to blow the bellow. . . . Pedlars and pack-horses were the means of locomotion and the medium of news in my day.'[9] By the end of his life railways and steam had arrived. He died in 1831, aged 107. Such people remained the exception. Even at the end of the eighteenth century old age started at fifty, and nearly three-quarters of the population had died by that age.

Compared to the trials of the seventeenth century, the eighteenth century saw fewer massive outbreaks of typhus and plague, but such outbreaks did occur. Food shortages were less serious in the eighteenth century but famine still killed in Europe.

There was no war comparable to the Thirty Years War, but armies still met, clashed, and decimated each other. Medical advances were being made, but most modern processes of antisepsis and the major anaesthetics were developed in the nineteenth century. Malthus' famous *Essay on Population*, warning of the effects of unchecked population growth, appeared in 1798. So it is not until the very end of the eighteenth century that people gained a perception of the radical changes in demography that the previous three generations had lived through. The difficulty is to convey the force of the change without misrepresenting it.

But by the end of the eighteenth century the change was evident. The population per square mile had increased. In England and Wales it had moved from 106 people per square mile in 1750 to 162 in 1800. Throughout Europe this change meant that not only were there more people, but more people living in larger groups. For as the populations grew so did the towns. London in 1700 had a population of under half a million, about the size of present-day Ottawa; by 1800 it was around the million mark, and by 1850 it was more or less the same size as present-day Montreal: 2,362,000. Even without any other alteration this basic demographic change would have altered the tenor of life. New demands were placed upon women, who were now involved in rearing the extra children. New demands were placed upon villages, as the number of people to be supported increased. The development of the towns meant new demands upon the political arrangements of the states. But these changes were not the only alterations in European life. Not only were more people settled in larger communities, but the pattern of agriculture changed, the place of industry in the economy altered, and the type and importance of commerce was transformed. At the same time more and more people became involved in the business of the state, and the state itself became active in spheres that had never before been considered to be the province of government. For example, the abuse of gin in London and other major cities, where placards read 'Drunk for a penny! Dead drunk for twopence! Drunk with straw to lie upon for threepence!' made people decide that in this area individual liberty must be curtailed. As a result the Gin Acts were introduced in England, and gave rise to a great debate in the 1730s and 1740s. These acts were the first attempt in British history to control the personal use of intoxicants, to prevent people being impaired by a drug, and they indicate that the duties of parliament were being considered from a different perspective than a hundred years earlier, when the business of parliament did not enter in this manner into people's social life.

One way of looking at the eighteenth century is to consider it as a seascape: the water itself the population; its tides, the ebb and flow of agricultural life; its currents, the pulse of industrial activity; and its weather—sunshine, wind, and rain—social, political, and intellectual activities. No single, simple linear organization of such a seascape is possible: the character of the sea is as much the result of any single one of these factors as it is of its basic make-up, people. Throughout the eighteenth century and in fact until well on in the nineteenth century the population of Europe was predominantly engaged in agriculture. But the changes that reached their height during the nineteenth century very definitely began earlier. Most of them are first noticeable in England and then found on continental Europe, although occasionally the discoveries that made the changes possible were European rather than English. New methods of crop rotation and of cattle breeding were developed in Holland, but their impact, in a radical form, was first seen in England, where they led directly to a revolution in landholding, so that land was no longer held by villagers in strips, scattered among large fields farmed in common, but was held in compact farms with fields hedged, ditched, and individually cultivated. This revolution can be traced in acts passed by parliament. In thirty-four years, between 1727 and 1760, 74,518 acres were enclosed by Acts of Parliament. In forty-one years, between 1761 and 1801, 752,150 acres were enclosed; and in forty-four years, between 1802 and 1845, 939,043 acres were enclosed.[10] On the continent of Europe agriculture was much more varied, both in the crops grown and in the ways in which land was held. Here the yield of cereal grain provides some indication of increased agricultural efficiency. Between 1500 and 1750 the yield was 6.4 grains harvested for every one sown; between 1750 and 1820 the yield rose more than ten-fold.[11] Further, all over Europe the amount of land under cultivation was increased. On the continent it was more often a matter of draining marshes and clearing woods. It has been estimated that between 1750 and 1790 the amount of arable land in France increased from nineteen million hectares to 23.9 million.[12] The change was cumulative. Better farming techniques and the greater amount of land under cultivation together produced more food, sufficient to allow the first stages of the urbanization of Europe.

The impact of these changes upon women has been looked at by a number of scholars in recent years, but one of the most stimulating approaches remains that of Ivy Pinchbeck in a work first published in 1930: *Women Workers and the Industrial Revolution, 1750-1850*. In the first two chapters she emphasized the essentially conservative nature of rural Europe, pointing out that changes came erratically, haphazardly, first to one farm in an area, then to another, taking several generations to spread. Old traditions gave way slowly before the innovations. She argued that until the end of the eighteenth century the life of the majority of Europeans outside the towns (and of course the majority of Europeans did live outside the towns at this time) depended upon a partnership of the sexes. Women in the household of a prosperous farmer were fully employed. The actual work done would vary from village to village, household to household, but as well as the purely household management, the farmer's wife usually 'had charge of the dairy—including the care of calves and pigs—the poultry, the garden, the orchard and all financial dealings connected with them.'[13] Further, 'On a smaller holding, the farmer's wife, having less assistance was more actively engaged in manual work', and this would include outdoor work. Pinchbeck quotes one report from the *Farmer's Magazine* for 1801 that said that a small occupier had 'the necessity of turning out his wife or daughter to drive the plough in the depth of winter'.[14]

The same pattern of equal participation can be seen, according to Pinchbeck, in all the myriad ranks and categories of village people. 'Among day-labourers women weeded, followed the harrow, and fed stock.'[15] For as another scholar has remarked, 'The system preceding the modern industrial regime based the family economy by the sternest necessity upon the labour of the mother and of the children of tender age as well as upon the labour of the man.'[16] In fact, as Olwen Hufton has shown in her recent work dealing in particular with France at the end of the eighteenth century, the worse the circumstances of a family, the more certain would be the work demanded from women.[17] While their presence in some areas of life may have been the exception, it was an exception not seen as an affront to custom but one acceptable because sex, after all, was neither the sole nor necessarily the most important characteristic of a human being.

But, as Pinchbeck went on to say, 'the second half of the eighteenth century saw the speeding up of those economic changes destined to sweep away the rural organization that had existed for centuries and to substitute the modern system of the large farm and the landless labourer.'[18] The immediate result of the larger farms was greater leisure for the women living on them. For, as G. E. and K. R. Russell have pointed out in their history of the English countrywoman, the new farms were grain and cattle farms, with no interest in dairies and in poultry. And at the same time as the agricultural revolution developed, ready-made cloth and the facilities for having it sewed or tailored became available. This meant that 'the richer farmers' wives were relieved at one stroke from the farm work that had been their mother's province, from the weekly visit to market to sell the produce of that work, and from the domestic tasks of spinning and clothes-making that had employed her mother's and grand-mother's indoor hours.'[19]

For one section of the rural population, then, large farms often meant new-found leisure, and this leisure led to demands for a particular type of education. Daughters of wealthy farmers required schooling in 'polite letter writing, and a smattering of French, history, geography, needlework, music and dancing.'[20] Schooling, in other words, that was expressly designed for a life apart from the management of a farm. The ideas of Fénélon in the previous century—that women should be educated for an independent life and taught how to manage money and its affairs —were ignored. Hannah More, an eighteenth-century author, remarked that the girls returned from school 'with a large portion of vanity grafted on their native ignorance, laughed at their parents' rustic manners ... and despised and ridiculed every home-bred girl in their native village.'[21] While only a few women had this experience, nevertheless their impact was considerable, for they set an example in the villages of social behaviour, that is to say of the manners and customs considered correct for people of a certain standing, although these manners and customs had little or nothing to do with the everyday life of the countryside. This trend in the countryside—to divorce women from the toil of the farm wherever possible and to educate them for leisure—encouraged the idea of women as incompetent and set apart from the serious business of life.

This alteration in life style affected primarily the lives of the wealthy, and the business of the smaller farms was carried on in the old way with the wife and daughters fully involved in its operation. But the agricultural revolution meant the decline of the small independent farmer, as *The Village Labourer*[22] showed so well, and the country population developed into large farmers and landless labourers. The enclosure of common lands, the removal of land that had been available to all villagers for pasture and fuel gathering, meant that the poorer country people found it less and less possible to manage. The Russells suggest that by the end of the eighteenth century 'in the south of England the cottagers were reduced to a diet of bread and tea.'[23] Without free fuel they frequently had no way of heating an oven, and this meant recourse to a village baker. But if baking was not done at home, the women would be able to take work outside, often at the home of the large landowner, now able to afford help for his wife. The contrast in life styles between the well-to-do and the poor became much more obvious than in a previous generation, when the farmer's wife had had responsibilities similar to those of the labourer's wife, if on a grander scale. Both women would have had responsibility for the poultry; very often the labourer's wife would have had a cow to look after, the farmer's wife a much larger dairy; and both would have had to provide clothes for the family by making the cloth and then sewing it.

So the gradual changes brought about by the agricultural revolution during its early stages meant that the image of women in rural areas began to alter. But the agricultural revolution cannot be considered in isolation: not only was the demography of Europe changing at the same time, but it was accompanied by the beginnings of the industrial revolution. Once more England led the way, but the rest of Europe experienced similar changes. The French economic historian Braudel calls the eighteenth century the time of 'revolutions and delays', since over and over again changes in industry and commerce were halted by difficulties of transport, of developing technological inventions, of finding capital. He points out that 'Newcomen's steam machine was invented in 1711. Only one was in operation in England thirty years later, in 1742; on the continent two had been assembled. Success came in the following thirty years: sixty machines were built in Cornwall to drain water from the tin mines. Nevertheless only five were in use for iron smelting in France at the end of the eighteenth century.'[24] Or, as another historian notes, 'The first Watt steam engine was installed in a German factory only in 1785. By 1790 when Britain possessed about two hundred factories for the spinning of cotton thread, there were only eight in France, all of them using British machinery.'[25] Even if in 1800 life over considerable areas of Europe was still as it had been for centuries, nevertheless 'there were important metal-working industries in parts of the Austrian Netherlands and western Germany, large linen and woollen industries in Silesia and Bohemia, a considerable cotton spinning industry developed in Catalonia.'[26]

The quantitative effect of the industrial revolution in the eighteenth century was small, but its potential impact was great. The new machines often meant that work that had been done in homes in the countryside was now carried out in factories in towns and cities. As Pinchbeck has noted, until the arrival of Arkwright's frame in 1773, 'the cotton industry was carried on entirely on domestic lines.'[27] Over the next sixty years Arkwright's invention and other machines helped to move cleaning, carding, roving, and spinning from the cottage to the factory, and spinning itself, 'for so many centuries a woman's industry was . . . performed by a class of skilled workmen on complicated machinery.'[28] This change in the world of work meant a very different type of life for women, for the fact that it caused them to move out of the home to a factory environment, coupled with the necessity of raising their children, faced many of them with difficult choices: should the mother work? Could the family survive economically without her work? How long could the family survive without the labour of the children? But the additional change in the role of women in the world of work implied by their exclusion from certain jobs meant a fundamental reorganization of the status of women generally.

The industrial revolution did not merely change the lives of the labouring classes, it also affected the wealthy. The emergent urban middle class, which did not need to have their women work, encouraged women to spend their lives in leisure activities, entirely separate from the world of work, which was the major preoccupation of the men. The question of what these women

Carding, sorting, and roving. *Courtesy Science Museum, London.*

Power-loom weaving. *Courtesy Science Museum, London.*

Workers at an iron works in South Wales, 1865.

Old lady with baby, 1877.

Housekeeper and domestic servants, 1886.

were to do with their lives, and what was considered the correct behaviour for them, was based on an idea of 'quality', a belief that there were leaders in society who made the rules for social conduct. The notion of class in this sense is part of the life of most of the countries of Europe by the middle of the eighteenth century. One writer noted in 1747 that in theatre-going 'we have ... three different and distinct Classes; the first is called the *Boxes*, where there is one peculiar to the King and the Royal Family, and the rest for the Persons of Quality, and for Ladies and Gentlemen of the highest Rank, unless some Fools that have more Wit than Money, or perhaps more Impudence than both, crowd in among them. The second is call'd the *Pit*, where sit the *Judges, Wits*, and Censurers ... in common with these sit the *Squires, Shapers, Beaus, Bullies*, and *Whores* ... The third is distinguished by the Title of the *Middle Gallery*, where the Citizens Wives and Daughters, together with the *Abigails*, Serving-men, Journey-men and Apprentices commonly take their places ....'[29] There was a tendency among the newly wealthy to model their lives on what they considered the lives of 'quality' to be.

In the eighteenth century many women of rank were still intent on leading independent lives—the Marchioness of Salisbury and Lady Melbourne, for example, who managed farms in Hertfordshire.[30] But the idea that women ought to be given a life of leisure without the responsibilities of work gained ground, particularly because the eighteenth century also saw the beginnings of yet one more revolution—that of communications: better roads, improved canals, and above all an increase in newspapers and books. The sheer increase of paper made in England alone is worth considering. At the opening of the eighteenth century England had 150 mills; by the end of the century there were 500 mills and their output had increased enormously.[31] With this improvement in communications ideas about social behaviour were able to reach a much greater number of people over a much wider area. The pronouncements of the court of Louis XIV about morals and general behaviour had affected a very small proportion of the population of France, those in attendance at the court itself, their family, friends, acquaintances, and servants. The structure of Europe, with small towns acting as centres of communication and control for the surrounding villages, had allowed if not actually encouraged a wide variety of acceptable standards of behaviour—social manners, questions of taste in music and literature, political and religious beliefs were all very much matters of local interpretation. By the time of Louis XVI, not quite half a century later, there is not only a hardening of attitudes about what is acceptable but an extension of such judgements to a wider sphere of human activity. Styles of dress, styles of life, and occupations were now subject not merely to neighbourly interest but looked at by people in the light of ideas about what proper conduct should be for someone of a particular background in a particular situation. For example, although peasant dress was still worn in Brittany, Paris fashions had already filtered down to people living in the local towns, and were seen and gradually being acquired by the peasants. This is not to deny the existence of community pressure before the eighteenth century. The bitter tyrannies of isolated villages could be both cruel and effective. But local customs would now confront a much more organized pressure of judgements made by people centred in a capital city. The disorganized, arbitrary nature of much of seventeenth-century western life and the predominantly self-regulating villages were being transformed into a tightly knit structure by the end of the eighteenth century.

But while the eighteenth century experienced one change after another, the new structure was little more than a scaffolding and its development was, as Braudel pointed out, a matter of half measures. Like the erosion of land by the sea, like the advance of the desert into grassland, this process moulded its own channels, completely over-running some parts of the previous order while leaving others relatively unchanged, moving along the line at its own chosen speed. The massive and relatively slow nature of this change makes it difficult to summarize, but the life of an Acadian woman, born in a tiny village on the shores of the Bay of Fundy and guillotined in her eighties in a village on the Atlantic coast of France, reveals some of the more powerful currents in this tide.

Her name was Anne and she was born in 1713, the eldest daughter of Antoine LePrince and Anne Trahan. She was an Acadian, a descendant of those Europeans who had first come to the Bay of Fundy during the seventeenth century. French-speaking and Catholic, the Acadians had nevertheless known both English rule and English migrants. The village in which Anne lived with her family was Pisiquit, and the lands that surrounded it were still called in international treaties 'Acadie or

Nova Scotia', territory divided up today between New Brunswick, Nova Scotia, southern Quebec, and northeastern Maine. The treaty signed in the year of Anne's birth brought these lands into the British Empire; during the previous four decades, since the Treaty of Breda, 1668, France had held the legal title to them. But the impact of England and France upon the colony's daily life was of comparatively little moment in the everyday concerns of the Acadians. Numbering about three thousand as the eighteenth century opened, used to being claimed as a colony both by the French and by the English, the Acadians' lives were bound up by farming, fishing, hunting, and smuggling.

There are no records of Anne's early life, and the first documents that mention her are those recording her marriage to Sylvain Leblanc, a man six years younger than herself, in the neighbouring village of Grand Pré, close to Pisiquit. Such a marriage, linking two villages, was typical of Acadian communities. Each village was not only a related entity in itself but connected to the next by all sorts of kinship lines.[32] As the Acadians settled their lands they developed into a clan, and the leading citizens in one community, such as Annapolis Royal, would have grandchildren in the next. The Acadians' marriage patterns were as extended as possible, given the limitations of a small group. As one traveller noted at the opening of the eighteenth century: 'No lines of social feeling bar the paths of those who wish to marry: daughters of the wealthy marry sons of the poor ....'[33] This traveller also noted something else: 'The work they do tire themselves with is breeding vast quantities of children.' Two neighbouring couples had respectively eighteen and twenty-two children. This characteristic was particularly evident during the early years of Anne's life, when the population more than doubled by natural increase: in 1710 the Acadians numbered under three thousand, and in 1748 more than nine thousand.

Two factors contributed to this growth: the abundance of food and the relative absence of disease. Agriculture was not only successful enough to provide for the local people, but at times both cattle and grain were exported. The Acadians supplemented their diet by game and fish. Epidemic diseases were rare, partly because of the relative scarcity of contacts between Acadians and potential carriers. Shelter and clothing were adequate, although neither particularly impressed the occasional visitor. To maintain their life style the Acadians worked much in the manner of modern-day peasant communities. The family was the basic unit of social organization, providing the labour on the farm, organizing relations between individuals and the village community, assuming responsibility for the aged as well as the young. The villages themselves often set about tasks as a unit, whether this was the complex use of dykes for flooding the land for fertilization, or the building of houses for those about to be married. There was a certain amount of division of labour by sex: the hunting was mostly done by men, and tasks involving spinning, weaving, dyeing, and sewing mostly by women. As important as such a division, however, was the fact that the work of the community involved both men and women equally.

Further, lines of power among the Acadians themselves were based on kinship, and were very different from the relations between the Acadians and the British or French. Kinship had meant the development of both matriarchal and patriarchal families. Marie Magdalen Maisonat, for example, the mother of five daughters, informed a British officer in 1720 that she was as just as good a subject of King George as he. Her influence throughout the colony was considerable, and one historian wrote that 'Soldiers arrested for breach of discipline often pleaded that they had been sent for to finish a job of work for Madame; and this excuse was usually sufficient to secure an acquittal.'[34] The extent to which women could develop at least as much as men among the Acadians was revealed in the 1750s, when the majority of the community was deported and scattered in exile through the British North American colonies, the Caribbean, and Europe. At the time of the marriage of Anne LePrince to Sylvain Leblanc, however, these events were some years in the future. The first intimations that the lives of the couple would be affected by events outside their village came in 1744, less than a year after their marriage. That was the year when the rivalry between England and France involved their North American colonies in formal hostilities. War reached from the French positions of Louisbourg and Quebec through to the British establishment among the Acadians, and the village of Grand Pré attempted to preserve a neutrality while visited by soldiers of both armies.

In 1748 the treaty of Aix-la-Chapelle imposed a truce; it was the year of the birth of Anne's daughter Marguerite. Anne's own birth had seen 'Acadie or Nova Scotia' defined as a British colony by international agreement. Her daughter's saw that same colony recognized, in the words of one of the men who negotiated in 1748, as 'the most important point to be Determin'd for settling the same Tranquillity in America as had been so happily established in Europe.'[35] Unhappily for the Acadians, Nova Scotia was a frontier of New England and the border of New France. For Massachusetts it was a place of questionable security that ought to be strengthened for the defence of the British in North America against French encroachments. For the people of New France it was a passage-way between Quebec and Louisbourg and Isle Royale that was held by their enemies and lived in by those who ought to be their friends. For the Acadians themselves it was home, it was life, it was family, and their policy was neutrality. During the 1740s this neutrality was recognized as a decisive factor by both French and English, and Mascarene, who was the lieutenant-governor of the British colony, wrote to his superiors that he had 'done all in my power to keep the French inhabitants in their fidelity who promise fair and as yet assist us in repairing our breaches.'[36] He considered that little more could be demanded of them, certainly not outright aid in fighting. He thought their situation parlous because 'those who pretend to be their Friends and old Masters have let loose a parcell of Banditti to plunder them, whilst on the other hand they see themselves threatened with ruin and Destruction if they fail in their allegiance to the British government.'[37] The French officers, defending their lack of success in capturing the province during these same years, remarked that it was because of Acadian neutrality that their efforts failed.[38] Once the negotiations of Aix-la-Chapelle were concluded, the Acadians hoped that their lives would be allowed to return to peaceful paths. But neither England nor France considered that the settlement arrived at was more than an uneasy armistice. Seven years later, in 1755, renewed hostilities between the great powers led the lieutenant-governor in charge of the British colony of Nova Scotia to set about the deportation of its French-speaking Catholic inhabitants, the Acadians.

As a result of these events Anne and her husband arrived in Liverpool, England, in 1756. They had been part of a group originally sent to Virginia, but that colony had reasoned that if

Acadians were a danger to Nova Scotia they would be no less a threat to a colony further south, and had despatched them across the Atlantic. Sylvain died that year in Liverpool and Anne found herself in exile, widowed, and with a very young child, Anastasie. She remained in England until 1764. The signing of the Peace of Paris that year paved the way for those Acadians who had reached England to go to the Atlantic ports of France. By the mid-1760s there were about two thousand such exiles scattered throughout Normandy, Brittany, the shores of the Charente-Maritime, and as far south as Bordeaux. Their lives over the next twenty years provide example after example of the differences between Acadian and French societies, and also show the pattern built by French government officials as they went about structuring a French state among the French people.

The Acadians had been used to a most comfortable physical existence; now, in Brittany, they complained about the lack of meat and milk, wanted wood to build houses, and scorned the local cider. The Acadians had been used to making their clothes to their own taste; now they found matters of fashion something to consider if they wished to blend with their new surroundings. The Acadians had farmed, fished, hunted, and turned their hands to carpentry and cloth-making as need drove and choice dictated; now they were members of communities where specialization had already put down long roots. Jean Babin, for example, tried to combine life as a merchant sailor with the working of a farm. He was brought before the courts for neglecting his land, even though his relatives were working it for him. The Acadians had been used to deciding important matters in village discussions; now they faced French officials who regarded such action as tantamount to base ingratitude, dangerous republicanism, and treason. The Acadians had been used to travelling the length and breadth of their lands with little difficulty; now they ran into demands for passports when trying to go from Bordeaux to La Rochelle, Nantes to St Malo, in search of relatives. In sum, the Acadians had lived in considerable independence, and politics had meant discussion between themselves on matters where they had local autonomy, and discussion and negotiation with the powers external to the community. Now they were beset by law and government to a degree they had never before experienced.

At one point, when French officials proposed the organization of all the exiles in four villages on Belle Ile just south of Brittany, they received the reply: 'On va discuter ça avec les chefs de notre nation.' Outraged, the French replied: 'il n'y a qu'une nation—c'est la France.'[39] The two groups misunderstood each other for twenty years before the Acadians left, with Spanish help, for Louisiana.

During the intervening decades the Acadians, men and women, complained and complained, writing to anybody they thought might render their lives more bearable. Old ladies wrote to the government officials asking for pensions. Young girls wrote asking for help in finding work. The exiles, as a group, criticized both the attempt to establish them on Belle Ile and a later attempt to settle them near Poitiers. There was some intermarriage between Acadian and French, but these couples were almost always brought into the Acadian group. This was true whether the Acadian partner was male or female. As a result, in 1785, when the exiles gathered themselves together to leave for New Orleans by way of Nantes, there was an acrimonious discussion. The French were willing to see French wives follow their husbands but not French husbands follow their wives.

Such discrimination struck at a fundamental strength of the Acadian community. Women had not been considered solely as wives, daughters, sisters, but as people with some individuality. When the French had set about listing the Acadian exiles in 1767, women as well as men came forward to testify as the elder of the family.[40] Acadians searched for sisters as well as brothers, and women as well as men initiated enquiries.[41] The strength of kin was the basis of the Acadian ability to survive in exile, and this strength was founded on recognizing maternal as well as paternal relationships, the call of sibling of either sex. While Acadian delegates to meetings with either French or English officials were male, decisions about policies had been matters for the community as a whole, discussed in the homes and villages. There women had the opportunity to speak as well as men. While the Acadians were officially Catholic, their religious practices were sustained by visiting priests as much as by priests in residence, so that even the religious influence was by no means overwhelmingly a matter of male prerogative. In sum, the Acadian communities had not institutionalized sexual discrimination against women in any major aspect of their life, except in the area of Acadian representation to other communities.*

Such was not the case in France by that period. While that country still allowed individual women, by virtue of hereditary rank, economic power, or intellectual ability, access to political and social leadership, it was becoming clear that both in government matters and the organization of daily life the place of women was being defined as something less free than the place of men. It must be borne in mind that France during the 1780s was an extraordinarily varied society and one cannot yet draw rigid lines to delimit the rights of women as opposed to those of men. But the work of structuring the nation-state of France, begun by Richelieu and continued by French monarchs and their ministers ever since, had resulted in a growing number of clear-cut controls over individuals. While such controls included the limitation of the rights of men, very often they also made a more drastic limitation of the rights of women. When Acadian confronted French official over what was seen by the former as a matter of family, a right of community, that same issue was seen by the latter as a matter of the state and of the obligations of the individual. The Acadians had farming, fishing, hunting, trading as their basic occupations, and their traditions were rooted in a society whose life was extremely simple, demanding little regulation for its orderly process. France had been developing a much more complex political structure, and the French moved in a society presenting problems of colonial administration and industrial development, of government and provincial bureaucracies, of widespread commercial enterprises and the growth of luxury. In giving France the structure necessary to develop in this manner, the leaders of France brought about a change in the importance of constitutional organization, of the written law, and of decisions made by administrators on behalf of the people, male or female, adult or child. By the end of the eighteenth century, on the eve of the French Revolution, France had woven together something approaching the bureaucracy of a modern state and, as a result, made the people in the provinces subject to the control of the

---

*This is written this way in order to leave comment about Acadian-Indian relations unrestricted, a subject that has suffered a great deal from the prejudices about white-Indian relations and on which a great deal of work needs to be done.

central government in a way that Louis XIV had dreamed about but never achieved.

But while the growth of restrictions upon a population can be explained by the development of a complex civilization, the question of why the rights of women were so often circumscribed more closely than those of men still remains to be answered. This question will be considered in more detail in the next two chapters. For present purposes suffice it to say that in the case of the Acadian exiles, the Acadian women won the right to be accompanied by their French husbands, but only because of the persuasive force of Spain, which paid the cost of the transportation (and indemnified the French government). The majority of the exiles left in 1785 by way of Nantes for New Orleans. Anne LePrince was seventy-two that year and she, her daughter Anastasie, and her great-niece, Marie-Modeste, stayed behind in Morlaix on the coast of Brittany. A scattered handful of Acadians chose not to cross the Atlantic one more time, and in one account of these years of her life Anne LePrince is spoken of as their 'Doyenne'.[42] She lived on a pension from the government of Louis XVI and additional resources obtained by knitting. When the Revolution broke out in 1789 she stayed where she was and continued to have her pension paid by various revolutionary government agencies until 1794.

That year, late in the evening of 19 June, the Abbé Le Clec'h arrived at her door asking for shelter. He was a priest who on 6 February 1791 had refused to take the oath demanded of the clergy by the civil constitution, and his action, while in accordance with the directives of the Pope, placed him at odds with the civil authorities. On 26 August 1792 the penalties for those priests who acted as had the abbé were increased. Those who refused the oath were to leave the country within fifteen days or suffer the consequences. It was now 1794 and Le Clec'h had finally come to the conclusion that flight would be best. In attempting to leave by boat for England he met with high seas and bad weather. Now he asked for help, food, and a hiding place until he could set out again. Anne Le Prince and her household set about providing refuge for the fugitive, but on the next day the municipal authorities discovered what was afoot. All four were arrested and sent to Brest, where they arrived on 23 June. On 1 July at 8 o'clock in the morning they appeared before the Revolutionary Tribunal, and

Anne and her daughter as well as the priest were condemned to death. At twelve o'clock that same day all three were executed: Marie-Modeste was released, no proof being given that she was an accomplice.

Thus ended a life begun eighty-one years before in a tiny village across the Atlantic. Anne had been born in 1713 into a community whose people thought they were almost entirely self-regulating. The impact of great powers, the policies of England and France, were questions of moment for the Acadians but not the most important questions of their existence. The demands of the British officials that the Acadians swear an oath of loyalty to King George, the demands of the French officials that the Acadians demonstrate their attachment to King Louis, these matters were seen by the Acadians not as peremptory demands carrying inescapable consequences but as matters for debate. In this context Anne's life could not be called more than exceptional: the idea of normalcy and of conventionality were not yet defined. But her death was conventional, that is to say it was something brought about by state policies, something sanctioned by a sense of social propriety within the community in which it occurred. That summer of 1794 the guillotine was used in France as a means of underlining social acceptance of political actions, not merely as an appropriate punishment for criminal deeds.

Anne's life both in time and in experience moved through those crucial decades when western civilization began the formalization of life to a hitherto unparalleled degree. Not merely certain aspects of it, such as religious belief, not merely certain groups of persons within it, such as nobles, courtiers, town-dwellers, guildsmen, and the like, but the whole panoply of existence was to be subject to new modes of organization and a new social judgement. Innis considered that the change was based on a shift in the forms of communication, and in fact thought the improvement of communication the parent of the new age. 'The Industrial Revolution', he wrote, 'followed the printing industry.' Another writer looked at the matter in much the same way but emphasized another aspect. Raymond Williams opened *Culture and Society, 1780-1950* by commenting that he had organized his writing with 'the discovery that the idea of culture, and the word itself in its general modern uses, came into English thinking in the period which we commonly describe as that of the Industrial Revolution.' What both are describing is the arrival of a new force in the lives of the majority, that of the nation-state with its bureaucracy, its ideologies, and its administration. To what extent this new organization was biased against women, to what extent it enshrined the rights of one half of the human race rather than those of all humans, and for what reasons, are the issues of the next chapters.

NOTES

[1] H. Nicholson, *The Age of Reason* (Panther, 1968), p. 19.

[2] M. Beloff; *The Age of Absolutism* (Hutchinson, 1966); C. B. Behrens, *The Ancien Régime* (Thames and Hudson, 1967).

[3] E. N. Williams, *The Ancien Régime in Europe, 1648-1789* (Penguin, 1972), p. 203.

[4] *Ibid.*, p. 18.

[5] C. Cipolla, *The Economic History of World Population* (Penguin, 1962), p. 31.

[6] W. Bowden, M. Karpovich, and D. Usher, *An Economic History of Europe since 1750* (Fergis, 1937).

[7] T. S. Ashton, *Economic History of England: the Eighteenth Century* (Methuen, 1955), p. 101.

[8] *Daily Courant*, 9 April 1706; quoted in A. Briggs, *How They Lived: 1700-1815* (Blackwell, 1969), vol. III, p. 22.

[9] Randall, *History of Mandeley*, quoted in Briggs, *op. cit.*, p. 22.

[10] Bowden, Karpovich, and Usher, *op. cit.*, p. 149.

[11] F. Braudel, *Capitalism and Material Life, 1400-1800*, Eng. trans. (Weidenfeld and Nicholson, 1973), p. 8.

[12] W. Abel, *Crises agraires en Europe XII-XX siècles*, ed. fr. (1973), p. 284.

[13] I. Pinchbeck, *Women Workers and the Industrial Revolution, 1750-1850* (Cass, 1969), p. 8.

[14] *Ibid.*, p. 9.

[15] *Ibid.*, p. 16.

[16] W. Bowden, *Industrial Society in England towards the end of the Eighteenth Century* (1925), p. 229; quoted in E. Richards, 'Women in the British Economy since 1700: An Interpretation', *History*, vol. 59 (Oct. 1974), 340.

[17] O. Hufton, *The Poor of Eighteenth Century France, 1750-1889* (Oxford University Press, 1974).

[18] Pinchbeck, *op. cit.*, p. 27.

[19] G. E. and K. R. Russell, *The English Countrywoman, a Farmhouse Social History, A.D. 1500 to 1900* (Melrose, 1953), p. 137.

[20] *Ibid.*, p. 138.

[21] *Ibid.*, p. 139.

[22] J. L. and B. Hammond, *The Village Labourer, 1760-1832* (Kelley, 1913).

[23] Russell, *op. cit.*, p. 147.

[24] Braudel, *op. cit.*, p. 323.

[25] M. Anderson, *Europe in the Eighteenth Century, 1713-1789* (Oxford University Press, 1966), p. 72.

[26] *Ibid.*

[27] Pinchbeck, *op. cit.*, p. 112.

[28] *Ibid.*, p. 117.

[29] *The Tricks of the Town Laid Open*, quoted in Briggs, *op. cit.*, vol. 3, p. 230.

[30] Russell, *op. cit.*, p. 136.

[31] H. A. Innis, *The Bias of Communications* (University of Toronto Press, 1964), 2nd ed., p. 42.

[32] The shortest available source about these people is N. E. S. Griffiths, *The Acadians: Creation of a People* (McGraw-Hill, 1973).

[33] Diereville, *Relation du Voyage du Port Royal de l'Acadie ou de la novelle France* (Champlain Society, 1968), pp. 72, 78.

[34] A. Doughty, *The Acadian Exiles* (Toronto, 1920), p. 39.

[35] Quoted in L. H. Gipson, *The British Empire before the American Revolution* (Knopf, 1958), vol. V, p. 304.

[36] Mascarene to Governor Philipps, 9 June 1744; printed in *Collection des Documents Inédits sur le Canada et l'Amérique* (1889), p. 80.

[37] Mascarene to Governor Shirley, 28 July 1744; *ibid.*, p. 81.

[38] De Gannes to the Minister for the Colonies, 28 Nov. 1744; PAC, Correspondence, Ile Royale.

[39] E. Martin, *Evangéline et la suite merveilleuse d'un poème* (n.p., n.d.).

[40] Declarations printed in M.P. and N. G. Rieder, *The Acadians in France* (Metairie, 1972), vol. II.

[41] Advertisements in the Gazettes of newspapers of the colonies; *c.f.* Boston *Weekly Newsletter*, March 1756.

[42] Noted in an unpublished account of her life compiled by the archivist of Rennes, Ile et Vilaine, France, c. 1850, and preserved there.

Four
Stereotypes and Politics

It is easy to write about past events as if they were always the product of deliberate intent. Because what's done *is* done it seems, after the event, probable that the result obtained was specifically desired. From the standpoint of the twentieth century, the organization of western civilization over the last two hundred years so that women as a group were placed at a disadvantage seems to have been brought about by deliberate, malicious plot. A closer look however shows that the impact of chance, ignorance, and short-sightedness were as much to blame as any other factor. What needs to be distinguished is the gradual process of actual events as opposed to the rationalizations provided to defend the process after it has occurred. There is no doubt about the growth of discrimination against women in the last two hundred or so years, but it is not a growth that has much internal cohesion, nor has it ever gone unchallenged both by men and women, and, of course, it is by no means the sole example of unfair discrimination among human beings during these years.

Prejudice against women did not appear for the first time during the eighteenth century. St Augustine, writing at the end of the third century, considered that 'woman herself alone is not the image of God; whereas the man alone is the image of God as fully and completely as when woman is joined with him.'[1] One can find example after example of such attitudes in the records left to us from the past. Yet at the same time there is also a heritage of opinions about the humanity of women and example after example of women whose lives were independent and influential. While Christian theology can be used to support beliefs in women's inferiority, the cry of the Puritan women in seventeenth-century England, 'Christ has purchased us at as deare a rate as He has done Men . . . '[2], was usually accepted. The great religious orders for women, from Benedictine through Franciscan and Carmelite to the Sisters of Mercy, the women accorded saint-hood by the Catholic Church, from St Monica who endured so much from her son St Augustine, through St Clare to that adviser of the Papacy, St Catherine of Siena, and that rare doctor of the Church, St Teresa of Avila, as well as the prominence accorded Mary, Mother of God—all helped to provide images of women that denied grounds for their oppression. As Mary Beard has shown in *Women as Force in History*, an examination of the laws in the Middle Ages in France shows conclusively that legally 'the subjection of women has been no general rule.'[3] 'The weight of documentary evidence is against any simple conclusion that men handed women around like chattels; that boys were free to make their own choices of mates, while girls were helpless creatures at the disposition of men.'[4] While some laws, especially in the field of sexual morality, discriminated against women, and while preju-dice against women can easily be documented, western civiliza-tion before the end of the eighteenth century did not accept the inferiority of women as unquestioned, nor was it enshrined auto-matically in custom, law, and action.

There is no doubt that ideas about women as the weaker sex and to be guarded against have almost always been present among western European people, but so have images of women as man's superior, as his guide, and as his partner. Human beings, as Peter Berger writes, have 'no species-specific environment, no environment firmly structured by . . . instinctual organization,'[5] and as a result they set about composing their own. This has led to an infinity of communities, as the basic needs of human beings are met in different ways. For, as J. A. C. Brown commented, when we discuss needs such as sex, hunger, sleep, and thirst, we explain why 'people initiate certain actions (why they want to eat, or drink, or obtain sexual satisfaction),' but we do not explain 'how they do these things, why they sometimes do them when they do not wish to, or do not do them when they do wish to. That people possess certain needs is a biological fact: how they are satisfied is a social or cultural fact.'[6] In social and cultural developments, which are both the definition and the despair of human beings, their glory and their curse, sexuality has been of overwhelming consequence; essential for the continuance of the species and momentous for the individual, all communities have surrounded it with their own concept of right action and conduct.

By the eighteenth century western Europe had acquired a wide variety of traditions for coping with this aspect of humanity. The most firmly rooted and widespread of these traditions ordained monogamy in marriage and celibacy for those who did not choose to bind themselves in this manner. Sexuality was to be channelled through family life, and penalties could be severe for people of either sex who were caught breaking these rules. Franz Schmidt, the public executioner of Nuremberg from 1573 to 1617, kept a diary. In the summer of 1584 he wrote that 'Anna Peyelstainin of Nuremberg, alias Moser Annala, because she had carnal intercourse with a father and son (who themselves both had wives, she having a husband) and similarly with twenty-one men and youths, her husband conniving: was beheaded here with a sword. Her husband, called Jeromes Peyelstain [sic] was whipped out of town.'[7] On 23 June 1612 he noted that 'Andrew Feuerstein, who kept a school with his father; debauched sixteen school girls. Beheaded as a favor instead of being hanged.'[8] Such scattered documentation does little but offer proof that penalties could indeed be severe for people of both sexes. But in many cases people's actions were not brought to public notice, or even when they were public knowledge, were not challenged. The sexual misdeeds of monarchs and aristocrats, for example, were rarely punished. In many localities, too, spring festivals or mid-winter celebrations were occasions for a general relaxation of sexual prohibitions without formal repercussions. Nevertheless by the seventeenth century the western idea of family was entrenched in Europe.

This did not, of itself, mean discrimination against women. As Mary Beard has pointed out, male heirs as well as female were considered negotiable assets during many centuries of English life. She quotes as an example: 'Ralph of Normanville offers [to the king—Henry III] one good destrier [war-horse] to have the land in his fee which belonged to Richard Labbe in Empingham with [the right to control] the marriage of the son and heir of the same Richard ... '[9] She also offers an example that shows the limitation of choice in marriage placed upon both sexes: 'Henry de Redeman offers forty marks to have the custody of the land and heir of Roger de Hedon and to have the marriage of the same heir to the use of his daughter.'[10] As was reported in a paper at the Canadian Historical Association meetings in Toronto in 1974, the marriage practices of the Italian cities during the thirteenth and fourteenth centuries made considerable provision for the continued control by the woman of the monies brought as dowry to her husband. There can be no doubt that during these centuries, from approximately the twelfth to the seventeenth, women were allowed to conduct all sorts of business. In fact during the period of the Crusades the number of women who remained behind and controlled huge estates while the men departed for several years at a time to foreign lands is considerable. When one considers that such distances, London to Jerusalem for example, meant the virtual absence of any form of continued advice and instruction, the position of the wife can be seen as one of considerable power.

Yet during these centuries the tradition of the predominance of the male line in tracing inheritance rights led to tight surveillance of the lives of married women. Every effort was made to ensure that children were legitimate offspring of the man whose property they could claim. An eighteenth-century comment on adultery notes that it is an action 'according to canon law [which] is as reprehensible in a husband as in a wife. But it is different in the secular [law], for a woman's infidelity has graver results. She gives her husband heirs who are not his children. It is theft to foist heirs born of debauchery on an entire family: it is the usurpation of the property, nobility and the name of the family.'[11] There is a story related by Madame de Pompadour at the close of the seventeenth century that shows clearly the particular relationship that existed in the minds of many concerning sexual morality and its most important consequences:

The Countess d'Egmont... inherited an immense fortune and, being young, beautiful and lovable was sought in matrimony after her husband's death, by the most distinguished men at court. One day her mother's confessor came and asked the Countess if he might see her in private and thereupon revealed to her that she was the fruit of an adultery which her mother had been trying to expiate for twenty-five years. 'Your mother', said the priest, 'was unable to prevent your first marriage although she trembled at it. God did not permit you to have children thereby, but if you remarry, Madame, you risk taking into another family an enormous fortune that does not belong to you and that has come to you as the result of a crime.' Madame d'Egmont listened to all this in terror. Her mother at that instant came in, flung herself to her knees, and through her tears, begged her daughter to preserve her from eternal damnation. Madame d'Egmont tried to reassure her mother and herself and asked: 'How?' The priest answered, 'Devote yourself entirely to God so as to efface your mother's sin.' The Countess, overwhelmed by all this, promised to do what he demanded and decided to become a Carmelite. I heard the story [Madame de Pompadour is talking] and spoke to the king of the barbarous treatment that this unfortunate woman was suffering at the hands of the duchess and her confessor. But we could not think how to help her. The King, in his generosity, persuaded the Queen to offer her a place as lady-in-waiting, and got some of the duchess' friends to try and persuade her to stop her daughter's entering the Carmelite Order. It was all to no avail.[12]

While this is an extreme case, it is not an exceptional one, and can serve as an example of the sorts of entanglements that ensnared people as they tried to balance private needs against the dictates of their particular society.

It has often seemed as if such snares trapped women more than men and dealt them graver wounds. Woman's lot of child-bearing often made sexual intercourse something other than it was for her partner, especially in ages without reliable methods of birth control. Not always, for birth within a legitimate family circle could bring as much emotional joy or pain to the father as to the mother. But even in these circumstances the physical travail involved in childbirth and the lack of knowledge of gynaecology and obstetrics could mean bodily misery for the woman, quite apart from any emotional or mental turmoil involved. Mrs. Alice Thornton was married in 1651 and during the next years, until her husband's death in 1668, she bore nine children. Her first entered the world on 6 August 1652, 'who lived not so long as we could get a minister to baptise it . . . after the miscarriage. . . . The hair on my head came off, the nails of my fingers and toes came off, my teeth did shake . . .'[13] On 10 December she wrote of the delivery of her first son and fifth child: 'the child stayed in the birth, and came crosswise with his feet first, . . . only living about half an hour, so died before we could get a minister to baptize him.' She wrote about the birth of her ninth and last child, Christopher Thornton, that he was born on Monday 11 November 1667 and that 'It pleased his Saviour . . . to deliver him out of this miserable world.' Of the nine children she carried, only three survived her: her sister, Lady Granby, carried sixteen, ten of them stillborn.[14] Yet for such wives and mothers discrimination against women was a meaningless term. The lives of men were not noticeably easier or longer. The first investigations into comparative longevity of men and women have revealed that, looking at European society as a whole, there was surprisingly little difference in life expectancy of the two sexes before 1800. The epidemic diseases—smallpox, measles, typhoid, and plague—struck both without favour. The terms of life themselves were a discrimination against the living, and if their sex exposed women to death through pregnancy, then their sex could also bring men to death on the battlefield.*

In sum, as the eighteenth century opened, discrimination against women was not yet built into the social structure of western Europe: it existed but it was not an inescapable barrier. As has been shown, one can discover discrimination against women in some of the legal practices of most of the communities, in that the rights of the family were defended for the advantage of the male and the detriment of the female. Further, if one moves from the lives of the élites into the lives of the common people, one can discover even more numerous examples of the way in which women's sexual transgressions were both more frequently and more severely punished than those of men. But what did exist was considerable prejudice against women. And unlike the trend noticeable in the twentieth century, from the late seventeenth century onward prejudice against women not only developed as a cultural attribute, acceptable in conversation, in literature and art, in philosophy and religion, but it was also supported by new laws and incorporated into the new political structures being developed. By the middle of the nineteenth century the structure of western society had produced that web of

---

*The actual battlefield was rarely a woman's field of action: Boadicea and Joan of Arc were exceptions, though not the only ones. But women did take part in army life, not merely as prostitutes but as cooks, launderers etc., and until the end of the eighteenth century appear as part of the personnel for whom the commanders take official notice when planning transport and living accommodation as well as ration strength.

oppression and exclusion that constitutes fundamental discrimination against women; it was a web that enmeshed a very large part of the population and covered an enormous range of human activity.

The force of this prejudice and the source of its strength can be found in two very different attitudes, one based essentially on a fear of human sexuality and the other on an inability to accept two different sexes as each other's equal. The first attitude considered women dangerous and evil, untrustworthy and insatiable, witches, the handmaids of the Devil. Here is the real beginning of an idea of women as sex-objects, because for people who thought this way, women were nothing but their sex. This is the view expressed, for example, by Phillippe de Navarre, sometime in the thirteenth century, when he wrote that 'Women have one great advantage: it is enough for them to cultivate a single virtue if they wish to be thought well of. Men, however, must have several if they wish to be esteemed. A man must be courteous, generous, brave and wise. But a woman if she keeps her body intact, all her other defects are hidden and she can hold her head high.'[15] The same theme is brought forward by Milton in the masque *Comus*, composed in 1634, and dealing with what Hayes calls 'chastity and the beastliness of sex.' Milton has a constant difficulty in admitting that human sexuality was really created by God. To quote again from Hayes: 'The marital relations of Adam and Eve in the great Protestant epic dramatize the basic conflict aroused by the sexual act. The couple come together

Straight side by side were laid; nor turned, I ween Adam from his fair spouse, nor Eve the rites mysterious of connubial love refused.

'In other words,' Hayes comments, 'this was the pure, unreal and idealized fantasy of sex which Milton entertained before facing the brutal facts of marriage. More light is shed on it when Adam innocently asks the archangel Raphael what is done about sex in Heaven. In defiance of the tradition that Heaven is sexless, Milton permits the angel to blush.'[16] Hayes, after considering the structure of *Paradise Lost* in detail, concludes that Milton was saying that 'after sexual knowledge the man feels castrated.'[17] Certainly even if Milton did not reach this level of psychosexual despair, his images of women in this poem have a content of hate never displayed in his image of Satan, fallen male angel. The fallen angel is portrayed in grandeur:

> Thus Satan talking to his nearest Mate,
> With Head up-lift above the wave, and Eyes
>   That sparkling blaz'd, his other Parts besides
> Prone on the Flood, extended long and large,
> Lay floating many a rood, in bulk as huge
> As whom the Fables name of monstrous size,
> Titanian, or Earth-born . . .
>   . . . with expanded wings he steers his flight
> Aloft, incumbent on the dusky Air . . .
> . . . moving toward the shoal: his ponderous shield
> Ethereal temper, massy, large and round
>   Behind him cast; the broad circumference
>   Hung on his shoulders like the Moon, whose Orb
>   Through Optic Glass the Tuscan artist views . . .
>   His Spear—to equal which the tallest Pine
>   Hewn on Norwegian hills to be the Mast
> Of some great Admiral were but a wand . . . [18]

Paradise Lost, Book I

His daughter, mistress, other and mirror-image, found at the gates of Hell, is described with loathing:

> . . . a formidable shape;
> The one seem'd Woman to the waste and fair
> But ended foul in many a scaly fauld
> Voluminous and vast, a Serpent armed
> With mortal sting: about her middle round
> A cry of hell hounds never ceasing barked
> With wide Cerberean mouths full loud, and rung
> A hideous Peal: yet, when they list, would creep
> If aught disturbed their noyse, into her woomb
> And kennel there; . . . [19]

Paradise Lost, Book II

Sex is horrifying; woman is sex; woman is horrifying. This is the syllogism at the root of this form of prejudice against women. Part of the horror comes because sex is felt as something uncontrollable, and therefore woman, seen as the embodiment of sex, is uncontrollable and so not only horrifying but also dangerous as a partner in a world that is, or ought to be regulated by reason.

To have a strong sexual appetite and to feel horror for the sexual act produces an ambivalence within a human being that leads easily to what Freud called 'transference'—the attribution of one's own characteristics to another. Men who felt their own desires evil could be solaced by believing that those desires were inflicted on them, aroused by the object, the result of external temptation, brought about without their volition or their responsibility. The process is a commonplace mental gymnastic. Nor is it to be found exclusively among men. Women could and did and do speak of men as beasts dominated by lust, centred only in their appetites, to be feared and if possible avoided. In the written records before the nineteenth century it is sometimes difficult to distinguish between dislike of men and dislike of pregnancies. Madame de Sévigné, writing to her daughter after the latter had conceived, sent 'a thousand kisses' to her son-in-law 'in spite of his mis-doings'. She continued the letter, 'I beg him at least, since he has caused the harm to cause the cure ... ' Two months later she returned to the subject and hoped that her daughter's confinement would end happily, and concluded that 'if M de Grignan (the son-in-law) loves you and has not undertaken to kill you, I know well what he will do—or rather what he will not do.'[20] Perhaps the closest parallel to Milton's outburst is the writings of some twentieth-century women, which represent all men as uncontrollable rape machines.[21]

Such sexual prejudice, then, is not confined to one sex nor is this type of sexual prejudice confined to any particular human community at any particular time. One might even consider it a given of the human community. It is, after all, the product of childhood experience. It is now a commonplace of psychology that all the events of childhood, not merely the family environment or the immediate community, but everything experienced, affects the individual. At any time within a community the actual experiences of people will be subtly different from others and will ensure the varied personalities that are to be found among people. Prejudice against the opposite sex that has its roots in certain childhood experiences is little different, in many ways, from prejudice against other groups for being a different colour or for holding different religious views. It is more destructive,

perhaps, because the people who hold such a prejudice are rejecting half the human race instead of a minority group, and because
they have lost the enjoyment of the human attribute of sexuality.
But this type of prejudice could be coped with when directed
against one sex if it did not co-exist with laws and customs based
on the second form of prejudice—the belief that women are inferior to men.

This belief in the inferiority of women comes in two forms.
The first is closest to that of Phillipe de Navarre and is based on a
view of women as some kind of toy or amusement created for the
diversion of men, gaining value only by value accorded. The second category allows a greater sphere to women, but is based on a
belief that the abilities of men and women are essentially different, coupled with a conviction that women are the inferior. This
form is the most complex, the most important, and the most difficult to summarize: it does not so much claim that men are the
superior sex as consider women the less important sex. Together
these attitudes become enmeshed in cultural definitions of gender
and concepts of the ideals of masculinity, and femininity. Both
forms of prejudice flourished and developed during the seventeenth century and helped to ensure the proliferation of legal and
political discrimination against women during the last decades of
the eighteenth century.

In some ways the view of woman as toy is just another variation of the sex = evil, woman = sex, therefore woman = evil
syllogism. In this case, however, the syllogism is sex = amusement
or status symbol; woman = sex; women = amusement or status
symbol. It is perhaps slightly less warped than the original, since it
admits sexuality as a possible source of human enjoyment. Further, while seeing women as having no value except that bestowed
on them by men, it nevertheless admits the possibility of something other than sexual intercourse as a link between men and
women. As Hayes has pointed out, that suave man-about-town of
eighteenth-century London, Lord Chesterfield, provides a first-
class demonstration of such ideas.[22] Women for this limb of the
aristocracy 'are only children of a larger growth: they have an entertaining rattle and sometimes wit; but not solid reasoning, or
good sense, I never knew in my life one that had it or one that
reasoned or acted consequently for four and twenty hours together. . . . A man of sense only trifles with them, plays with

them, humors and flatters them, as he does a sprightly forward child.'[23] In spite of his disdain Chesterfield admitted that women could be entertaining and could have wit, attributes other than physical appeal. But in essence this is still a prejudice that denies women an inborn share of human value in the same measure as men, and betrays a fundamental wish to see sexual activity separated out from the rest of life. Those who subscribe to such views would have Don Juan as their patron, to whom sex is a game, women merely part of the equipment.

Although women also could apply to men the hate threading through the ideas of Milton, they could scarcely until very recently envisage men as toys, pleasant things with which to while away an hour, because the result of playing with them involved such a high risk of pregnancy. Sexuality could not be envisaged as an end in itself when intercourse could give a child to be carried, to be born, and to be nurtured. Instead the woman's equivalent reaction has been either to use sex as a tool, a method to obtain what was denied through other channels, or to see sexual pleasure as a quite unnecessary human attribute and sexual attractiveness as a quite unnecessary complication of human life. Ninon de l'Enclos, the great French courtesan of the late seventeenth century, used sexuality to gain fame, fortune, and influence. She amassed a large fortune, which she left to her lawyer, M. Arouet, and which educated his son Voltaire. Her lovers, she remarked, 'never quarrelled over me; they had confidence in my inconsistency; each awaited his turn.'[24] Saint-Simon, a member of the French aristocracy, remarked that 'It was useful to be received by her, on account of the connections thus formed.'[25]

Margaret Cavendish, Duchess of Newcastle, lived from 1623 to 1673 and published a wide variety of writings—plays, biography, and philosophical treatises. In one of her letters she remarked:

> 'But nature be thanked, she has been so bountiful to us as we oftener enslave men than men enslave us. They seem to govern the world, but we really govern the world in that we govern men. For what man is he that is not governed by a woman more or less? None, unless some dull stoic, or an old miserable usurer, or a cold, old withered bachelor, or a half-starved hermit, and such like persons which are but here and there one. And not only wives and mistresses have prevalent power with

men but mothers, daughters, sisters, aunts, cousins, nay, maid-servants have many times a persuasive power with their masters, and a landlady with her lodger or a she-hostess with her he-guest. Yet men will not believe this, and 'tis better for us, for that we govern as it were by an insensible power, so as men perceive not how they are led, guided and ruled by the feminine sex.'[26]

In other words, the relationship between men and women has to be one of manipulation. Here indeed is sex war.

Such women had little in common with those who became prostitutes for want of alternative means of maintaining life. The exploitation of women in brothels, as street walkers, or in positions where their sexuality was considered to have been sold along with their services as shophands or domestic servants, brings a new question into the discussion, for it is a different type of abuse and needs to be considered in the context both of the suppression of the poor and the exploitation of sexual appetite for profit.

Sex as game, sex as tool, and sex as saleable commodity all continuously challenged the place of sex as communication and as pleasure and comfort for husband and wife. But the greatest blow to the latter came from the women who were outraged at the very notion of such a possibility. Their attitude—that sexual pleasure was an encumbrance and at best something for the man alone—led to the vicious belief that legitimate motherhood was incompatible with a loving sexual relationship. This idea did not reach its full destructiveness until the nineteenth century, when society would harbour the belief that experiencing sexual pleasure was the mark of the morally degenerate woman, but its roots are to be found in the traditions of eighteenth-century Europe. Lady Mary Wortley Montague, travelling in Vienna in 1716, remarked that she had 'not seen any such prudes as to pretend fidelity to their husbands, who are certainly the best natured set of people in the world and they look upon their wives' gallants as favourably as men do upon their deputies, that take the troublesome business off their hands, though they have not the less to do; for they are generally deputies in another place themselves; in one word, 'tis the established custom for every lady to have two husbands, one that bears the name, and the other that performs the duties.'[27]

Here it is clear that the enjoyment of physical love is not to be expected by anyone within the bonds of legitimate marriage—pleasure is to be found only in illicit relationships. This is the first step, and the least destructive form, of the idea that sex should not be a source of pleasure within the marriage bond. Lady Mary further remarks that the woman is always paid, and in fact a woman's judgment 'would be called in question, if they should be mistresses for nothing ... '[28] In sum, the prejudices against women that spring from an attitude towards sex as merely entertainment give rise not only to that present-day cliché, woman as sex object, but to a denial of sex as valid for other than entertainment and to all the myriad abuses attendant upon the exploitation of sex as a saleable commodity, including the denigration of sexual pleasure as a valid human attribute.

All the prejudices so far discussed have been rooted in the physical aspect of human sexuality, what might be considered its psychophysiology. The step from such considerations to the prejudices based upon a view of women as being of the weaker or the inferior sex is across a narrow but significant divide. In some ways the concept is linked very closely with the point of view of Lord Chesterfield. The Duchess of Newcastle reveals in her writings the complications of these beliefs. She was convinced of the inferiority of women. In her book *From the World's Olio*, she remarked 'men have great reason not to let us into their governments, for there is great difference between the masculine brain and the feminine ... women have no strength or light of understanding that is not given them by men. This is the reason why we are not mathematicians, arithmeticians, logicians, geometricians and the like.'[29] She continues the list of things that women are not for a considerable time and goes on to paint the innate characteristics of women in torrential sentences. Her theme is the old one of 'if you would know what has been achieved, look around', and she writes:

And thus we may see by the weakness of our actions, the constitution of our bodies; and by our knowledge, the temper of our brains; and by our unsettled resolutions, inconstant to our promises, the perverseness of our wills; by our facile natures, violent in our passions, superstitious in our devotions, you may know our humours: we have more wit than judgment, more active than industrious, we have more courage than conduct, more will than strength, more curiosity than secrecy, more vanity than good housewifery, more complaints than pains, more jealousy than love, more tears than sorrow, more stupidity than patience, more pride than affability, more beauty than constancy, more ill nature than good.[30]

Yet even after this tirade there is a distinct ambivalence, for she concludes that Nature, if she had made women without

heroic gallantry, yet she has laid in tender affections, such as love, piety, charity, clemency, patience, humility and the like, which makes them nearest to resemble angels, which are the most perfect of all her works, where men by their ambitions, extortions, fury and cruelty resemble the devil.[31]

Rousseau, that tormented eighteenth-century French intellectual whose emotional life was so chaotic, described woman from much the same standpoint as that of the Duchess of Newcastle and Lord Chesterfield. Once more the value of women was not inherent but endowed. Once more the nature of human bisexuality was seen as hierarchical and the mutual interdependence seen as a dominant-inferior relationship. 'Men and women', wrote Rousseau in his influential pamphlet on education published in 1762, 'are made for each other, but their mutual dependence is not equal. . . . We could survive without them better than they could without us. In order for them to have what they need . . . we must give it them, we must want to give it them, we must consider them deserving of it. They are dependent on our feelings, on the price we put on their merits, on the value we set on their attractions and on their virtues. . . . Thus, women's entire education should be planned in relation to men. To please men, to be useful to them, to win their love and respect, to raise them as children, care for them as adults, counsel and console them, make their lives sweet and pleasant: these are women's duties in all ages and these are what they should be taught.'[32] The prejudice apparent in this extract, and developed at length in the author's work, is much more complex than that of Chesterfield. Women are seen as useful and necessary and the influence accorded them is considerable, the tasks allotted to them attractive. There is a basic value in caring and a genuine satisfaction in making lives 'sweet and pleasant' that recently has too often been overlooked. But the flaw is that these actions, while accorded importance, are neither seen as accomplishments of intrinsic worth nor seen as the heritage of all human beings; they are to be undertaken solely in order to please men (and again it is forgotten that women did, do, and can care for other women—including their daughters).

Further, in making women the sex given to please and to love, Rousseau automatically denies men as much interest in these attainments. Instead he considers the strength of the men precisely that: 'son mérite est dans sa puissance; il plait par cela seul qu'il est fort.'[33] Rousseau thus perceives men and women as having qualities that are distinct and exclusive to their sex. Women are but a malleable substance, and from their birth must be trained to their task while men, it seems, need only be encouraged and developed, having innate characteristics not given to women. Women are men's reward, not in the old medieval sense of 'My arms your defence, your arms my recompense', but in the sense of distraction, of something without independent existence, a creation not solely for men but by and of men.

Incalculable damage has been done to human beings in the name of these beliefs. In ascribing to one sex qualities that the other cannot by nature possess, and in making these qualities those that the world's great religions have postulated as the necessary ingredients for spiritual life, and in separating the possession of these qualities from the ability to hold authority, the scaffold is raised for the death of morality. Not only women, who may at least know the pleasures of love and charity, but also men, who may not be merciful nor be able to be compassionate, are crippled by this idea. When society accepts such a division of potential it sees the qualities of sanity divorced from the exercise of power and the way clear for government without ethics. Here is the ground for the elevation of whim into Buchenwald. Questions of right and wrong, the proper consideration of human beings, the right valuation of human life, are no longer a concern of those who act: action is its own justification. Schemes and plans will be evolved with no consideration other than the wishes and ambitions of their instigators for worldly success. No attempt will be made to understand the necessities of humanity in any other than strictly material terms, for all such considerations are women's work and women's virtue, out of place in a 'man's world'.

What is being attacked here is not the value of a cultural

definition of gender, the development of concepts of what is masculine and feminine. Such concepts are a social norm of human communities, and represent among other things an imaginative translation of a physiological reality, the application of the human mind to the conditions of human life. But it is suggested that definitions of masculine and feminine must start from the root, the human person, whose intellectual and emotional capacities are not determined by sex. Neither men nor women have a monopoly of any human characteristic, whether this be the capacity to love or the capacity to destroy. In discussing the differences between men and women and in structuring the acceptable social limits for their behaviour, the distinction has to be made between the potential capacities of the sexes that are demonstrably different for all males and all females and those abilities that may more often be the provenance of one sex than the other. Women bear children as men provide the spark, but both men and women can be intelligent or stupid, wise or foolish, courageous or cowardly, loving or rejecting, compassionate or ruthless as and when circumstances determine. It is not necessary to deny the possibility of certain attributes in either men or women to fight against the exclusion of all men or all women from an activity. That human communities should wish to socialize one sex or another to concentrate upon the development of particular characteristics does not, of itself, mean more than that the community is arranging for a broad organization of human effort. If however such channelling is accompanied by the belief that the development of certain characteristics is the mark of the inferior, or if it is denied that both men and women have such characteristics in some measure, or if it is considered a warping of the right order of a human being for one person to display characteristics more often observed in that community as the provenance of the other sex, then the pattern becomes vicious. In such circumstances there is no real attempt to chart that line between the social and the biological, between hereditary and environment, so tentatively envisioned by Freud. A human community becomes a hive and society becomes the despot of its components instead of their servant.

The prejudice that divided the sexes by attributes, making certain characteristics the monopoly of one sex or the other, gained more and more ground during the seventeenth and eighteenth centuries. But in many ways it was the introduction of the concept of a 'man's world' as something separate from the world lived in jointly by both men and women that is the critical turning point in the transformation of prejudice against women into widespread discrimination against women. Once more it is something that reaches its full growth in the nineteenth century but, once more, its roots are to be discovered, well-developed and spreading, in the century before. It is the link between the sorts of prejudice talked about above and the institutionalization of discrimination against women. It is revealed in action through, for example, the letters of John and Abigail Adams. He was to become the second President of the United States, and one of the histories of that country noted: 'If he is loved at all, if he is considered at all, it is for his wife, and the brightness of Abigail Adams has dimmed such lustre as historians might have been prepared to give her husband.'[34]

During the spring of 1776, as the constitution for the United States was being formulated, Abigail wrote her husband a letter that has become a treasure of American feminists ever since. 'I long to hear that you have declared an independancy,' she wrote, 'and by the way in the new Code of Laws which I suppose it will be necessary for you to make I desire you would Remember the Ladies, and be more generous and favourable to them than your ancestors.... Men of Sense in all Ages abhor those customs which treat us only as the vassals of your Sex.'[35] His reply, sent two weeks later, was jocular and facetious and reads, in part: 'As to Your extraordinary Code of Laws, I cannot but laugh. We have been told that our Struggle has loosened the bands of Government everywhere. That children and Apprentices were disobedient—schools and Colleges were grown turbulent.... But your Letter was the first Intimation that another Tribe more numerous and more powerful than all the rest were grown discontented ...' He continued: 'Depend upon it, We know better than to repeal our Masculine systems. Altho they are in full Force, you Know they are little more than Theory. We dare not exert our Power in its full Latitude. We are obliged to go fair and softly, and in Practice you know we are the subjects. We have only the name of Masters, and rather than give up this, which would completely subject Us to the Despotism of the Petticoat, I hope General Washington and all our brave Heroes would fight. I am sure every good Politician would plot, as long as he would against Despotism, Empire, Monarchy, Aristocracy, Oligarchy or Ochlocracy.'[36] Abigail considered this reply 'very sausy'[37] and she returned to the attack. While John Adams did not apparently yield on this point in letters to his wife, his immediate reply did not present more than a panic-stricken defence. It is in a letter he wrote to James Sullivan six weeks later, that is to say two months after his wife has brought the question forward, that one catches a glimpse of how he really thought of votes for women.

The question being discussed is the proper base of the electoral franchise. 'It is certain, in theory,' he wrote, 'that the only moral foundation of government is, the consent of the people.'[38] Having put that sentence down he then went on to consider: 'But to what extent shall we carry this principle?' or, in other words, when do humans stop being people? 'Shall we say that every individual of the community, old and young, male and female, as well as rich and poor, must consent, expressly to the act of Legislation?' He found this proposition unacceptable and concluded that 'the right of the majority to govern and the obligation of the minority to obey' came 'From Necessity.' 'But', he wrote bluntly, 'why exclude women?' He continued: 'You will say, because their delicacy renders them unfit for practice and experience in the great businesses of life, the hardy enterprises of war, as well as the arduous cares of the state ... True. But will not these reasons apply to others? Is it not equally true, that men in general, in every society, who are wholly destitute of property, are also too little acquainted with public affairs to form a right judgement and too dependent on other men to have a will of their own? If this is a fact, if you give to every man who has no property a vote, will you not make a fine encouragement for corruption, by your fundamental law? Such is the frailty of the human heart that very few men who have no property have any judgment of their own ... ' After a burst of exasperation with the difficulties of the problem, which caused him to write that government is basically only machinery, he continued: 'The same reasoning which will induce you to admit all men who have no property, to vote with those who have for those laws which affect the person, will prove that you ought to admit women and children: for generally speaking women and children have as good judgments, as independent minds, as those men who are wholly destitute of property. ...

Depend upon it, Sir,' he concluded 'it is dangerous to open so fruitful a source of controversy and altercation as would be opened to alter the claims of voters . . . '

Adams was caught in the common trap of eighteenth-century constitution-making—the clash between the contemporary vision of human equality and the right of the governed to assent to the government, and a society that was made up of people who were not merely unequal in physique and abilities but also in economic status and in the social standing accorded them by their communities. His solution was a retreat, a comparison of government with an army, which he saw as 'a piece of clock-work, and to be governed only by principles and maxims, as fixed as any in mechanics . . . '[39] This method of cutting the debate was the one most frequently used by those involved in constitution-making and general legislation for western society over the next two hundred years: it admits the basic validity of an argument in the intellectual sphere but contends the impossibility of its translation to the here-and-now. Desegregation of schooling must come, but not now. Apartheid must be ended, but in another generation. Anti-semitism must be outlawed, next year. Women must be legislated into the Rideau Club, but not in the twentieth century.

Behind this stance on women, however, is less an overwhelming sense of superiority than an odd combination of duty, pride, and self-trust. There was a basic opinion that the woman's place as wife and mother entitled her to the protection and care of her husband, and that the man should look upon this role as a duty. There was an inability to concede that political equality ought immediately to spread through the heterogeneous elements of the society, through the ranks of the economically and socially indigent as well as through those of the propertied. There was also the belief in the rectitude of those men who held power, of their commonsense, of their wish to look after those who had no direct access to authority, in essence a belief in themselves as 'honourable men'.

Abigail's reaction to this stand was twofold. To her husband she threatened that the home would, indeed, become the battlefield for women's rights. There, she agreed, the women would overwhelm 'our Masters, and . . . "Charm by accepting, by submitting sway" . . . '[40] In other words manipulation would become the sole method for action. To her friend Mercy she commented that she had wished that the rights of women were considered, since 'there is a natural propensity in Human Nature to domination, I thought the most generous plan was to put it out of the power of the Arbitrary and tyranick to injure us with impunity by Establishing some laws in our favour upon just and Liberal principles.'[41] The temptation to oppress would be great enough to overwhelm the good intentions of those who held unrestrained power. Further, Abigail was well aware of the tradition of discrimination in English jurisprudence, which was against considering the wife capable of acting as a separate legal entity. Blackstone, the eighteenth-century English jurist, might feel that even such 'disabilities, which the wife lies under, are for the most part intended for her protection and benefit. So great a favourite is the female sex of the laws of England,'[42] but Abigail saw the same system as producing 'the Laws of England which gives such unlimited power to the Husband to use his wife Ill.'[43] For her the only corrective continued to be access to political power.

In sum, during the seventeenth and eighteenth centuries western society began to find solutions to problems of organization brought by the changes that occurred in technology, agriculture, industry, commerce, all complicated by the demographic revolution that began towards the middle of the 1700s. Discrimination against women as opposed to prejudice against women and injustice dealt women by particular legal practices became part of the new structures that emerged, and as these new structures emerged and as they affected the lives of more and more people in more and more ways, so discrimination against women became more and more widespread, more and more accepted, and more and more difficult to combat. At this stage there is less need to impute malice than muddleheadedness, less need to see brilliant plots for oppression than the results of lazy minds faced with complex problems. During the next decades, however, those that bring us from the eighteenth century into the nineteenth, the situation is changed. These years see the construction of a particular culture throughout western society, and this results in new and particularly damaging levels of discrimination against women.

NOTES

[1] Quoted in J. O'Faolain and L. Martines, eds., *Not in God's Image—Women in History from the Greeks to the Victorians* (Harper, 1973), unpaged.

[2] Women's petition to Parliament against Popery, 1642, quoted in S. Rowbotham, *Women, Resistance and Revolution* (Allen Lane, 1972), p. 15.

[3] Mary R. Beardd, *Women as Force in History: A Study in Traditions and Realities* (Collier, 1962), p. 186.

[4] *Ibid.*, p. 249.

[5] P. L. Berger and T. Luckman, *The Social Construction of Reality: A Treatise in the Sociology of Knowledge* (Penguin, 1966), p. 65.

[6] J. A. C. Brown, *The Social Psychology of Industry: Human Relations in the Factory* (Penguin, 1954), pp. 46-7.

[7] Master Franz Schmidt, *A Hangman's Diary*, ed. by A. Keller, trans. by C. Calvert and A. W. Gruner (P. Allen, 1928), quoted in O'Faolain and Martines, *op. cit.*, p. 228.

[8] *Ibid.*

[9] M. Beard, *op. cit.*, p. 104.

[10] *Ibid.*

[11] François Serpillon, *Code Criminel*, quoted in O'Faolain and Martines, *op. cit.*, p. 224.

[12] Madame Hausset, *Memoires de Madame Hausset, femme de chambre de Mme. de Pompadour* (Bruxelles, 1825), p. 221, quoted in O'Faolain and Martines, *op. cit.*, pp. 241-2.

[13] *The Autobiography of Mrs. Alice Thornton of East Newton, Co. York, 1627-1707.* First published London, 1875. Quoted in Joan Goulianos, ed, *By a Woman Writt: Literature from Six Centuries by and about Women* (Penguin, 1973).

[14] *Ibid.*, p. 34.

[15] *Les Quatres Ages de l'Homme* (1888), quoted in O'Faolain and Martines, *op. cit.*, p. 141.

[16] H. R. Hayes, *The Dangerous Sex: The Myth of Feminine Evil* (Pocket Books, 1966), p. 159.

[17] *Ibid.*, p. 164.

[18] C. Brooks, *Complete Poetry and Selected Prose of John Milton* (Modern Library, 1950), Bk. I, pp. 97, 99.

[19] *Ibid.*, Bk. II, pp. 132-33.

[20] Quoted in O'Faolain and Martines, *op. cit.*, p. 240.

[21] Monique Wittig, *The Guerilleres* (Picador, 1972) comes to mind, but this work is more a paen to women than a denigration of men. But the idea that humanity would be better off with a single sex comes through this work.

[22] Hayes, *op. cit.*, p. 168.

[23] *Letters of Chesterfield to his Son*, quoted in Hayes, *loc. cit.*

[24] Madame de Sévigné, Marie de Rabutin-Chantal, Marquise de, *Lettres* (London, 1927), vol. I, p. 80.

[25] Saint-Simon, Louis de Rouvriy, Duc de, *Memoirs of Louis XIV and the Regency* (Washington, 1901), vol. I, p. 344.

[26] Quoted in Goulianos, *op. cit.*, p. 61.

[27] Lady Mary to Lady R., 20 Sept. 1716, quoted in Goulianos, *op. cit.*, p 129.

[28] Lady Mary to Lady R., 20 Sept. 1716, quoted in Goulianos, *op. cit.*, p. 130.

[29] This work is not dated. Cited in Goulianos, *op. cit.*, pp. 56-7.

[30] *Ibid.*, p. 59.

[31] *Ibid.*, p. 60.

[32] Rousseau, *Oeuvres Complètes* (Ed. Seuil, 1971), vol. III, p. 247.

[33] *Ibid.*, p. 243.

[34] R. B. Nye and J. E. Morpugo, *A Historyy of the United States* (Penguin, 1955), p. 207.

[35] Abigail Adams to John Adams, Braintree, 31 March 1776, quoted in A. Rossi, ed., *The Feminist Papers, from Adams to de Beauvoir* (Bantam, 1974), pp. 10-11.

[36] John Adams to Abigail Adams, 14 April 1776, Rossi, *op. cit.*, p. 11.

[37] Abigail Adams to Mercy Otis Warren, Braintree, 27 April 1776, Rossi, *op. cit.*, p. 12.

[38] John Adams to James Sullivan, Philadelphia, 26 May 1776, Rossi, *op. cit.*, p. 13.

[39] *Ibid.*

[40] Abigail Adams to John Adams, Braintree, 7 May 1776, Rossi, *op. cit.*, p. 13.

[41] Abigail Adams to Mercy Otis Warren, Braintree, 27 April 1776, Rossi, *op. cit.*, p. 13.

[42] Quoted in Beard, *op. cit.*, p. 89, from Blackstone, *Commentaries on the Laws of England*, 7th ed., 1775.

[43] Abigail Adams to Mercy Otis Adams, Rossi, *op. cit.*, p. 13.

Five
European Attitudes

McNeill, whose work *The Rise of the West* is one of the most stimulating attempts to talk about all of western civilization in a single book, considers that by the time of the French Revolution Europe was 'a giant society, straddling the Atlantic, reaching deep into the Eurasian steppe, and extending to the antipodes.'[1] This quotation gives the geographical extent of European influence, perhaps, but the hallmark of that civilization is much more difficult to establish. As has been suggested in the two previous chapters, changes in agriculture, industry, and communications, as well as changes in the population base had presented European peoples in the eighteenth century with a new series of problems to solve. But as this century came to an end the organization of life was still along traditional lines, and innovations in laws and institutions, as well as social conventions, were slow to appear. Goubert, trying to make a twentieth-century audience understand seventeenth-century France, wrote 'Looked at objectively, France at this period could be described very simply as a rich and varied agricultural country, extremely backward technically, with large but unexploited national resources.'[2] If one were to describe western civilization in 1789 in similar terms, one could say again that it was a rich and varied agricultural territory, just beginning to develop technology, just about to exploit commercial possibilities with the rest of the world, but one with varied and complex political and social structures. In the decades leading up to Canadian Confederation in 1867, this same civilization came to command more wealth and power than any other organization of people, and while in some ways western civilization remained as varied as it had ever been, certain ideas and attitudes had acquired considerable authority and widespread popularity.

In particular ideas of the weakness and ineffectiveness of women, as well as the concept of femininity as something implying, in the words of Lord Tennyson, 'the lesser man', were widespread. The year after Confederation Ruskin, the English essayist, could paint in his work *Sesame and Lilies* a belief in the rightness of woman's submission based on theories that Ronald Pearsall summed up: 'a) because it was good for them; b) because it was good for men; c) because it preserved the social *status quo*; d) because it stopped women from getting above themselves; e) because it kept the home running smoothly; and f) because it perpetuated a sentimental notion of the man-woman relationship.'[3] These ideas were part of the beliefs that led Queen Victoria to write her oft-quoted words condemning 'this mad, wicked folly of Woman's Rights with all its attendant horrors.' A belief that had in earlier centuries been diffuse and only one opinion among many had come to dominate. While one can always find challenges to this attitude, there is no denying the strength of a belief in women's inferiority to men in the mid-nineteenth century.

This change in attitude was partly because of a change in culture. Raymond Williams considers that the alteration in the nature and influence of European culture between 1780 and 1850 was so cataclysmic that it should be looked upon rather as the first arrival of the culture itself than as its metamorphosis. He comments on the changes in the use of words, remarking that five key words—industry, democracy, class, art, and culture—are all redefined during these years, 'witness to a general change in our characteristic ways of thinking about our common life; about our social, political and economic institutions; about the purposes which these institutions are designed to embody; and about the relations to these institutions and purposes of our activities in learning, education and the arts.'[4]

He noted that industry, once used to describe a human quality —diligence—changes during these years to encompass another meaning and becomes 'a collective word for our manufacturing and productive institutions, and for their general activities'.[5] Democracy stops being a word used only by philosophers or those interested in the ideas and activities of the ancient Greeks. It becomes common coinage, an everyday term for a form of political representation. Class adds to its meaning of category or division into particular groups—classes of diamonds, classes of schoolchildren—a meaning with a particular social sense. Williams notes, 'First comes lower classes, to join lower orders, which appears earlier in the eighteenth century. Then in the 1790s we get higher classes; middle classes and middling classes follow at once; working classes in about 1815; upper classes in the 1820s.' He considers that 'Class is a more indefinite word than rank, and this was probably one of the reasons for its introduction.'[6] Art suffers the same change as industry, and from meaning a skill common to almost any human activity—the art of beekeeping, or weaving, or boat-building, or ploughing—becomes instead a name for a particular group of skills, those linked with literature, music, painting, sculpture, and the theatre. Finally the word culture had meant, as Williams comments, 'the tending of natural growth', and by analogy, a process of human training. But in the eighteenth and nineteenth centuries this comes to mean 'first "a general state or habit of mind"...; Second, "the general state of intellectual development in the society as a whole"; third, "the general body of the arts"; fourth, later in the century, "a whole way of life, material, intellectual and spiritual."'[7]

For Williams Europe in general and England in particular are not only creating new meanings for old words in order to speak about the changed circumstances of human lives, but are also creating a new centre of judgement within society to consider proper patterns of human behaviour. It is this idea of culture as a way of life that produced the idea of a 'cultured' person—one who acted rightly, in the sense of a code of correct social behaviour, rather than in the sense of a particular moral or religious ethic. In many ways this was not a new birth. There had been the medieval tradition of courtly love that implied the existence of culture in this same sense. During the Italian Renaissance books of manners such as that written by Baldassare Castiglione envisioned rules of conduct in social life based on culture rather than on religious beliefs. His description of the qualities of a lady—that she should 'have knowledge of letters, of music, of painting, and know how to dance and how to be festive...in everything be most graceful'[8]—are hardly prescripts based upon a belief in Christianity or any other major ethic, but a view of the human community as a place for role playing, for deliberately chosen codes, in short, for culture in the meaning given to it by Williams. The etiquette required at the Court of Louis XIV and imitated at smaller courts throughout Europe was much the same sort of activity. Culture in this sense was also responsible for the development in seventeenth-century France of the idea of the 'précieuse', a woman whose intellect, wit, and manners were such that she could entrance a man entirely without the help of any physical attraction between them. A contemporary remarked that the précieuses 'have transferred a live palpitating passion from the heart to the brain, and converted impulses into ideas.'[9] Here is the creation of particular ways of living among a small group of people, in this case women of the court of Louis XIV, that contain the idea of propriety, of a relationship with men that did not involve overt sexual behaviour and so would not expose them to religious censure.

It was not possible in seventeenth-century Europe for such mannered behaviour to involve many people. But with the new communications of the nineteenth century the tyranny of proper ways of behaviour could spread very much further. If the arbiters of society accepted rules of behaviour that restricted both men and women, the threat to the status and position of women would be very great. And this was precisely what one of the consequences of the change in culture perceived by Williams meant. For while Williams is talking mainly about the development of common forms of response and of the building of particular codes of signals among the literate, the idea of set prescriptions of behaviour permeated even to the more mundane level of everyday life.

During the nineteenth century there was a widespread acceptance by all types of people, in all sorts of circumstances, of the notion that there did exist proper patterns of social behaviour, of carrying on conversations, of eating and drinking and greeting one another. Further it was widely accepted that these patterns should be known, learnt, and obeyed in order to obtain full acceptance, not merely with a particular coterie, but with an important element of society. Previously such knowledge and acceptance of the conventions of manners had been restricted to members of the court circles of Europe, while people whose lives were passed in isolated communities greeted one another according to local usages, local interpretations of Christian belief perhaps, but rarely according to well-known formalized and written codes of behaviour. In 1861 Thackeray, whose social observations made his novels so popular, could comment thirty years after the death of George IV:

> He is dead but thirty years and one asks how a great society could have tolerated him? Would we bear him now? In this quarter of a century, what a silent revolution has been working! how it has separated us from old times and manners! How it has changed men themselves! I can see old gentlemen among us, of perfect good breeding, of quiet lives .... That gentleman of the grand old school ... [who] dined at the prince's table, would fall under it night after night .... If in petulance of play or drink that gentleman spoke a sharp word to his neighbour, he and the other would infallibly go out and try to shoot each other the next morning .... That gentleman, so exquisetly [sic] polite with the ladies in a drawing room, so loftily courteous, if he talked now as he used among men in his youth, would swear so as to make your hair stand on end.[10]

Manners had changed indeed. But there was more than merely a change in manners. There was an alteration that brings together the ideas of Williams on the birth of culture and the implications of the question asked by Thackeray: how a great society could tolerate certain types of behaviour—drunkenness, duelling, crude speech.

What developed in the early decades of the nineteenth century was the belief in the regulation of much community life by the ideas of a part of it, and that part of it called 'society'. Again this is not new except both in the number of people who accepted the proposition and the extent of human activity covered by the arbitration of this new force. 'Society' was now not merely the social life of a few but an entity that laid down rules of conduct for all levels of the community—what will people say? The idea of 'society', a judge that somehow connected patterns of speech, fashion of dress, daily behaviour, economic standing, and religious belief into a rigid formula determining moral worth was a related creation, but one that could not have existed in the old context of undeveloped, illiterate, rural Europe. It was the product of industrialization, of the innovations in transport, of urbanization, and of the growth of literacy.

Williams remarks on the way in which the new consciousness

of community is shown by a number of novels published in a twenty-month period, 1847-8: *Dombey and Son, Wuthering Heights, Vanity Fair, Jane Eyre, Tancred, Town and Country, The Tenant of Wildfell Hall*. In these works and those in French, such as *Le Rouge and Le Noir* of Stendhal, published in 1831, or *Père Goriot* of Balzac, published 1834, there is a self-conscious examination of what a community is about, 'of what it has been, of what it might be; how community relates to individuals and relationships; how men and women, directly engaged, see within or beyond them, for but more often against them, the shape of society.'[11] It is in these works, again to use the words of Williams, that 'Society from being a framework could be seen now as an agency, even an actor, a character. It could be seen and valued in and through persons: not as a framework in which they were defined; not as an aggregate of known relationships; but as an apparently independent organism, a character and an action like the others. Society, now, was not just a code to measure, an institution to control, a standard to define or to change. It was a process that entered lives to shape or to deform; a process personally known but then again suddenly distant, complex, incomprehensible, overwhelming.'[12]

In estimating the power and status of women during these decades it is this creation—society—that one finds so often approving and ensuring discrimination against women, both tangibly and intangibly. It can be seen in the laws enforced by government action, for example acts strictly enforcing the right of husbands to control the property of their wives. It can be seen in terms of employment, in work conditions and equal pay, questions that are discussed later in this chapter. It can be heard through the columns of newspapers such as the *Saturday Review*, which considered 'It is no small thing that half the human race should habitually take a purer and more sentimental view of life than those who have to do the dirty work.'[13] That was written, of course, when women working in the mines was still an unremarkable feature of the European scene. It can be heard in the books of sermons, the letters of advice about the right lives and conduct of women. 'A woman's position is one of subjection', wrote the Reverend F. W. Robertson in 1849, and in 1853 in *Letters to a Young Man About Town* Thackeray wrote: 'An exquisite slave is what we want for the most part; a humble, flattering, smiling, tea-making, pianoforte-playing being, who laughs at our jokes, however old they may be, coaxes us and wheedles us in our humours, and fondly lies to us through life.'[14] But above all, discrimination against women became part and parcel of theories about childhood training and the development of formal education for the young.

Once more it is not the birth of a new idea but of an idea becoming dominant over others and one that deeply affects the lives of girls and women. Until the middle of the eighteenth century youth was not recognized as a stage of development that demanded much attention. Children were expected to fit in with the norms of their environment and little care was taken to soften the demands of life. Children of the nobility quickly picked up the impression of rank: Louis XIV aged five refused to permit his three-year-old brother to eat at a table set at the same height as his own. Children in the countryside were soon expected to help guard the sheep and cattle, and those of the town to run errands. Education in a formal sense was minimal and consisted for the vast majority in an acquaintance with the precepts of Christianity, taught through Church schools, and, in some of the towns, some knowledge of ciphering and the alphabet.

For the nobility and the wealthy, learning was an accomplishment. In both France and Holland educated women were considered an aid to their husbands. The solid gains in commerce made by Holland in the seventeenth century were seen by one English traveller as due in large measure to the education of women, not only because of the help women could be in business but because 'the women are as knowing therein as the men, it doth encourage their husbands to hold on to their trades to their dying days, knowing the capacity of their wives to get in their estates . . . whereas a merchant in England . . . must loose one third of it, through the unexperience and unaptness of his wife to such affairs.'[15] As has been stated, Fénélon, writing about the education of women in 1683, considered that it was disgraceful for women not to be taught reading and writing, bookkeeping, and general management of an estate. Education was not generally used to inculcate a sense of inferiority and incompetence among women. While some might consider it their best interest to follow the example of a fifteenth-century Italian, Leon Battista Albertia, and keep wives ignorant in order to keep them obedient, there was a wide variation in the educational opportunities available to both men and women. It is true that by the sixteenth century universities had become male preserves, but it is also true that few attended them and that university education had little effect upon social standing.

By the end of the eighteenth century, however, structured education was beginning to assume more and more importance. The new institutions of the state and their attendant bureaucracies required educated people for their operation. The new techniques in industry required knowledge for their adoption. Restriction of educational opportunities meant a barrier to career advancement. As the nineteenth century opens Europe begins to respond to new needs for formal education by the development of state school systems linking primary to post-secondary education to provide people whose training would allow them to cope with the organization of the new political and economic structures and to implement the new technical inventions. The process was not constructed to produce equal opportunities, even in Napoleonic France.* There was no belief in educating the poor of either sex for such tasks. Writing in 1785, a commentator expressed a prevailing opinion: 'The Ignorance of the Poor', he wrote, 'affords their masters the best security of their unremitting Utility, Faithfulness and Obedience. That to instruct them in Reading and Writing generally puffs them with Arrogance, Vanity, Self-Conceit and . . . unfits them for the menial stations which Providence has alloted them.'[16] Barriers against the education of women, then, were not the sole injustices in the systems of education established during the early decades of the nineteenth century.

But if discrimination against women was not the sole injustice in educational matters, the idea of keeping women ignorant of important areas of human learning was one of the most damaging for the status of women. It ensured that comments about women's lack of reasoning powers, learning ability, and mental capacities were in the nature of self-fulfilling prophecies. The effect of this had been foreseen by Mary Wollstonecraft, and in Chapter II of her work *A Vindication of the Rights of Women*, first published in

---

*Even now most educational systems favour one section of society rather than another. As Anthony Sampson points out in his work *The Eurocrats*, in 1973 only 2 per cent of the children attending French universities came from working-class homes.

1792, she summed up the damage being done by 'the prevailing opinion, that (women) were created rather to feel than to reason' and therefore barred from having their minds trained. '[M]ade by this amiable weakness (that of having power only by their charms) entirely dependent, excepting what they gain by illicit sway, on man', she wrote, 'not only for protection but advice, is it surprising that, neglecting the duties that reason alone points out, and shrinking from trials calculated to strengthen their minds, they only exert themselves to give their defects a graceful covering, which may serve to heighten their charms in the eyes of the voluptuary, though it sink them below the scale of moral excellence.' Her comment foreshadows the bitter remark of Henrik Ibsen: 'You make women into sideboard ornaments and then complain of their shallowness.' It was not merely that exclusion from the new educational programs automatically meant exclusion from careers based upon such instruction, but that neglect of women's minds rendered them, as Mary Wollstonecraft wrote, 'more artifical, weaker characters than they would otherwise have been; and consequently, more useless members of society.'

As has been suggested already, there never was a time when western society presented a unified agreement about the inferiority of women, but the pressure of general belief in this proposition had been on the increase throughout the eighteenth century. *The Vindication of the Rights of Women* was a visible challenge to the unthinking support of such prejudice. If it did not receive universal approval, if some of her intelligent women contemporaries refused to read it on grounds rooted in their own prejudices, her work nevertheless sold widely and before the end of 1792 had sold out the first edition. It was published not only in England but also in the United States and was translated into French and German. While repetitious and disorganized, it had the outstanding virtue of commonsense and presented arguments for the education of women as much on grounds of utility as upon ideas of natural justice. Its fundamental importance lies less in the brilliance of its argument than in the fact that at a time when Europe was organizing its beliefs about society into a structured culture, the arguments for the inferiority of women did not go unchallenged.

Madame de Stael, 1766-1817, a contemporary of Mary Wollstonecraft, has left a vivid impression of the miasma of social prejudice against women. 'I soon noticed', she wrote, 'that the feelings I expressed were turned into jests, and that my intelligence was silenced, as if it was improper for a woman to have any. Thus I locked up in myself everything I felt, I early acquired the art of dissembling and I stifled my natural sensibility...I was, and still am convinced that women being the victim of all social institutions, are destined to misery if they make the least concession to their feelings and if in any way they lose control of themselves.' Here is the daughter of one of the most influential men in the French government during the 1780s, someone capable of making her house a meeting place for men of political power, herself seen as wielding considerable authority during one of the more critical stages of chaos in the French government, nevertheless aware of disdain for herself based not on her personality but on her sex. Rousseau had expressed the beliefs of a considerable part of the educated European population when he had pictured women as something weaker than men.

As is often the case, ideas that are new at one time become the accepted norm of people a generation or so later. In trying to explain the character of western civilization one has to choose constantly between emphasizing when an idea first appeared and when it became, in some interpretation or another, the commonplace of many. Freud lived and died in the last decades of the nineteenth century and the first decades of the twentieth century, yet the greatest impact of his ideas has occurred in recent years. So ideas that were not generally accepted throughout western civilization in the eighteenth century became the underpinning of policies of wide application in the nineteenth century.

By the end of the eighteenth century, then, ideas were being articulately expressed that were to become almost unarguable premises in the nineteenth century. Even Immanuel Kant, who, as the editors of *Not in God's Image* remarked, 'comes as close as any man ever had to acknowledging a perfect equality between the sexes,'[17] was infected by the arguments of political expediency that John Adams had earlier advanced. For Kant the sexual act was 'the enjoyment for which one person is given up to the other,' and he made no distinction here between male and female prerogative, no argument about active and passive enjoyment, male need and female sufferance, male right and female duty. But when he examined the question of authority within the family, he felt that one ought perhaps to accept the legal definition of the husband as representing the entire household because of the greater faculties accorded him by that law (the tautology is Kant's).[18] In other words, if society considers the male to have a better civil status than the female, the couple should not strive to correct the injustice but accept the argument of 'needs must'. Fichte, writing during the same years, the 1790s, did not even reach this clarity of vision. On the one hand he wrote: 'The question whether the female sex really has a claim to all the rights of man and of male citizens could be raised only by persons who doubt whether women are complete human beings. We do not...' On the other hand he could immediately add: 'But the question may certainly be asked whether and how far the female sex can desire to exercise all rights...'[19] However convinced of the equality of humanity, however dedicated to principles of political democracy, minds twisted and turned to avoid the conclusions that would follow from granting that women were human first and women second.

It is not unjust to summarize opinion about women at the end of the eighteenth century as being not merely something other than men but something less than men. William Cobbett, known for his work on behalf of the rights of the working poor, could nevertheless announce that 'God has said it is the duty of wives to be obedient to their husbands; and the very nature of things prescribes that there be a *head* of every house and an *undivided* authority.' He advised the young husband, 'You want no *comité*: reason, law, religion, the marriage vow; all these have given you the full power to rule your family, and if you give up your right, you deserve the contempt that assuredly awaits you, and also the ruin that is, in all probability, your doom.'[20] Further, the shadow of Milton still touched some thinkers and Hegel could write during these years that 'With regard to sexual relations, we should note that in giving herself to intercourse the (unmarried) girl renounces her honor. That is not, however, the case with men, for they have yet another sphere for their ethical activity beyond that of the family. Girls have their essential destiny in marriage and there only; thus the demand that their love take the form of marriage...'[21] But while this idea had damaged human lives in the seventeenth century, its impact in the nineteenth and twentieth centuries was even more harmful. It is this theory that permits a justification of a double standard of morality for men and women and allows the sexual exploitation of women to be carried on without any moral qualms. The first act of seduction, the taking of virginity, is still considered indefensible, but once betrayed the woman is lost for good and one cannot, after all, degrade that which has already fallen.

It is important to realize that what is being said concerning European attitudes during the early nineteenth century does not imply that no men were exploited, that all women were exploited, and that all writings and actions were essentially anti-feminist. During these decades immense suffering was visited upon count-less men, women, and children. For example, the report of one of the earliest enquiries into the conditions of employment for chil-dren in the textile industry, set up in Britain in 1816, gave the following evidence about the working conditions of eight- and nine-year-olds:

> What were the hours of work? From five o'clock in the morn-ing until eight at night.
> Were fifteen hours in the day the regular hours of work? Those were their regular hours of work.
> Was that the regular time all the year through? Yes.
> What time was allowed for meals? Half an hour for breakfast and half an hour for dinner. . . .
> Did they, beyond working these fifteen hours, make up for any lost time? Yes, always. . . .
> Did the children work on Sundays as cleaners of the machi-nery? Yes.
> Did they do this regularly? Regularly every Sunday; I do not know that they missed one Sunday while I was there.
> Through the year? Yes.
> How many hours did they work on Sunday? Their orders were from six to twelve.[22]

It should be emphasized that these conditions were to become generally accepted during the next decades; Lord Ashley's investi-gation into mining in the 1840s and enquiries carried out by French government committees during the same years report much the same conditions. These conditions bound children of both sexes and in effect amounted to slavery, since the children were usually legally contracted to work a set number of years in a particular factory and were often housed and fed by the owner. In the case reported above, the sleeping room was less than a hundred yards from the workshop. While a fair proportion of the children would be órphaned or abandoned by their parents, there were also children committed to such lives by parents too poverty-stricken or too unimaginative to cope with their young in any other fashion.

The indictment that can be drawn up about the textile industry in England at this time can be drawn up for industry after industry, country after country, as industrialism became the norm of European life. Mantoux quotes an example from one of the German states where 'two hundred little girls, under a matron's rod, sat spinning without a moment's relaxation and in complete silence, and were beaten if they did not spin quickly or well enough.'[23] Nor can any great distinction be drawn between the sufferings of children and those of adults. Leaving aside the question of health, the incidence of crooked backs, crippled limbs, tuberculosis, and other miseries produced by childhood work, the conditions of employment for adults were very little, if any, improvement on those of the children. Further the fluctuations of market demand for labour meant that for all, unemployment was a constant spectre and a frequent reality. The alternative of complete destitution often meant work accepted in spite of inhuman conditions.

Without suggesting that Europe was one complete sink of human misery during these decades, the dark Satanic mills like bolts holding down the squirming mass of living souls, one cannot doubt that technology and urbanization combined to provide a bitter life for many Europeans at this time. Ashton and others have suggested that the disasters of the industrial revolution have been much exaggerated. It is true that throughout this period, 1789-1867, in no one decade was there massive exploitation of all the working force of Europe simultaneously. Further, much of Europe retained its rural character during these years: the countryside continued to be populated and the towns had definite limits. Even while, as one contemporary observer wrote, 'the animal machine—breakable in the best case, subject to a thousand sources of suffering—is chained fast to the iron machine which knows no suffering and no weariness',[24] efforts were made to legislate better working conditions and to control the impact of the new machines. The transformation of Europe to an industrial economy, while extraordinarily rapid when placed in the context of the history of western civilization, nevertheless happened over a number of decades. While it was, and in many ways still is, an intensely swift reorganization of life, it nevertheless was, and is, haphazard. It left some parts of Europe relatively untouched, such as the Shetlands, the Basque country, villages in other mountain-ous or forested regions, and it also left unmarked some occupa-tions and some beliefs. Some goods were still made with the old methods, especially those linked to the accoutrements for horses —harness work, coachwork and such like, and to luxury items such as jewellery, lace, and perfume. Some occupations such as farming and fishing were very slow to feel the impact of the new ways. In spite of the new agricultural techniques, parts of the Auvergne still used wooden ploughs in the second half of the twentieth century.

But even though the life of the countryside of Europe remained relatively unchanged over these decades compared to the trans-formations made in urban living, fewer and fewer people lived there. Further, total isolation of villages from the events of the larger political entities became the exception. The thrust for national unity, combined with improvements in transportation and literacy, brought to an end much of the local autonomy that had been the hallmark of so much of Europe in the seventeenth century. By the middle of the nineteenth century Europe had created an industrial civilization that, if not fully fledged, was an obvious change from the traditions of previous eras, and its nature can be the better discerned because remnants of the older dispensations were still present in the 1850s.

While changes in agricultural techniques, in communications, and in life expectancy altered European villages during these years, the basic demands continued. Farming and fishing still required the same sort of human endurance as in the past. Few men or women had considerable political or economic power in the community at large. The work of the wife was frequently as important as the work of the man. It is true that Pinchbeck has noticed the decline of women employed as day-labourers in Eng-lish farming communities during the first half of the nineteenth century. One witness remarked in 1843: 'I remember formerly when girls turned out regularly with the boys to plough, etc., and were up to the knees in dirt, and in the middle of winter, in all kinds of employment. Now you never see a girl about in the fields.'[25] One can find other changes in dairy-farming, haying and reaping, owing to the introduction of machinery. But looking at Europe as a whole, the life of the villages saw the general continuance of women in the work world on much the same terms as in the past, that is to say as necessary and valued partners. Whether it was in specialized activities such as tending the vegetable garden or keeping poultry, or whether involved in the central concern of the village, such as the oyster-industry of Brittany, women were caught up as a vital part of the economy. To a very considerable extent the power and status of women in European village life was still governed by the traditions and needs of the particular locality. What is changing is not so much the life of the village as an entity, but the life of particular villagers who leave the communities.

For the individual there were alternatives, and Bavarian records are full of complaints of 'how female servants and hired hands would squander their entire wages in buying expeditions to the cities, returning to the farms with clothes alien to native folkways.'[26] In some sense the picture is expected: the old ways existing as ever while the new emerge. The new roads and the merging railways made possible a relationship between countryside and town that helped to preserve, rather than destroy, village family life. Whether trips to urban centres were no more than a safety-valve, or whether they were the basis for a final migration from countryside to town, the new ease of travel meant a less drastic pace of change. But the continued existence of the traditional was precisely that, its existence not its development, and the new Europe of the industrial towns was the thrusting, absorbing arbiter of the life of the continent.

In the great manufacturing centres, the Black Country of England, the industrial north of France, the towns of Belgium, and the factories of the Ruhr, the new patterns were made. Here the economic worth of women was recognized as both necessary and valuable, but as of something less than that of men. Almost without exception women were paid less for the same work: the returns from a number of Lancashire cotton mills in 1834 show this.[27] While the wages were marginally higher for females than for males in the early years of the working life, they were consid-

erably lower over the whole lifespan. As was remarked in the
Factory Inspectors' Report for 1843: 'The small amount of wages
paid to women acts as a strong inducement to employ them
instead of men, and in the power loom shops this has been the
case to a great extent.'[28] Similar statistics can be brought together
for women in the metal trades, such as nail and chain making.
These differences in wages were to be found on the continent as
well as in England. The principle of unequal pay for equal work
was the established rule of labour during these decades and, as
Ivy Pinchbeck remarks, called forth no adverse comment. This
form of discrimination is undeniable.

AGE	NO. OF WOMEN EMPLOYED	AVERAGE WEEKLY WAGE		MEN'S WAGE FOR CORRESPONDING AGE GROUP	
Below 11	155	2s	4 ¾d	2s	3 ½d
11-16	1123	4	3	4	1
16-21	1240	7	3 ½	10	2 ½
21-26	780	8	5	17	2 ½
26-31	295	8	7 ¾	20	4 ½
31-36	100	8	9 ½	22	8 ½
36-41	81	9	8 ¼	21	7 ¼
41-46	38	9	3 ½	20	3 ½
46-51	23	8	10	16	7 ¼
51-56	4	8	4 ½	16	4
56-61	3	6	4	13	6 ½
61-66	1	6.	0	13	7
66-71	1	6	0	10	10

Source: I. Pinchbeck, *Women Workers and the Industrial Revolution,
1750-1850* (Cass, 1969), p. 193.

What is very much less clear is the percentage of the total
population of women employed in such occupations. One survey
conducted in Britain in 1851 shows that, of all females over ten,
2,832,000 were 'occupied' and 5,294,000 were 'unoccupied'.[29] Yet
many contemporary statements about factory work gave the
impression that, as Pinchbeck remarks, 'every woman in a factory
above the age of eighteen was a wife or mother.'[30] But in the
textile industry in the north and west of England comparatively
few married women worked in the factories. The Factory Commissioners Supplementary Report of 1834 shows that the majority
of women operatives were aged from sixteen to twenty-one, and

that there was a 'prodigious diminution immediately after.'[31] The statistical evidence is, at present, inadequate for any precise statements, but Pinchbeck considered that perhaps a quarter to a third of the women employed were married, and that 'the detractors of the factory system overestimated and exaggerated its effects on home life.'[32] Or, in other words, the evidence at present collated and discussed shows the conditions of work of only a part, albeit a significant part, of the female population of Europe during the first half of the nineteenth century. While it is possible to say that a considerable number of families needed the labour of husband and wife, not to speak of children, for their survival, and this whether they lived in country or town, the precise categorization of occupation is a much more tangled problem than was once thought.[33]

Despite the complexity of the matter, however, and the need for many more specific studies of the European labour force in the nineteenth century, there are two or three points that can be made about the status and position of European women during the first half of the century. These decades were first of all a time of child-rearing. Richards believes that 'the mid 19th century probably experienced the highest average size of family in British history.'[34] The population curves of other European states show a very similar trend towards large families.[35] By the 1840s Europe had accepted its new demographic pattern, its increased and increasing population, and considered that 'The sphere of Domestic Life is the sphere in which female excellence is best displayed.'[36] The extent to which this was making a virtue out of necessity is a matter for debate. What is not debatable is that during these decades, roughly 1800-1850, the care and nurture of children, on a scale hitherto unknown, preoccupied European women no matter what their social standing.

Among the destitute of the urban societies of London, Paris, Antwerp, and Vienna a pregnancy most often meant abortion or child murder.[37] In such circles of despair the alternative was often the scarcely less dreadful one of baby-farming, the boarding out of children in foster-homes. While some homes looked after infants well, the generality either educated the more prepossessing for a life of crime, allowed them to die by malign neglect, or committed outright murder.[38] In London in 1867 the death rate among illegitimate children was eight times that of children born in wedlock.[39] At the next level of society, the poor, where the wages of all possible labourers were needed to sustain the family, women coped either with other people's children or with their own and other people's children. While factory work, work in the mines, and in trades such as dressmaking and allied crafts absorbed the energies of many women, by far the greatest sphere of their activity was domestic service. The employment of nursemaids, nannies, governesses, tutors, laundry-maids, housemaids, kitchen-maids enabled the wives of the well-to-do to have a wide social life.

The discovery that during the years of increased child-rearing domestic service was the major field for the employment of women is scarcely surprising. In a world without labour-saving devices and peopled by numerous children, servants are not merely domestic conveniences and a symbol of social success, they are a key to parental freedom. Without automatic washing machines, and when clothes were made of linen, cotton, and wool, the laundry was a major item in the work of a household. Heating by coal meant, for many European homes, not only the work of tending the fires but also additional dusting and sweeping without the aid of the vacuum cleaner. The basic minimum for the middle-class European household in the 1840s was 'three domestics, cook, parlour maid and housemaid, or cook, parlour maid and nursemaid . . . beyond this point extensions were variations on a basic theme. The cook was provided with a kitchen-maid and later a scullery maid . . . [in England] during this period of middle class expansion [1840s and 1850s] . . . Whereas the number of general servants increased no faster than that of house-occupiers, the number of cooks, housemaids and nursemaids grew more than three times as fast and housekeepers nearly six times.'[40] There were regional variations in Europe as to the work that the wife of the householder would do, cooking being considered a much more serious activity in France than in England. On the whole, however, the pattern is substantially the same from the households of the north of England to those of northern Italy: the women of the labouring classes worked directly to produce the leisure of the economically more fortunate.

If the first two elements in the lives of European women at the middle of the nineteenth century were children and domestic service, the third is the flood of debate about their rights and duties. Hegel could use philosophy to reduce women's field of

moral responsibility to their sexual conduct, while John Stuart
Mill argued how much the 'world would gain by ceasing to make
sex a disqualification ... consisting in an increase in the general
fund of thinking and acting power ... '[41] Jane Austen might write
in *Pride and Prejudice* of homes where it was a matter of congratu-
lation that daughters had nothing to do but amuse themselves. At
roughly the same time Elizabeth Fry, a Quaker, began her
arduous work in the prisons of England to ensure more human
conditions for the prisoners. If the older established universities
such as Oxford and Cambridge, Berlin and the Sorbonne, refused
to admit women, London University had two colleges established
for their benefit by 1849. If the idea of woman as the cloistered
but subordinate wife and mother was continuously placed before
the public in work after work, then the life and work of women
such as Harriet Martineau showed the right of women to a wider
responsibility and a broader sphere of action. Her life spanned
the years 1802 to 1876, and her work as a social observer and her
account of American society has earned her, in the minds of
many, the title of the first woman sociologist.

By the middle of the nineteenth century the arguments for the
inferiority of women were well articulated, but arguments were
already marshalled on the other side. The organization of many
of the institutions of society severely restricted the field of action
of many women, but already organizations for reform of property
laws and for educational opportunities existed in England and
France. The established conventions of many social circles within
the community gave women peculiarly complex roles to play, and
these were frequently used by women for their own benefit. If
women were poor, defenceless, weak playthings, they could nevertheless ensure that men obeyed them by acting out that role
and using emotional blackmail. If woman was supposed to be
both purer and more delicate than the male, she had the right to
dissolve in tears and to cry 'Unfair! Immoral! Brute!' Or, as Ronald Pearsall remarks, there is a 'road of husband baiting, the road
that begins with petulance, continues with bitchiness and presum-
ably goes on to jealousy raising, and then mental torment.'[42]

If discrimination against women can be seen as one of the
major aspects of early nineteenth-century European culture, it
would be false to view European society at this time, in either
attitudes or action, as some kind of totalitarian community where

men alone controlled. Once more, western civilization is complex, varied, and has to be understood as a tension of conflicting forces rather than as the inexorable development of particular trends. At any moment in time a variety of ideas and beliefs is available to support any action contemplated. Of course certain ideas and beliefs will have more support than others, but ideas never seem to die. Instead certain beliefs have periods of popularity while people still hold their opposites, still argue for their acceptance, and still demand that the laws and institutions should reflect them. Canada, for example, is not supposed to have any discrimination on the grounds of religion, colour, or sex. The recent Green Paper on immigration clearly showed the number of people who would like to discriminate against others on such grounds. So one way of looking at the period 1789 to 1867 is to see it as the years when discrimination against women gained acceptance, but an acceptance that was always criticized and that provoked its own movement for alternatives, its own critics.

In this area, as in so many others, the French revolution left a heritage to be exploited. While governments in the early decades of the nineteenth century condemned anything that looked remotely as if it might lead to a similar upheaval, nevertheless 'Liberty, Equality, Fraternity' remained ideals that might lead to a different future. As Rowbotham has written:

> In the French Revolution the feminist aspirations of the privileged and the traditions of collective action of the unprivileged women encountered each other. They regarded each other uneasily and never really combined. But each emerged tinged with liberty, equality, and fraternity and the memory of revolution. Things could never be quite the same again. Women rioting over prices in Normandy in 1789, women of the third estate in Grenoble taking action in favour of the States General, women demanding in the lists of grievances presented, better medical provisions and improved education, protection of trades from male competition, women marching to Versailles to confront the baker and the baker's wife, pamphlets and petitions about divorce, prostitution, are all indications of a great acceleration of activity and consciousness.[43]

In all parts of the European community there were traditions of action for women, even if discrimination against women emerged during these years as the dominant trend within society. The suffragette movement that developed in the last half of the nineteenth century was not some kind of Athena from the head of Zeus, born with no past, an instantaneous creation of the moment's needs. It was a natural and infinitely stronger force, as much part of the texture of European civilization as its opponents. It would never have gained the success it did had it been the superficial creation of a discontented few. Nowhere is this more obvious than in the story of the obverse of Europe's urban industrial sprawl: the story of her emigrants.

NOTES

[1] W. H. McNeill, *The Rise of the West: A History of the Human Community* (University of Chicago Press, 1963), p. 656.

[2] P. Goubert, *Louis XIV and Twenty Million Frenchmen* (Allen Lane, 1970), p. 27.

[3] Ronald Pearsall, *The Worm in the Bud. The World of Victorian Sexuality* (Pelican, 1971), p. 109.

[4] Raymond Williams, *Culture and Society, 1780-1950* (Penguin, 1961), p. 13.

[5] *Ibid.*, p. 13.

[6] *Ibid.*, p. 15.

[7] *Ibid.*, p. 16.

[8] Baldassare Castiglione, *Il Cortegione* (1828), C. S. Singleton, ed. (Anchor Books, 1959), p. 213.

[9] Saint Evremond, *Oeuvres* (Paris, 1927), vol. I, p. 47.

[10] 'The Four Georges: Sketches in Manners, Morals, Court and Town Life, 1861', in Kenneth and Miriam Allot, *Victorian Prose, 1830-1880* (Penguin, 1956), pp. 53-5.

[11] Raymond Williams, *The English Novel from Dickens to Lawrence* (Paladin, 1970), p. 11.

[12] Williams, *Culture and Society, op. cit.*, p. 12.

[13] *Saturday Review*, 6 May 1871, quoted in Pearsall, *op. cit.*, p. 110.

[14] Both excerpts cited Pearsall, *op. cit.*, pp. 115 and 110-11 respectively.

[15] Sir Josiah Child, *A New Discourse of Trade* (London, 1694), pp. 1, 4.

[16] J. Fawel, *The Principles of Sound Policy (1795)*, quoted in A. Briggs, *How They Lived. An Anthology of Original Documents . . .* , vol. III, p. 342.

[17] I. Kant, *The Principles of Laws (1797)*, quoted in J. O'Faolain and L. Martines, eds., *Not in God's Image: Women in History from the Greeks to the Victorians* (Harper, 1973), pp. 285-6.

[18] I. Kant, *The Science of Laws* (1795), quoted in O'Faolain and Martines, *op. cit.*, p. 287.

[19] Fichte, *Advice to Young Men . . . 1829* (italics in original), quoted in Allot, *op. cit.*, p. 136.

[20] Allot, *op. cit.*, p. 137.

[21] *Grundlinien der Philosophie des Rechts*, pp. 240-9, quoted in O'Faolain and Martines, *op. cit.*, p. 289.

[22] *Reports of the Minutes of Evidence taken before the Select Committee on the State of the Children Employed in the Manufactories of the United Kingdom*, 25 April-18 June 1816, pp. 178-91.

[23] P. Mantoux, *The Industrial Revolution in the Eighteenth Century* (Eng. trans., 1928), p. 420.

[24] Quoted in L. and B. Hammond, *The Rise of Modern Industry* (1926), p. 196.

[25] I. Pinchbeck, *Women Workers and the Industrial Revolution, 1750-1850* (Cass, 1969), p. 169.

[26] Edward Shorter, 'Female Emancipation, Birth Control and Fertility in European History', *The American Historical Review*, vol. 78 (June 1973), 618.

[27] Pinchbeck, *op. cit.*, p. 193.

[28] *Ibid.*, p. 194.

[29] Quoted in E. Richards, 'Women in the British Economy since 1700', *History*, vol. 59 (October 1974), 348. However, 'Well over a third of all working wives in Preston in 1851 were employed in non-factory occupations, but were not recorded.'

[30] Pinchbeck, *op. cit.*, p. 197.

[31] *Ibid.*

[32] *Ibid.*, pp. 198-9.

[33] E. Briggs, 'Women's Employment: Problems of Research', Society for the Study of Labour History, *Bulletin*, No. 26 (Spring 1973).

[34] Richards, *op. cit.*, p. 349.

[35] E. Shorter, 'Illegitimacy, Sexual Revolution and Social Change in Modern Europe', *The Journal of Interdisciplinary History*, vol. II (Autumn 1971), pp. 265-72 has curves for both legitimate and illegitimate births in Europe.

[36] J. A. Banks, *Feminism and Family Planning in Victorian England* (Liverpool, 1964), p. 58.

[37] An analysis of London's coroners reports for 1856-60 showed a yearly average of 226 deaths of infants under two by foul play. K. Chesney, *The Victorian Underworld* (Pelican, 1972), p. 417.

[38] *Ibid.*, pp. 414-21.

[39] *Ibid.*, p. 415.

[40] Banks, *op. cit.*, p. 69.

[41] John Stuart Mill, *The Subjection of Women*.

[42] Pearsall, *op. cit.*, p. 131.

[43] S. Rowbotham, *Woman, Resistance and Revolution* (Allen Lane, 1972), p. 37.

Six

Canadian Experiences

As the eighteenth century drew to a close—at a time when Mary Wollstonecraft published her *Vindication of the Rights of Women* and Anne Le Prince died on the guillotine—the status and position of women in what is now Canada were structured by factors much like those that had regulated the life of women in seventeenth-century France—the locality controlled everyday life, and the impact of larger politics came through a network of structures that might or might not involve present and immediate concerns. As S. F. Wise has pointed out,

> there were no British North American people in the 1790s, nor even, except in a technical sense, Nova Scotians or Upper Canadians. Although most colonists or *Canadiens* were involved in farming, fishing, or the fur trade, economic similarities were less significant than the cultural, religious, and geographical isolation that divided colonial groups from each other. For the many little particularisms of British North America, the horizon, intellectual as well as social, extended only to the bounds of a parish, along a stretch of coast, within the limits of a river valley settlement, or to the edge of the ever-present bush.[1]

For most people the bounds of their lives were family opinion and the strength of village custom. And in this respect the lives of women were not greatly different from those of men.

First and foremost, the elementary necessities of human existence—food, shelter, and companionship—usually depended upon the efforts of all—men, women, and children. While some environments, such as the fishing villages or lumbering camps, encouraged a division of labour according to age and sex, in many others tasks could be allocated more generally. In villages such as Buctouche or Cocagne, Acadian establishments on the

New Brunswick coast, people were involved in lumbering, farming, fishing, as well as a certain amount of general commercial activity. If few women took a boat out to sea and few men stayed home to garden, spin, weave, sew, cook, and care for the children and the aged, it was not unknown for such to happen. Joseph Gueguen, for example, wrote from Cocagne in October 1796 to the ecclesiastical authorities in Quebec about the difficulties of caring for four children after the death of their mother.[2] Oral tradition speaks of widows and orphans, when death removed husband or father, taking up pursuits more commonly delegated to men. It would be possible to describe the lives of these men and women in terms of sex-role typing, but such a description would convey very little of the real texture of these communities. In the small settlements of the colonies the personality of the individual and the immediate challenge of the day were more important than social conventions about gender-roles.

Yet however pragmatic village life might be, however scornful of modes and manners brought by outsiders, there were at least two major areas of life where women were treated on a different footing from men solely because of their sex. The organization of direct political power, the right to vote and be considered for election barred many men but excluded almost all women.* Their political power depended upon indirect influence, on persuading a man to act in the way they wished. While the question of political rights might seem relatively unimportant at the end of the eighteenth century when the activities of government bodies were relatively circumscribed, the matter became more serious in the nineteenth century when the elected officials became responsible for a greater and greater amount of public policy. Even during these early years the barrier meant more than just the denial of a minor opportunity. The exclusion of almost all women in the colonies from participation in an essential element of the political process helped to encourage a general belief in the incapacity of women to undertake an active political life. It was an encouragement to accept discrimination against women and it set up a reinforcing mechanism: barred from responsible action, women were not encouraged to become informed or to comment upon political life, and their absence from this sphere came to seem a natural phenomenon.

*A handful of widows in both Upper and Lower Canada voted.

The institutional structures of most of the Christian churches also discriminated against women, and this discrimination is a much more complex matter. Among the Quakers the position and status of women was often equal to that of men; in many of the Methodist congregations the influence of women could be considered perhaps greater than that of men; while the Catholic hierarchy barred women from the priesthood, the encouragement of religious orders open to women provided opportunities for work in education and medicine not otherwise available. Yet if Christian belief did not mean automatic relegation of women to a lesser category of humanity, nevertheless much Christian teaching about the organization of the family supported a patriarchal system, with women always seen as the responsibility of the male, the charge of father, brother, husband. But in practice the incidence of death very often gave women a greater freedom than that propounded by theory. Further, the impact of religious belief in small villages was a variable quantity. At the beginning of the nineteenth century the Abbé Sigogne organized the Acadians of Baie St Marie, Nova Scotia into parishes that accepted not merely his theological teachings but his authority in many secular matters.[3] The Acadians around Caraquet, on the other hand, argued with their priests during Sunday sermons, a habit noted as late as 1837 when they argued strenuously against a sermon on the necessity of lay obedience.[4]

Perhaps the least misleading generalization that can be made about the lives of women in British North America at the opening of the nineteenth century is that their position and status depended as much upon the circumstances of the individual as upon generally accepted beliefs concerning the nature and capabilities of the female sex. Yet such a generalization ignores one important component of colonial life: the towns. The importance of these larger settlements can scarcely be overemphasized. It was within their boundaries that people could discover, as well as a market for their goods and a supply of those articles that the smaller settlements were unable to produce, a wider world. In towns one heard of happenings elsewhere, learnt of the debate on the political issues of the day, discovered ways of life other than the farm, the fishery, the lumber camp, and the village.

There might not be in Halifax, Quebec City, Kingston, and Montreal the complexity of convention or the level of unquestioned authority that the court of Louis XIV had established in France. But in these centres, both before and after Confederation, there was a social life concerned with morals and manners and a political life and institutions that would have an important influence on the future direction the colonies would take. People in the towns were concerned with the legal disposal of property within the colony, the granting of land, the question of inheritances, the ideas of the government of the mother country for the colony, and the proper exploitation of the colony itself for their own economic benefit. Directives from them might be questioned, their demands might be resisted by the smaller settlements, but their influence was undeniable. It was an influence, moreover, that makes the question of the role of the sexes in the colonies a most complex matter.

The towns were the seat of the apparatus of government, the organizational centres for political, ecclesiastical, and commercial enterprises, webs of communication linking many quarters, the forces that brought cohesion and conformity to colonial life. Halifax, St John, Fredericton, Rivière-du-Loup, Quebec, Montreal, or Kingston, none can stand alone as the symbol for the life of a colony in the way that London might serve for the British Isles or Paris for France. Yet in each of them the threads of colonial life made a dense weave, acquired a rich colour. Their very existence meant that the colonies possessed not merely institutions and conventions for the regulations of their affairs but also the possibility of the development of social and cultural distinctiveness. People in the villages had few resources and little leisure to spare, but in the towns some people were engaged almost wholly in the establishment of norms, whether shaped by a vision of society derived from the mother country or worked out of immediate personal experience within the colony. Those who lived in new settlements or in isolated villages followed the practices of religion and the observances of social manners as time permitted and their individuality dictated. Those who lived in towns were conscious, willy-nilly, of the pressure exerted on a community by a sophisticated élite.

S. F. Wise has used the term 'official culture' to describe the social and political activities of those engaged in the apparatus of government in the colonies, 'the governor, the civil and military bureaucracies, the members of the legislature and local office holders', together with 'such other members of society who had the wealth, the leisure, the education or some similar qualification of admittance.'[5] It was in such circles that views from outside the colony were brought together with the preoccupations of those who had settled within its bounds. Here ideas of correct and incorrect conduct mattered. But if one can identify powerful social groups within these towns, their influence was a matter of flux. Within the town itself the disposition of power between varying groups was subject to change—one might distinguish the arbiter of society in Halifax or Quebec in one particular year, only to find that within six months a subtle shading of judgement had occurred. Perhaps one of the most constant features of the towns was the ebb and flow of their population: officials were sent for a set number of years, emigrants paused briefly before yet another stage in their journey, settlers came to buy, to sell, or to transact legal business.

The result was that while some dominant cultural ideals can be distinguished—the idea of the saintly life within the confines of a religious order cherished by some sections of the Catholic populace, for example, or the model of the self-reliant pioneer woman praised in most groups within the colonies—it is impossible to select any single vision of femininity to represent the approved norm for women within British North America at the opening of the nineteenth century. As the years of the nineteenth century go by and the colonies absorb ever increasing numbers of immigrants with their concepts about the proper organization of life already formed by their experience in another land, the diversity of models increases. Already by the end of the eighteenth century Nova Scotia was combining pre-Revolution Yankee with later Loyalists, returned Acadians with established Germans, not to mention Protestant and Catholic Highlanders as well as a number of Indians. New Brunswick at the same time contained Loyalists and Acadians, while each of the other colonies could point to almost as rich a mixture of components. As Michael Cross has written:

> The great folk movement that was British migration after the Napoleonic wars began to transform British North America in the 1820s. While the total was modest by the standards of the flood which would follow in the two decades ahead, over 125,000 Britons left their homes for the North American colo-

nies in these ten years. They filled in the settled areas, they pushed back the frontier, they brought large amounts of cash into an economy chronically short of specie. Their skills built Canadian businesses, from Nova Scotia's Albion coal-mines to York's wholesale houses.[6]

The story of women's experience in these years cannot be reduced to a few types—the politician's wife, the settler's wife, the daughters of the lawyers, the sisters of the lumbermen, the mothers of the explorers, or the self-denying sisters of the religious orders. Instead, while one or two careers might be closed to the direct participation of women, because women comprised half the population of the colonies no aspect of life escaped their influence. There were some women who would pass into legend in any age, the equivalent of Chaucer's Wife of Bath with her 'gat teeth' and her five husbands and many travels. Such a character was the keeper of a tavern in Bytown during the 1820s, of whom the balladeer wrote:

> She kept the reckoning, ruled the roost
>   And swung an arm of potent might
>   That few would dare to brave in fight;
> Yet she was a goodnatured soul
> As ever filled the flowing bowl;
> In sooth she dealt in goodly cheer
> Half pints of whiskey, quarts of beer.
> And when a man had spent his all
> She chalked the balance on the wall.
> And woe to him, who soon or late
> His tally did not liquidate.[7]

Some looked after their own interests, not perhaps seeking to alter existing circumstances but definitely seeking justice within them. Such a woman was Almira Dow. Before her marriage to Bradish Billings in 1812, one of the first settlers of Gloucester Township, she was a schoolteacher. 'Her salary was $7 a month in notes payable in wheat at Brockville. On one occasion she walked there from Merrickville to collect her money, but was refused as the wheat had not arrived; so she returned, gathered the wheat from the settlers, took it to Brockville and collected her account in goods!'[8] Others endured with grumbles because they must, immigrants who had crossed the ocean and found the new land, with all its promise, no substitute for the known. Such a woman was the anonymous soul reported in *The Backwoods of Canada, 1836*:

> One poor woman that was lamenting the miseries of this country was obliged to acknowledge that her prospects were far better than they ever had or could have been at home. What, then, was the cause of her continual regrets and discontent? I could hardly forbear smiling when she replied, 'She could not go to a shop of a Saturday night to lay out her husband's earnings, and have a little chat with her *naibors*, while the shopman was serving the customers,—*for why?* there were no shops in the bush and she was just dead-alive. If Mrs. Such-a-one (with whom, by the way, she was always quarrelling when they lived under the same roof) was near her she might not feel so lonesome.'

The author comments with some scorn on a woman who could demand 'a dish of gossip' at the price of 'the advantages, real solid advantages of having land and cattle, and poultry and food and firing and clothing.' But this woman found no comfort in a better physical state and looked back to the friendly known, however squalid.

Her situation, unglamorous and unsung, was one faced often enough by women, was borne without a nervous breakdown, and endured because needs must. The courage necessary to cope is the hidden theme behind the stories of so many immigrants, men and women, who formed part of this movement of peoples. Nostalgia gnawed at many a heart, and the 'Canadian Boat Song' expressed in the symbols of one group the ache of many:

> From the shieling of the misty island
> Mountains divide us and the waste of seas.
> Yet still the blood is strong,
>   the heart is Highland,
> And we in dreams behold the Hebrides.

Migration meant not merely a new life in a new land, but a life in a strange land reached only by a most difficult passage, with, more often than not, the possibility of return ruled out. The very voyage away from the known hills of Ireland, the familiar lanes of England, the communities of childhood was an ordeal in itself and one where illness and death might strike before the new land was even seen. Lasting anything from six to nine weeks, the passage across the Atlantic was usually made in a ship that was considered 'unfit for carrying *dry* cargoes, but perfectly fit for the conveyance, *on any voyage*, of cargoes not in their nature subject to sea damage.'[9] A contemporary wrote: 'Before the emigrant has been a week at sea he is an altered man. How can it be otherwise? Hundreds of poor people, men, women and children, of all ages, from the drivelling idiot of ninety to the babe just born, huddled together without light, without air, wallowing in filth . . .'[10] There is no room to go into the details of the ravages of epidemics at sea, the lack of provisions, the general misery of these voyages that landed their passengers exhausted in the ports of the New World. There is little to choose between the sufferings of men and women. Often the husband had gone on ahead to earn the money for the rest of the family. How can one compare the lot of the man, alone, lonely, looking for work and worried about those who would follow, with the lot of the wife, left behind to bring on the children, and say which was the hardest? Thomas Sligo, who arrived in St John, New Brunswick in 1847 and went on to the United States to find work, wrote to his wife: 'Be on watch at the Post Office day after day I wont delay in Relieveing yous . . . I long to see that long wished for hour that I will Embrace yous in my arms . . .'[11] May Jane Johnsons followed her husband with her two children, only to find, on arriving in Quebec, that he had died of cholera.[12]

If the lot of married people cannot be divided into two disparate parts, one much more enviable than the other, neither can that of single people. Both sexes suffered the possibilities of exploitation by the unscrupulous, but both men and women found opportunities for employment. It might be argued that domestic service was the more probable fate of women, and that should a woman wish some alternative life, then her choice would have to include marriage, the opportunities of her partner being the real gauge of her own. However this is much too simplistic a view of life in either the United States or the British North American colonies during the second quarter of the nineteenth century. The complexity of the situation, at least in Upper Canada, can be grasped at least partly through the writings of a number of women who were themselves emigrants during these years.

Mary Gapper crossed the Atlantic in 1828 at the age of thirty, expecting to stay for a year. Instead she married Edward O'Brien and spent her life in Upper Canada. Her journals were edited by Audrey Saunders Miller and published in 1968. Anne Langton was thirty-three when she came over to join her brother in 1837. Remaining unmarried, she spent the rest of her life in Upper Canada, and her journal and letters were edited by the descendant of her brother's children, H. H. Langton, in 1950. Susanna Moodie and Catharine Parr Trail have been called 'the gentle pioneers'. These two sisters, their husbands, and their brother Samuel Strickland established themselves in Upper Canada in the 1830s. Catharine Parr Traill wrote not only an account of her own experiences, *The Backwoods of Canada*, but also a work called *The Canadian Settler's Guide*, an invaluable compendium of advice on how to cope with pioneer life. Her sister, Susanna Moodie, wrote a vivid narrative of her experiences, *Roughing it in the Bush*. Together these works provide a mine of information about the experience of a group of women pioneers, those who might be called 'the female of the middling class.'[13] All the writers were talented, perhaps Susanna Moodie most capable of expressing bad-tempered exasperation, Anne Langton of displaying cheerfulness in adversity, Catharine Parr Traill of explaining how to make do with the material at hand, and Mary O'Brien of conveying the day-by-day texture of life.

Mary O'Brien wrote a journal that commented on everything. On 26 May 1829 she noted that she had mosquito bites, 'six active and eight dying away'; on 29 May she comments on household affairs, having to supply 'the deficiencies of the new girl by making a pie'; on 30 May she is dealing with literature and politics: 'I have been reading the Quarterly Review which I still find stupid enough. . . . We have just heard of the settlement of the Catholic question, at least it is to be hoped.'[14] What comes through these pages is a kaleidoscope of people, their competency to confront life not in any way determined by sex. Perhaps because she herself did not see marriage as a necessity but as an option, perhaps because she felt no constraint about moving round the world on her own, her pages breathe both self-confidence in her abilities and concern for others. From the pages of her journal for the first year of her marriage, 1830, comes the picture of a woman helping with the hay, keeping the house, commenting on *Guy Mannering*, considering how to ensure the right man gets sent to the legislature from the area, helping to choose where she and her husband should settle on the shore of Lake Simcoe, being entertained by the Governor and his wife.[15] The discrimination against the direct participation of women in the political process is softened by the very obvious indirect influence exercised. Mary O'Brien was not one to question the organization of society, partly because she did not consider that its control over her actions was in any way total. Her attitude seems to have been that the organization of the state and the pressures of society were among the matters with which human beings had to cope. Like the weather, such factors existed, could be helpful, might be harmful, but above all required intelligent appraisal.

When the present research being carried out by historians such as S. F. Wise and others on the social and intellectual attitudes of the British North American colonies during these decades is completed, it will be far simpler to place women such as Mary O'Brien in context. The work will hopefully reveal the precise strength and interconnections of each of the components of the society. In the meantime one can only distinguish the points of view of women like Mary O'Brien and perhaps suggest that the acceptance of the structures of life that one finds in her Journals is part and parcel of the belief within the British North American colonies that 'law, order and good government' is the right end of political institutions. At any rate, the life of Mary O'Brien herself shows the ability of some women in certain circumstances to face existence without feeling particularly 'cabin'd, cribbed and confined' because of her sex. Perhaps one of her great strengths was her sense of the fragility of human existence for men, women, and children. As her *Journal* shows, sickness and death, the need to protect the weak, these are matters that are as much part and parcel of her thoughts and actions as housekeeping, reading, and delight in beautiful flowers. Her strength came from an ability to distinguish what, for her, were those things she could alter and what had to be endured.

Anne Langton, living in a more restrained circle and with less resources, was much the same type of character. As Lower has pointed out, the Langtons were people who had had a 'good up-bringing and some education',[16] and in England they were very much of the 'middling class'. From the pages of Anne Langton's memoirs and letters comes the idea of settlement in Upper Canada as an adventure, the place of women in it an accepted necessity. But there is an attitude to the roles of men and women that is a straw-in-the-wind for the direction of sex-role typing at a later stage in the development of the society. John Langton is portrayed as taking an important part in community affairs in attending to his duties at Peterboro as Councillor.[17] Anne herself is shown as preoccupied with establishing schooling for the children and in organizing the lending library.[18] On first reading the impression is that there is an 'equality of difference' in their actions. Anne had frail health, which hindered her efforts; John was the instigator of action within the family. Reading the book over again, however, the concern for a structured form of social behaviour, for the 'right' ordering of life becomes more striking. The letter from John Langton to his father, written in the summer of 1834, noted 'I must address myself and tell you what *you* will miss here. You will miss society of which you are fond, at least you will find no-one of your own age with whom you would like to associate much . . . '[19] While this is only a very minor reference, nevertheless the concern with types and ranks of people is there.

So it comes as no surprise to find in Anne Langton's writings a concern with ideas of femininity based upon an image of women as having a proper code of social behaviour, one that, if not followed, destroys the woman. Within a year of her arrival in Upper Canada she wrote:

I am sometimes reminded of my early years and companionship with boys only; perhaps you would think my feminine manners in danger if you were to see me steering a boat for my gentleman rowers, or maybe handling the ropes a little in sailing, but don't be alarmed: though such things do occur occasionally, they are rather infrequent, and my woman's avocations will always, I think more than counterbalance them. I said I was often reminded of my early years. I have caught myself wishing an old long-forgotten wish, that I had been born of the rougher sex. Women are very dependent here, and give a great deal of trouble: we feel our weakness more than anywhere else.[20]

Here is evidence of the tangled connection between ideas of social hierarchy and a class-ordered society, and of the right conduct for the female of the species—the insidious belief that to be feminine one must be a lady.

Catherine Parr Traill and Susanna Moodie both reflect this attitude in their works, although both accord women a wide field of action. The ambivalence that these ladies felt is shown by two paragraphs in the former's work, *The Backwoods of Canada*.

> Our society is mostly military or naval; so that we meet on equal grounds, and are, of course, well acquainted with the rules of good breeding and polite life; too much so to allow any deviation from those laws that good taste, good sense, and good feeling have established among persons of our class.
>
> Yet it is considered by no means derogatory to the wife of an officer or gentleman to assist in the work of the house, or to perform its entire duties, if occasion requires it; to understand the mystery of soap, candle, and sugar making; to make bread, butter, and cheese, or even to milk her own cows, to knit and spin, and prepare wool for the loom. In these matters we bush ladies have a wholesome disregard of what Mr. and Mrs. So-and-so think or say. We pride ourselves on conforming to circumstances; and as a British officer must needs be a gentleman and his wife a lady, perhaps we repose quietly on that incontestable proof of our gentility, and can afford to be useful without injuring it.[21]

It is difficult to decide whether what is wanted is the life of comfort and servants, or a particular mode of life for women, and this attitude comes from the spur that brought these people to emigrate. Whereas the majority of those who crossed the Atlantic did so from sheer necessity, softened only partly by the hope of a life of greater freedom, emigrants like these sisters left to better their status. As Susanna Moodie wrote: 'We were not compelled to emigrate. Bound to England by a thousand holy and endearing ties, surrounded by a circle of chosen friends, and happy in each other's love, we possessed all that the world can bestow of good—but *wealth*.'[22] In other words, the new land was seen first and foremost as a land that would provide the means of sustaining a way of life already known and cherished. It is interesting that the reaction to the actuality of Upper Canada by these two sisters was quite different. Mrs Traill could admit that 'Not to regret my absence from my native land, and one so fair and lovely withal

Women at work in J. W. Woods Ltd., 1909. *Courtesy Public Archives Canada.*

Filling cans with Damson Plum Jam c. 1911. *Courtesy Public Archives Canada.*

Susanna Moodie. *Courtesy Public Archives Canada.*

Catherine P. Traill. *Courtesy Public Archives Canada.*

would argue a heart of insensibility; yet, I must say, for all its roughness, I love Canada and am as happy in my humble log house as if it were courtly hall or bower.'[23] But her character was very much one to make the best of things, as Clara Thomas has pointed out in the Introduction to Catherine's *The Canadian Settler's Guide*. Having expounded on fire and its dangers, for example, Catherine Traill writes firmly, 'In cases of emergency, it is folly to fold one's hands and sit down to bewail in abject terror: it is better to be up and doing.'[24]

In this work Catherine Parr Traill set down what she had painfully learnt about life in the backwoods, warning the prospective emigrant what ought to be considered before the journey was undertaken. In particular she stressed the necessity of both husband and wife agreeing on the question of emigration and having the health necessary to undertake the project, for 'a sickly, discontented person will make but a poor settler's wife in a country where cheerfulness of mind and activity of body are very essential to the prosperity of the household.'[25] Her work then sets out not only to help with questions of housekeeping, of gardening, of coping with illness in isolated places, but of making these tasks bearable. Housekeeping for Mrs Traill meant not only bread-making and preserving, it meant flowers and curtains and, of course, 'A little taste displayed about the rudest dwelling will raise the inmates in the eyes of their neighbours.'[26] One is alternately enchanted and exasperated by Catherine. Her ability to cope, to set about soap-making, to make use of foods not common in her earlier circumstances such as large eels, to bake bread, beginning by making the yeast from 'half a pail of potatoes', all such activities arouse admiration.[27] At the same time her concern for social prestige is aggravating. How fortunate she considered the 'many young women who were formerly servants in my house (and) are now farmers' wives, going to church or the market towns with their own sleighs or light waggons and in point of dress, better clothed than myself.'[28] One leaves her writings with the impression that she suffered from that British disease, the belief that status mattered, yet was really too intelligent to allow it to hamper her life.

Her sister was of a much different persuasion and one wonders what it must have been like to have been an acquaintance of hers. She had tremendous pride in her family, asserting that she 'was

the youngest in a family remarkable for their literary attainments.'[29] She was convinced of the right ordering of a society
based on rank. One wonders whether her favourite hymn would
not have been 'All things Bright and Beautiful.... The rich man
in his castle, the poor man at his gate,' for she remarks upon 'the
saucy familiarity of servants, who, republican in spirit, think
themselves as good as their employers.'[30] By the time one is
half-way through *Roughing it in the Bush* the suspicion is very
strong that Susanna's and her husband's decision to emigrate, if
quite definitely not because of imminent starvation, was because
they were unable to maintain a particular style of living without
emigrating. But while Susanna revealed herself as a snob of the
first water, concluding that Canada "To the poor industrious
working men ... presents many advantages; to the poor gentleman, *none*,'[31] she also revealed a delight in life, an exasperated
ability to cope with circumstance, and a great talent to convey her
view of society and its happenings. For example she described the
events of a cold day in February 1837 with pith and wit and less
self-pity than total exasperation. The temperature was thirty
below zero and 'it would have been much colder if the thermom-
eter had been longer.' It 'was so intensely cold', she went on, that
everything liquid froze in the house. The wood that had been
drawn for the fire was green and it ignited too slowly to satisfy
the shivering impatience of women and children; 'I vented mine in
audibly grumbling over the wretched fire, at which I in vain
endeavoured to thaw frozen bread, and to dress crying children.'[32] It was this day that the house burnt down. Since she wrote
with exasperation rather than self-pity, one can maintain interest
in her adventures, with three small children to manage and her
husband from home. Yet her statement: 'It was always a humiliat-
ing feeling to our proud minds, that hirelings should witness our
dreadful struggles with poverty ... '[33] makes one gasp at the mixture of courage, commonsense, and snobbery.

It is difficult to assess the influence of women of this sort upon
Upper Canadian society. The sharp division seen by Leo Johnson
in his article 'The political Economy of Ontario Women in the
Nineteenth Century'[34] is too clear cut. One cannot divide the
people of any part of British North America during the first half
of the nineteenth century into toilers and aristocrats with any
precision. Marxian analysis, developed for an urban, industrial

society within the institutional structure of a nation-state, has little to reveal about societies built around rural life. But even if one decides to rely upon Marxian terminology, the analysis breaks down because of the immense variety of social groups within Upper Canada. The idea of the 'ownership of the means of production' can be used to divide people in the community into the 'haves' and the 'have-nots', but the groups in Upper Canada were so heterogeneous that such a division falsifies. There were the people who lived on the fringes of all organized structures, the kin to those today who register neither birth nor death, so remaining outside the census. Statisticians compute that almost 10 per cent of the population are not covered by the census. Even in countries such as the present-day Soviet Union people of this character preserve their independence by refusing to fill any form: not being 'born' on a certificate they have no legal existence, and while this means no welfare benefits from the state it will also mean no identity for the state to control. Gypsies in earlier centuries and even today are the prime example. Here is one description of a girl seen by Susanna Moodie: 'seventeen or eighteen years of age, with sharp knowing features, a forward, impudent, carriage, and a pert voice, standing upon one of the trunks, and surveying all our proceedings in the most impertinent manner. The creature was dressed in a ragged dirty purple stuff gown, cut very low in the neck, with an old cotton hankerchief tied over her head; her uncombed tangled locks, falling over her thin, inquisitive face, in a state of perfect nature. Her legs and feet were bare, and in her coarse dirty, red hands, she swung to and fro an empty "glass decanter".'[35] There were also the hardworking immigrants of the lumbering towns, not merely those who made Bytown, now the federal capital, a rowdy and lawless settlement, but people like Thomas Need of Bobcaygeon, who in the 1830s owned the saw-mill that established the village. There were those who came to work on the Welland Canal, those who came to serve an exile, such as the Tolpuddle martyrs, as well as individuals of wealthier backgrounds. The Tolpuddle martyrs were men accused of fomenting revolution in England because of their attempt to form a union for agricultural workers. Three of these families, Loveless, Standfield, and Brine, settled in Upper Canada.[36] The variety of groups seems endless: those who established themselves in York or Kingston, owning what one *Emigrant's Guide* called 'elegant private residences'; the Cartwright family, with clear-cut ideas of why the wrong side had won the American Revolution; Colonel Talbot and his settlers, with martinet views on the proper conduct of life; let alone the groups of Mormons, of Methodists, and other people intent upon creating an earthly reflection of envisioned Paradise. Arthur Lower remarked that in the Ontario county he knew best there were 'Highland townships, North of Ireland townships, Catholic Irish settlements, a French township and other minor French settlements, one or two German communities, many miscellaneous English, a few Negroes, and various odds and ends.'[37] To analyse this patchwork quilt for general attitudes to women demands not merely that distinctions are perceived but an ability to understand their importance.

There are only two general assertions that can be advanced about women in Canada in the first half of the nineteenth century, the rest has to be thought of in terms of particularisms. Firstly, the dominance of rural life meant that the value of woman as economic partner in the struggle for existence was a matter of general agreement. Secondly, as the century advanced the moulding of everyday life in the colonies meant the strengthening of conventions of behaviour, and these conventions very often worked against women. There is a poem by Isabella Valency Crawford that has caught the most optimistic mood of women who helped to settle British North America during these decades. The heroine of the poem looks at the land around her and declares:

And these wild woods and plains are fairer far
Than Eden's self . . .
I would not change these wild and rocking woods
Dotted by little homes of unbark'd trees
For the smooth sward of Eden bowers . . . [38]

If the evidence of Susanna Moodie's unhappiness has to be set against this 'home in the clearing', it must nevertheless be recognized that these lines did mirror part of reality.

The status and position of women on the farms and in the small villages of the colonies was determined above all by personality and kin. Leo Johnson suggests that one can look at woman in these circumstances as defined by her economic role, her labour necessary to the success of the family, her reproductive capacity essential for the advancement of all, since numerous children were so many potential money makers.[39] Johnson considers that 'Men remarried quickly, not merely because of loneliness but because of economic necessity', and 'adult females without husbands and families were persons without a clear cut economic or social role.'[40] Such a tidy world does not adequately convey the vigour of normal human life. It suggests that there is no such thing as love between human beings or contentment without vaulting ambition. It omits entirely the force of human character. Susanna Moodie relates the story of a young man completely under the thumb of an old woman who had less education, less prospects, breeding, 'class' than himself. One of the contentious issues between them was the lad's washing when he arrived from work:

> Och! my dear heart, yer too particular intirely; we've no time in the woods to be clane.' She would say to him in answer to his request for soap and a towel, 'An' is it soap yer a-wantin'? I tell yer that that same is not to the fore; bating the throuble of makin' it's little soap that the misthress can get to wash the clothes for us and childher, without yer wastin' it makin' yer purty skin as white as a leddy's. Do, darlint, go down to the lake and wash there; that basin is big enough, anyhow.' And John would laugh and go down to wash in order to appease the wrath of the old woman ... '[41]

But once the countryside and fishing villages are left, the question of discrimination against women becomes a matter of growing importance. It is in the towns that one can discover the roots of a class structure. In St John, New Brunswick, for example, by the middle of the century affairs were organized with reference to a social hierarchy. As C. N. Wallace has pointed out, 'An attempt to eliminate the property qualification for voters was rejected in the House of Assembly through the efforts of people like Tilley who "condemned the principle of allowing those to vote who had not paid their taxes".'[42] Edith Firth has found that by the 1830s York had a very obvious social structure, a strong middle class, 'articulate, keenly aware of the world beyond their immediate surroundings' as well as 'men connected with industry ... small shopkeepers, clerks and skilled tradesmen, plumbers, paperhangers, ice-cream makers, lapidaries and truss makers ... and a significant body of urban poor.'[43] In these circumstances one can begin to trace the impact of a much more rigid image of the proper social behaviour for women.

Even as early as 1817 morality had become a matter of social concern. In other words the private behaviour of people within the community was seen as something that ought to be structured by rules and regulations; the state or those holding power within the community had every right to be in the bedrooms of the nation. Such an attitude was shown in the dispensation of charity in York: need alone was not the test for receiving charity; charity was dispensed to the virtuous, the deserving poor. For example Mrs Powell, wife of Judge Powell, would work on behalf of 'a poor woman far advanced in her pregnancy'[44] who was abandoned by her husband. But in the case of one of her own unmarried servant girls who became pregnant, Mrs Powell's reaction was severe and unyielding.

It needs to be underlined that what is happening here is that sexual morality is no longer a matter of punishment by members of a religious society, the demand of a group for adherence to its ideas by those who have committed themselves to its principles. It is now the exercise of power by members of the community at large over the conduct of individual people, the belief that people ought to abide by certain rules even if they have made no formal commitment to do so. Whatever the views of the majority of people within the community of Upper Canada, the society, those holding positions of power and influence, would act along particular principles. As a result, charity is now merely a matter of something to be deserved, 'love thy neighbour' becoming 'love thy neighbour if worthy.'

The acceptance of class distinctions is also developed. At one point Mrs Powell remarked to her brother that 'you know I am not addicted to extravagance in any personal indulgence, but in an aristocratical Government, expences must be incurred according to the station held.'[45] The question of sex-role typing in Upper Canada involves, as the nineteenth century continues, the organization of the whole society. There is an obvious link between belief in privilege and rank and belief in particular attributes of men and women. There is little difference in the curriculum of studies offered to girls and boys in the common school. There both boys and girls were taught grammar, reading, spelling, parsing, writing, and arithmetic.[46] The lives of the working people did not permit the discrimination that becomes apparent when one looks at the studies offered in private schools, where girls were not offered the rigorous mental training that their brothers received. In Mrs Cockburn's Girls' School under the patronage of the Rt Honorable Lady Sarah Maitland, the duties of a particular life style were taught rather than subjects that might lead to employment. The pupils at Mrs Cockburn's establishment were taught 'the English Language, Gramatically, History, Geography, the use of Globes with plain and fancy Needle Work ... Drawing and Painting on Velvet' as well as 'Music, Dancing, Flower and Card-work.'[47]

But, as has been suggested earlier, one cannot make the towns stand for the colonies. The conventions that one finds emerging in the small societies of the urban centres are constantly modified by the impact of the hinterland, of the backwoods, the settlements elsewhere within the colony. The status and position of women in British North America during the nineteenth century has yet to be fully told in the context of the general political and social development of these colonies. It can only be suggested that those conventions that particularly restricted women's activities were less effective than elsewhere because of the nature of life in the country. As the community established formal institutions for the organization of life, the explicit exclusion of women from direct influence in certain areas becomes more and more burdensome. Nevertheless, even though these restrictions are undeniable, the exclusion of women from the franchise being only the most noticeable of these, it is also undeniable that the idea of women having a role to play in society is still in existence, e.g. among the Methodists who still used women school teachers. The continued existence of this attitude provided the jumping off point for the subsequent fight at the end of the century to permit women to attend universities and to gain the vote.

Once more the question is one of tension and dominance. Of the many ideas struggling for expression within the community, which ones were to gain the acceptance of those who held the power to influence the conventions and institutions of the society? Which ones were to be the basis of laws? Of the ordinary accepted standards of social interchange? As the nineteenth century passed these questions gain a greater importance because the new methods of communication made it possible for some ideas to become dominant in a way not possible before Confederation. Yet the beginnings of constraints existed earlier in the century. At this time it is important to realize that if what can be called a 'middle-class ethic', a belief in the classification and categorization of people based on appearance or behaviour, was growing stronger, there also existed alternative ideas about the organization of society.

For the growth of prejudice and discrimination against women is part and parcel of an attempt to cope with the problems that faced people as their lives were affected by actions over a wider territory and in a wider sphere. Government of a small number of people in a small area of land, rarely visited by other peoples, is a very different matter from the government of many millions over wide areas, whose economic existence depends on the general effort of all.

It is against this background that one has to envisage developments in the nineteenth century. People are seeking the right ordering of society, looking for some way to simplify the problems to be solved. At first categorization of people seemed to be the best way of working. Sex-role typing was an obvious, discernible categorization, but it was only one line of discrimination emphasized in western civilization, others being language, religion, money, colour, aesthetic sense. The complexity of what is happening is visible above all in Europe at the middle of the nineteenth century, and, of course, European developments were of immense importance to Canadian experience.

NOTES

[1] S. F. Wise, 'The 1790's', in J. M. S. Careless, *Colonists and Canadians, 1760-1867* (Macmillan, 1968), p. 62.

[2] Joseph Gueguen to Mgr Hubert, Archives de l'Archveque de Quebec, New Brunswick, Vicaires/2.

[3] Nova Scotia Historical Series prints Sigogne's rules for villages in *Reports*, vol. 23, pp. 113-17.

[4] Archives de l'Archeveque de Quebec, N.B., VI/96: V.G., X:139.

[5] Wise, *op. cit.*, p. 63.

[6] M. Cross, 'The 1820's', in Careless, *op. cit.*, p. 150.

[7] A. H. D. Ross, *Ottawa, Past and Present* (1927), p. 113.

[8] Edwin C. Guillet, *Early Life in Upper Canada* (University of Toronto Press, 1933), p. 53.

[9] Quoted in T. Coleman, *Passage to America* (Penguin, 1974), p. 101, from Lloyd's Register of British and Foreign Shipping, London, 1851.

[10] Quoted in *ibid.*, p. 120, from the *First Report from the Select Committee of the House of Lords on Colonization*, 1847.

[11] Quoted in Coleman, *op. cit.*, p. 29.

[12] *Ibid.*, p. 26.

[13] All these works are at present, 1975, in print. A. S. Miller's edition of Mary O'Brien is published by Macmillan of Canada, the Langton work by Clarke Irwin, and the works of Moodie and Traill are part of the New Canadian Library series, McClelland and Stewart. Morris' work is printed by a division of General Publishing Co.

[14] M. O'Brien, *op. cit.*, p. 52.

[15] *Ibid.*, pp. 121-20.

[16] A. R. M. Lower, *Canadians in the Making* (Longmans, 1958), p. 201.

[17] H. H. Langton, ed., *A Gentlewoman in Upper Canada* (Clarke Irwin, 1964), p. 167.

[18] *Ibid.*, p. 170.

[19] *Ibid.*, p. 4.

[20] *Ibid.*, p.60.

[21] Catherine Parr Traill, *op. cit.*, pp. 98-9.

[22] S. Moodie, *op. cit.*, p. 137.

[23] Catherine Parr Traill, *The Backwoods of Canada, op. cit.*, p. 144.

[24] *Ibid., The Canadian Settler's Guide, op. cit.*, p. XIII.

[25] *Ibid.*, p. 1.

[26] *Ibid.*, p. 55.

[27] *Ibid.*, pp. 166 and 92.

[28] *Ibid.*, p. 10.

[29] S. Moodie, *op. cit.*, p. 138.

[30] *Ibid.*, p. xvii.

[31] *Ibid.*, p. 236.

[32] *Ibid.*, p. 192.

[33] *Ibid.*, p. 198.

[34] L. Johnson, 'The Political Economy of Ontario Women in the Nineteenth Century' in *Women at Work in Ontario* (Canadian Women's Educational Press, 1974), pp. 12-31.

[35] Quoted in Lower, *op. cit.*, pp. 204-5.

[36] J. Marlow, *The Tolpuddle Martyrs* (Panther, 1971), p. 256.

[37] Lower, *op. cit.*, p. 207.

[38] D. Sinclair, *Nineteenth Century Narrative Poems* (McClelland and Stewart, 1972), p. 190.

[39] Johnson, *op. cit.*, pp. 16-17.

[40] *Ibid.*, p. 17.

[41] Moodie, *op. cit.*, p. 199.

[42] C. N. Wallace, 'St. John', in 'The Canadian City in the 19th Century', *Urban History Review*, 1975, p. 120.

[43] E. Firth, *The Town of York: A Further Collection of Documents of Early Toronto, 1815-1870* (Champlain Society, 1966), p. 1xvi.

[44] Mrs W. D. Powell to George Murray, York, 19 Oct. 1817, in Firth, *op. cit.*, p. 222.

[45] Powell to Murray, York, 27 Feb. 1819, *ibid.*, p. 304.

[46] Quarterly Report of the Common School, 1828, in Firth, *op. cit.*, p. 149.

[47] Advertisement in the Upper Canada *Gazette and Weekly Register*, 23 May 1822, in Firth, *op. cit.*, p. 152.

Seven

European Conventions and Regulations

W. H. McNeill has underlined two themes as dominating the development of the last two hundred years: 'the growth of human control over inanimate forms of energy; and an increasing readiness to tinker with social institutions and customs in the hope of attaining desired goals.'[1] As far as the status and position of women in society are concerned, both these themes were important. The first meant that the circumstances of everyday life, the working world of many people, was rapidly changed. Between them industrial development and technological advancement created a new environment for people and changed the appearance of Europe. At the same time many people were aware of this change and were making considerable efforts to organize reaction to what was happening. Debate over what the old traditions of life had been, what could, or ought to be preserved from them, and what were the inescapable consequences of the new industries and towns shook gathering after gathering, university common-rooms, drawing rooms in country houses, and political meetings.

It was during these years that the historical perspective came to be considered important, and historical tradition was used as a forceful argument to sustain certain beliefs. It is not merely that social philosophers such as Marx framed their arguments in terms of a schematization of human history and destiny. In many disciplines the historical point of view was used to explain the present. Renan's *Life of Jesus* attempted to come to grips with problems of Christianity within the context of historical events: how reliable was the documentary evidence for His life? What was happening at the time of His birth and death? The publication of Charles Darwin's *The Origin of the Species* in 1859 meant that the idea of evolution was extended, not merely through biological and geological time, but by implication, through the historical development of humanity.

It is important to realize that this emphasis upon the historical vision was developed in a period when stereotyping of sex-roles was accepted by many of those who influenced the conventions and structures of the society. Further, while some women had been admitted to some universities, such as the University of London, as early as 1839, the new discipline of history was very much the preserve of the male sex. It is not surprising that the depiction of the role of women in history tended either to substantiate what the writer considered to be a reflection of the proper order of life, or to be non-existent.

Macauley, for example, in his multi-volumed *History of England* made few references to women. He wrote about men, whether artisans, gentlemen, members of the nobility, or the poor. Even when talking about national character at the end of his chapter on the 'State of England in 1685', his conclusions are concerned with a once 'rude and thoughtless schoolboy who became 'a refined and accomplished man'. To prove his contention that 'our ancestors were less humane than their posterity', one of his examples concerned 'Husbands of decent station [who] were not ashamed to beat their wives.'[2] Macauley made the assumptions that women were subordinate to men, and that people in the lower classes will obviously indulge in less civilized behaviour than their 'betters'.

Thus as Europe undertook a tremendous self-examination, trying to discover from what had happened how to make decisions about what ought to happen to the organization of society, the contribution of women was frequently ignored except as helpmeet within the home, as a member of a family unit whose social and political personality was generally that of the male. Nevertheless it must be remembered that what was under consideration was the examination of the human condition and that, even if the particular experience of women was neglected it was not, and could not be, completely ignored. Every European state set about compiling evidence on its citizens, and the volumes of documentation—government enquiry, joint commissions, private investigation—that began to come forth from the press in the 1820s and 1830s reached flood proportions in the last decades of the nineteenth century. While the final analysis of all this evidence has not yet been made, it is quite obvious that its main burden is a story of considerable human misery that, to a very great extent, was the lot of men as much as of women, of children as much as of adults.

There was no single agreed answer to these ills, but there was a consensus that some action was needed. By 1891 his Holiness Pope Leo XIII was sufficiently exercised over the sufferings of the poor to write an encyclical *Rerum Novarum*, 'The Condition of the Working Classes', in which he called attention to 'the need for some opportune remedy [to be] found quickly for the misery and wretchedness pressing so unjustly on the majority of the working class.'[3] He went on to affirm that 'It is neither just nor human so to grind men down with excessive labour as to stupefy their minds and wear out their bodies.' Working from very different premises that discounted organized religion as a force for social change, Sidney and Beatrice Webb, English reformers, believed that society, while in need of change, *was* being changed, and the future really demanded little more than the reinforcement of trends for social reform that were already visible. They believed that by the 1890s Europe had reached an 'unconscious acceptance of this progressive Socialism', and could poke fun at

> The Individualist Town Councillor [who] will walk along the municipal pavement, lit by municipal gas and cleansed by municipal brooms with municipal water, and seeing by the municipal clock in the municipal market that he is too early to meet his children coming from the municipal school yard by the county lunatic asylum and municipal hospital, will use the national telegraph system to tell them not to walk through the municipal park but to come by the municipal tramway, to meet him in the municipal reading room by the municipal art gallery, museum and library, where he intends to consult some of the national publications in order to prepare his next speech in the municipal town hall, in favour of the nationalization of the canals and the increase of government control over the railway system. 'Socialism, sir,' he will say, 'Don't waste the time of a practical man by your fantastic absurdities. Self-help, sir, individual self-help that's what's made our city what it is . . .'[4]

Others such as Lenin would work for drastic but planned revolution, and yet others such as Anarchists gave way to final despair about the life of the community and wished to destroy everything that humanity had achieved in Europe, hoping total destruction might provide the ashes for a new phoenix.

What bound all these attitudes together by the end of the

nineteenth century was the power and the reality of the organization and institutions of the society. Whether its claims were accepted or denied, everywhere society was recognized, perceived as an actor in human affairs. The earlier writers of the 1830s and the 1840s had largely envisaged society as something important to all but controlling very few. In *Le Rouge et Le Noir* Stendhal presented society as one of the controls over people's lives, as important as the religious control of what God expects of them. He made his hero seek wordly honours because these were what the human community had been led to believe were important. With Flaubert's *Madame Bovary* as with Thackeray's *Vanity Fair*, the same theme is central: here are the lives of those who wish 'to gain the whole world' because they do not believe they have souls to lose. By the end of the nineteenth century this worldliness had been explored fully by writers such as Trollope and Proust.

At the same time a new perception had emerged, the idea of society as juggernaut, as the manacles of the community. While earlier writers had depicted the human community as containing 'society', as having this as one arbiter of human destiny but still only one, later writers see society as containing the community. Zola in *Germinal*, published in 1885, writes of society as having swallowed the community whole, as a machine that ground together employer and employee without much distinction. The theme of this novel is not merely the despair of the victim but the impotency of the powerful. Zola wrote of the wretchedness of the mining towns of northern France not only to show the suffering of particular individuals but the final sterility of all life led in their confines. The accident in the mines, the strike, the acts of sabotage are presented as matters out of the control of both the workers and the company. No human hand can grasp the sorry state of things and set it right. The struggle by the workers is crippled by their very possession of the most vital attribute of human beings—the ability to love one another. Defiance is ended because workers have wives, mothers, children, and 'one must eat'. Zola was quite conscious that his novel was more than a work of art. He saw it as 'un roman socialiste',[5] something that would make the reader accept workers as people—men, women, and children. He tried to make *Germinal* more than a story and more than a tract: it was to be actual life. So the people of the comfortable houses and the easy days were to be as human as the oppressed, the owner of the small factory defending 'his skin, his life, that of his family', who is ruined by the end of the book, is no less a person than 'le vieil ouvrier ... et la raccommodeur, fumant, hochant la tête, élevant leurs mains tremblantes.'[6]

What Zola is talking about is the eternal task of human society —to define what it means to be human and to determine what the community must do to make its social arrangements allow people to be fully human. In the last pages of *Germinal* he catches this intent magnificently and poses for the reader the problem of how much can be excused by the phrase 'this is the way things are', when the result is the mangling of human lifes. Two of the major characters in the novel are Etienne and Catherine, whose lives have been determined by the poverty of their families, the lack of any opportunity other than going down the mine, the demands of their responsibilities to those they love, and their own needs. At long last they are brought together but only when trapped in the mine, buried below ground in the more-than darkness of the pit, with the company of a corpse. Zola wrote:

> With a rush [Catherine] clung to him, she sought his mouth and pressed her own passionately to his lips. The shadows seemed to lift, she saw the sun again, she discovered once more the tranquil mirth of the loving. He, trembling to feel her this way against his body, half-naked under the shirt, his trousers in shreds, took her, in an awakening of his manhood. And this finally was their wedding night, at the bottom of this tomb, on a bed of mud, the need not to die without having happiness, the desperate need to live, to know of life one last time. They loved in despair of all, in death.
>
> Then, there was nothing else. Etienne sat on the ground, always in the same corner, and he had Catherine against his knees, crouched, immobile. Hour after hour went by. He thought for a long time that she slept; then he touched her, she was very cold, she was dead. Yet he did not stir, fearful to wake her.[7]

Etienne is finally rescured two days later, days in which 'she never moved, he touching her with his mechanical caress, reassured to feel her so tranquil.'

The reader is given not categories—worker, owner, man,

woman—but human beings and the grief and sadness of human suffering. Somehow Zola managed to make *Germinal* a statement of the crisis of the community, with nothing of the agony softened and yet not ending in nihilist despair. The final pages of the novel look to the future as a believable time when the machine will have come under control, when the society that now chews humanity for fuel will be made to work by other means. In spite of human frailty, in spite of 'the way things are', in spite of blindness, wilful and as well unwitting, a new dispensation would be wrought. There is only one precondition: to value the individual.

Zola's work is only one account of the late nineteenth-century perception of the dilemma, the constant dichotomy in human affairs—the need to strike a balance between individual freedoms and group needs. The urban, industrial society of late nineteenth-century Europe, linked by rail and steamship, flooded by newspapers, journals, books, debated the claims of morality and expediency with tremendous passion. How, where, when, to what extent, for how long, must a part suffer for the whole? While there was little doubt in most minds that the social organization of the community was a necessity, whether to control people by the dominance of conventions alone, or by the structures and institutions of the state, there was much debate about how much organization was necessary, and over what sectors of experience that organization should be enforced. On one side were those who had accepted the methods evolved at the opening of the century to contain the new: the rigidity of the state, the creation of categories to help manage the press of people and their demands. Humanity was typed into exclusive units—the unwashed, the destitute, the poor, the middle class, the aristocrat —and assigned predictable behaviour—dishonesty, moral degeneracy, limited ambition, limited intellect, social insensitivity. On the other side were those who insisted that such categories were a stumbling block to humanity, and that the solution could be found in some social structure built on an intepretation of human equality. This is not to say that those who believed in dividing people into categories necessarily denied the need to reform many aspects of the organization of society, and when dealing with legislation on what might be called improvement of living conditions, the debate was usually about questions of timing, of priorities, of the practical possibilities. But when the debate was

over some question of human equality, and particularly legislation to improve the lot of women, these people were opposed to
such drastic reform and based their arguments on unalterable
characteristics, basic principles, and fundamental capacities. Lord
Brabazon, writing in 1882 on the need for the House of Lords to
impose regulations for the work hours of shop-assistants,
appealed to 'the common cause of humanity'.[8] He supported his
argument by describing their working conditions and his conclusion was hammered home by an appeal to economics. He stated
that he knew 'individual girls working in shops where the rule is
from 8 a.m. to 10 p.m. every day, and on Saturdays, and when
stock-taking (which they seem to do twice a year), to 11 and
11:30.' He pointed out that their 'only time for a walk (was) between 10 and 12 p.m., and that, too, when heated, excited, and
over strained! and some very young, many but fourteen!' Lord
Brabazon concluded by pointing out that the employer in one
shop 'said how much he would close earlier, for the expenses, gas,
labour, all was more than his profit, only he dared not close when
others were open!'

The tone of Lord Brabazon's argument is one of reason and an
appeal for action, not to alter the basic structure of society, but
merely to adjust it somewhat. Similarly debates about the treatment of orphans, about the need for workhouses for the old run on
more humane principles, about the need to regulate home industries such as fur-pulling, artificial-flower making, and match-
box glueing are based on the same premise. In the business of the
fur-puller, for example, whose work was 'broadly speaking—to remove the long coarse hairs from rabbit skins: the skins and the
collected hairs having each their further uses',[9] the demand for
action is based on the argument that such lives, once known
about, must be improved. The account of the lives of women engaged in this occupation, published in the November 1897 issue of
The Nineteenth Century, contained little argument—it simply assumed that the need to change these conditions was obvious and
the possibility of changing them good. The writer, Edith Hogg, is
concerned not only with the conditions of work—long hours in
appalling rooms—but also with the authorities—the London
County Council, the School Board, those administering Poor Relief
—that should interfere 'for the fur-puller's benefit'.

The point of the account is made by contrast, the lives of the fur-pullers being set against what the writer assumes without question is the norm. The streets of London where the work is done are described as being without any intimation of 'the worth and dignity of that human nature made after the image of the Divine', and it is asserted that 'to apply the word "homes" to dens such as these is cruel mockery.' The 'home' is then described: 'the room barely eight feet square, even less because of its accumulation of dirt: it has to serve for day and night alike. . . . The window is tightly closed, because such air as can find its way in from the stifling court below would force the hairs into the noses and eyes and lungs of the workers. . . . To the visitor, indeed, the choking sensation caused by the passage of hairs into the throat, and the nausea from the smell of the skins, is at first almost too overpowering for speech.' The text is packed with figures—numbers of hours worked, wages paid—and is brought alive by 'personal histories' such as that of the elderly woman who 'had been left an orphan at ten years old, and had done the pulling ever since. Her husband was a waterside labourer, never in regular work, and his earnings did no more than pay the rent. Out of a family of eight she had "buried" five, but did not apparently see any connexion between this and the pulling, though it was "dreadful unhealthy work".' The conclusion is a call to improve these '"homes" in which leisure was unknown, or if it comes as the rarest of visitors, comes as a curse.' There is no philosophical argument except the reference to the idea of motherhood as something normally associated with joy, here merely a matter of toil.

This attitude towards demonstrable misery is found in all European states at the end of the nineteenth century. Few people, of whatever rank, wealth, or ambition, were completely insensitive to the sight of human suffering, especially suffering that could be staunched by some measure that would not cause a major alteration in the accustomed pattern of life. This is the attitude that ensured the passage through assemblies peopled by the wealthy of legislation shortening working hours; it is the attitude that provided state schools, that accepted the need for housing regulations, and gave a measure of public-health care in state after state by 1900. But it was not an attitude that would seek any fundamental reorganization of the accepted conventions of life. One would feed the poor: starvation was wrong. This did not imply that one should seek an egalitarian society. One would fight for better working conditions for poor women: it was not proper that inhumane treatment be accepted without question for those whose lot in life was less than fortunate. This did not imply that one should support careers for women, nor the active participation of women in direct political power.

The vital difference in attitude towards change in the structure of the community, as opposed to legislation affecting a segment of society, legislation whose purpose and effect could be carefully calculated, can be illustrated by the story of the campaigns waged by Josephine Butler against the inhumane treatment of the prostitute and the sexual exploitation of women. She had been born in 1828 in Northumberland, one of seven children of John Grey, who was determined to bring up his daughters to be as independent as his sons.[10] Beautiful, intelligent, educated, wealthy, she married in 1851 George Butler, the son of one of the headmasters of Harrow and himself of brilliant intellect. Throughout her life until her death in 1906, she fought for the right of women to consideration as human beings, morally responsible for their lives.

Her struggle was much more bitter than that waged by Wilberforce against the slave trade earlier in the century, or by Charles Booth against urban slums at the century's end. Wilberforce after all was working against only a small number of people who were actually engaged in the trade, and since there were no slaves in England the trade was hardly approved of there. Charles Booth was merely demonstrating something people had tried not to notice, although it was visible enough: the appalling living conditions of the big cities. It was far easier to appeal for better working conditions in mines and factories, to ask for educational reforms, to demand plumbing and sewage improvements, than to ask for changes in the law, changes that implied a statement about men and women and human sexuality. As has been suggested, there is a considerable difference between the sexual exploitation of women and political and social discrimination against women, although frequently all three are found operating in the same community and reinforcing a general disdain for one sex by the other. Nineteenth-century Europe, whether Catholic or Protestant, whether German or English, French or Italian, had experienced the development of a vision of sexual morality enshrined in laws and in convention that encouraged the sexual exploitation of women.

By the time of Josephine Butler's campaigns the tradition of monogamy was now more than just the commonly accepted social structure of the family within Europe: it was represented in civil laws in most states as the sole legitimate means of sexual expression. On its own this might not have meant the exploitation of women, but it was allied with a particular interpretation of political right and sexual appetite that together produced a witches' brew of contradictory images of the proper ordering of human sexuality. Women were too pure to feel sexual appetite, but woman was the temptress. Women were the guardians of all that was worthwhile in human civilization, but woman was too stupid to be considered the political equal of man. Women must be protected within the family environment, and the problem of those orphaned and unmarried was in some mysterious manner their own fault. Since many of these ideas were developing at the same time that beliefs about the right and proper nature of social stratification into classes were commanding acceptance, and therefore it was doubtful whether women of differing social classes could be expected to act in similar fashion, the resulting vision of the proper behaviour to be expected from women was a very muddled one.

The changes wrought by urbanization and industrialization had made the family both more important and more fragile to many people. The demands of the new age were such that many agreed with the words of Ruskin: 'the man . . . must encounter all peril and trial; to him must be the failure, the offence, the inevitable error; often he must be wounded or subdued; often misled and *always* hardened. But he guards the woman from all this; within his house, as ruled by her, unless she herself has sought it, need enter no danger, no temptation, no cause of error or offence. This is the true nature of home – it is Peace; the shelter not only from all injury, but from all terror, doubt, and division.'[11] Home as sanctuary from the working world was the concept that the industrial changes brought. It was, of course, particularly the vision of those families that could manage without the labour of the wife, and of those families where work was removed from the living quarters. It could scarcely apply to farm life, fishing villages, the actual urban poor where men, women, and children had to contribute labour to buy food and shelter for the family. Yet by the end of the nineteenth century this idea of home led one man to insist to Josephine Butler that 'no occupations should be opened to women, not even the light trades, they ought never to work, nor have the means of working'.[12] Her reply was a careful presentation of the reality: 'There are more than two million and a half of unmarried women in England, working for their own bread.... They would marry, but they cannot; there are many more women than men in the country.... According to your theory of shutting them out of trades, and not suffering them to work at all for subsistence, you have two million and a half of women for whom there is no alternative but starvation or prostitution.'[13]

By the middle of the nineteenth century the pattern was clear: the ideal of family, of home, was linked to the idea of the proper and sole occupation of women as homemakers, wives, and mothers. In this context sexual appetite was looked upon as something that could destroy the one safe refuge. It became not merely the one human appetite that should be regulated, but in being regulated it also became the moral foundation of social life. What evolved out of this attitude was a vision of sexual appetite as a male need and something to be endured by the female. While there were some who maintained in print that 'sexual enjoyment was more delicious and protracted for women',[14] the force of written opinion was that 'woman is naturally and organically frigid.'[15] As Ronald Pearsall has shown in his work *The Worm in the Bud: The World of Victorian Sexuality*, the impact of these beliefs meant, inevitably, a great gulf between public appearance and private indulgence. It resulted among other things in the general acceptance of the 'double standard' – that the sexual conduct of a man need be neither as continent nor as circumspect as that required of a woman. This was an attitude that Josephine Butler, a logical thinker and convinced Christian, could not accept. In 1878 she wrote to her husband from Oxford: 'Fancy Talbot (the Warden of Keble) saying to me "but do you really think that sin is equal in men and women?" And an archdeacon said to Rawlinson, "But you know it is absurd to suppose that the seventh commandment is as binding on men as it is on women".'[16]

At the same time there was a social decision that, since women did not suffer the force of sexual desire, their sexual indulgence was a worse transgression. Women ought to be strong enough to resist seduction. As the sexual object, without which there would be no sin, women were the most guilty party in any illicit sexual relationship. Thus there was a moral condemnation of prostitution not merely on the grounds of the sinfulness of incontinent sexuality, but also on the grounds of the moral wickedness and degeneracy of the prostitute. The harlot, having chosen a life of sin that with industry and prayer could easily have been avoided, was hated as the wilful occasion of the sin of others, the temptress without which there would be no filth. At the same time the man was excused. As the preamble to one Royal Commission dealing with matters relating to prostitutes commented: 'There is no comparison to be drawn between prostitutes and the men who consort with them. With one sex the offence is committed as a matter of gain, with the other it is an irregular indulgence of a natural impulse.'[17]

The inevitable result of this peculiar notion of human sexuality was the undeniable exploitation of prostitutes and of women suspected of such activities. A woman considered unchaste was a woman excluded from all legal consideration, her rights as a person nonexistent, and her claim to reform considered worthless. Josephine Butler met this attitude in Paris, where she was informed of the case of a young girl, about to bear an illegitimate child, who was being pressured to register as a prostitute. Josephine went to the chief of the morality section of the Paris police about the matter, and described the interview to her husband.

> M. Roux's view is, the girl has been *debauched*. In such cases it is well – it is indispensable – that these girls should be registered at once and without delay before they have time to pursue their career any farther, and become diseased and communicate the disease to *honest men* (I am quoting the very words spoken to me) to *honest men!* – Yes, it is necessary to lose no time but at once to register and submit to medical surveillance a debauched girl. A girl young, perhaps, and ignorant is seduced by a man of higher rank . . . . Lecour and his men say she must *at once* . . . be made public property – a thing not a woman.[18]

The attitude of the police chief was one that society in general accepted, and Josephine Butler's mission was to make the community realize the essential iniquity of such a view and to change its laws, whether in England, France, Italy, or Switzerland (the countries in which she was most active). She realized that many people, both men and women, thought that society needed prostitutes to ensure 'a reserve of healthy women who are depraved beyond redemption for the use of . . . men'.[19] She considered that this accommodation reduced such women to the level of slaves and was 'the most open denial which modern times have seen of the principle of the sacredness of the individual human being'.[20]

Her first major campaign was the repeal of the Contagious Diseases Acts in the United Kingdom. The first of these Acts had been passed in 1864, the second in 1866, and a consolidating Act in 1868. The aim of the legislation was to control the spread of venereal disease in garrison towns by instituting the medical inspection of prostitutes or women suspected of being prostitutes. Among the effects of the acts were that the police in towns such as Aldershot and Dover were given power to bring before a magistrate any woman they had cause to suspect of being a prostitute, and such women had to submit to medical examination, no matter what evidence might be brought forward to establish their innocence. Servant girls talking to soldiers, girls of twelve years old were detained 'on the grounds they had been seen loitering in public places . . . and were subject to a medical examination which was, in the context of a Victorian up-bringing, at best degrading and, for the children particularly, incomprehensible . . . '[21] Josephine Butler did not attack these acts solely because of their impact on the innocent. In her appearance before the Select Committee of 1882 she said that she believed that 'the habitual outrage of any class of woman, however degraded that class may be (brings) the demoralisation of society . . . I am not here to represent virtuous women,' she continued, 'I plead for the rights of the most virtuous and the most vicious equally.'[22]

She conducted her campaign against the Acts, which was finally successful in 1886, with every imaginable weapon. She openly charged that 'the real reason why men are not here treated in the same way as women is that Parliament would not endure that men should be put in prison for solicitation on such slight evidence before a summary court, as is the case with women; for the men of the upper classes would be laid hold of by the Bill, and it would be a terrible thing indeed to the hearts of our present legislators to think that one of themselves or their sons might be touched . . .'[23] By making military and naval surgeons testify publicly that 'while they would object profoundly to inspecting soldiers and sailors for symptoms of venereal infection, as being degrading both to themselves and to the Service to which they belonged, they saw nothing degrading in inspecting queues of young girls for signs of such diseases,'[24] she showed that their ideas of propriety were untenable. Josephine Butler believed that a prostitute could be raped quite as firmly as she believed that innocent women and girls could be brought to prostitution against their will. She had been brought up by parents who saw people as human beings first, and could remember her father exploding over the Poor Law Amendment Act (1835): 'Do you think to treat men or women exactly as you do one pound notes, to be used or neglected as you think proper?'[25]

In sum, men like Shaftesbury, who worked for better conditions for miners, women like Florence Nightingale, and Elizabeth Fry, who worked for prison reform, fought to have society repair the demonstrable ills of certain conditions; the sufferings of the soldier at Scutari were real, bitter, and remediable in the sense that policies could be instituted, oversights corrected, and righteous anger appeased. But the cause of prostitutes meant that Josephine Butler confronted in England and on the Continent the entrenched convention of a supposedly moral order. While the work of improving working conditions and organizing the protection of children might meet with obstruction, the campaigns of Josephine Butler met with vilification. Her biographer, Glen Petrie, whose work has proved invaluable for this chapter, notes that 'Sir James Elphinstone M.P. declared that she was "worse than the prostitutes".' The *Daily News* stated in an editorial that women like Mrs Butler 'are so discontented in their own homes that they have to find an outlet somewhere, they have to be noticed at all costs, and take pleasure in a hobby too nasty to mention.' Another journalist described Josephine as 'an indecent maenad, a shrieking sister, frenzied, unsexed and utterly without shame'.[26] Dr Jowett, the redoubtable Master of Balliol College, Oxford, to whom Josephine once appealed for aid, considered that 'Mrs Butler takes an interest in a class of sinners whom she had much better have left to themselves.'[27]

But Josephine Butler's life is not merely a reproach to late nineteenth-century European society, it is also an accolade. She could not have achieved her results without support. The need is so real, so demonstrable, and frequently so desperate, that the response to the reformers' zeal seems at best slow and insensitive, at worst malicious, wilful obstruction. But, as in the case of Florence Nightingale and her reform of the nursing profession, Josephine Butler was helped by the encouragement of men and women from all walks of life. As one of her French supporters wrote: 'One feels, dear Madame, that God is with you in your heroic crusade against what you have so well called "the typical crime, the gigantic iniquity". God is with you Madame; it is necessary that men should be with you also. I beg that you will count entirely upon my weak but sincere services.'[28] Further she had the support of a deeply loving marriage, one strong enough to survive the tragic death of a five-year old daughter. While her struggle was much more controversial than that of Florence Nightingale and her reform of nursing, or of the work of Sidney and Beatrice Webb for sensible town planning, she did not work singlehandedly. She not only undertook the campaign, she could and did elicit support throughout society to obtain her ends.

In other words, it is not enough to describe Europe at the end of the nineteenth century as a repressive, sexist, and exploitive society. It was also a society that could be roused to defend individual rights, the liberties of women and the needs of the powerless. While all European states enacted legislation closing the doors on direct political power for women, the fight for votes for women occured in all these states. If in all European languages there is literature representing women as defined by their relationship to men, their work circumscribed by the home, their minds limited to non-intellectual pursuits, and their moral beings summed up by their sexual conduct, there is a considerable body of literature arguing the opposite. Further, if the story of European attitudes to prostitution in the nineteenth century is a story of exploitation and complacency, it is also the story of a campaign to alter social attitudes. At the end of the nineteenth century, as at any other time, European civilization was complex, combining not merely patterns of traditional belief with the evolution of new standards of human behaviour, but also containing many different groupings of people whose lives and circumstances enforced different priorities on them, and who therefore emphasized different values in changing circumstances. The Sicilian peasant, the Scandinavian fisherman, the Welsh miner, the English lacemaker, the French soubrette, the German musician, the Swiss clockmaker, all these lives and more have to be provided for in the picture of European civilization. If it can be done at all, descriptions that link together their experiences must be built on an acceptance of variations of human behaviour, even on the assumption that whatever is asserted, the opposite must also exist in some degree. While one particular view can be said to dominate social customs and to influence political decisions at a given time, it can usually be discovered that the opposite belief exists in the community both in theory and in practice. Victorian sexuality encompassed rigid marriage patterns and the bawd. The mountains of evidence about European life in the late nineteenth century transcribe more easily into theme and variations than into symphonic orchestration. It is easier to show that questions of human behaviour were considered of greater or lesser political and social importance at a given time than to show a continuous and uniform development of a particular attitude in European society towards any one question. It is easier to show that the human need for love was circumscribed by a particular structure at a given time than to show that its expression has followed a progression through the years. It is easier to show that Europeans have always been concerned with the existence of right and wrong than to show the linear development of the assertion of right, as for example objections to the use of torture for political ends from the time of Judge Jeffreys, the sadist of late seventeenth-century England, to the time of the French Algerian crisis of the 1950s. G.M. Young in his outstanding essay on Victorian England, *Portrait of an Age*, saw that culture changed by means of tension between the generations—the older generation is the 'voice of society in equilibrium and bent on maintaining its equilibrium. The judgements of the younger generation are,' he considered, 'on the whole, the voice of society dissident and exploratory.' While this conflict is undeniably part of the social process, by the end of the nineteenth century Europe had other equally powerful sources of dispute. The 1880s and the 1890s were years when the populace was informed by politicians as well as artists, by economists as well as social workers, by revolutionaries as well as by the Pope, that the present organization of the community needed to be restructured. The agitation about women's working conditions was part of the general debate on conditions of labour. The dispute over prostitution was part of the interest in the bonds of human conduct. The issue of votes for women was part of the general discussion about the source of political power within the community.

One of the earliest English suffragette leaders saw the question of votes for women very much in this light. Millicent Garrett Fawcett wrote in 1886 in the May issue of *Nineteenth Century*:

> Women's suffrage will not come, when it does come, as an isolated phenomenon, it will come as a necessary corollary of other changes which have been gradually and steadily modifying during this century the social history of our country. It will be a political change, not a very great or extensive character in itself, based upon social, educational and economic changes which have already taken place. It will have the effect of adjusting the political machinery of the country to the altered social conditions of its inhabitants. The revolution has been quietly taking place for at least two generations; the political change will not be a revolution but a public recognition by the State that the lot of women in England is no longer what it was at the beginning of the century.[29]

For Mrs Fawcett, whose daughter Phillippa came top of the mathematics examination at Cambridge University in 1890, the nineteenth century had been a period when the rights of women to political power grew because of the extension of that power. She considered that the nineteenth century had demonstrated women's participation in the general activities of European society, and that as political rights were extended to men, women would have to be treated equally.

For Mrs Fawcett the question could be argued on the lines suggested a hundred years ago by Abigail Adams – the need to recognize that the political nature of women in no way differed from that of men. The advance of manhood suffrage during the nineteenth century made the position of Mrs Fawcett stronger. There were as obviously men of poor judgement and little moral character who had the vote as there were women with good judgement and fine reputation who did not have it. Further, while the right to participate in political life through the electoral process had been denied women, many European states had involved women in politics by appointing them to committees and boards set up to cope with the needs of society. It was because of these developments that the suffragette movement found supporters among people who were by no means convinced of the equality of the sexes but who were becoming more and more persuaded that political rights had little to do with quantifiable, measurable equality.

Such a viewpoint was expressed by M. Dilke, who wrote in the July 1889 issue of the *Nineteenth Century* an article replying to those who argued against female suffrage. 'Woman may never be intellectually fitted for the position of minister of the Crown or ambassador,' he wrote, 'though with her present rate of progress he would be a rash man to predict exactly how far she will go; but that does not affect one way or another her right to vote .... Why should she sit on a School Board, and in that capacity make recommendations to the Government on the Education Code, and yet when that same Code is before Parliament have no power to support its provisions or secure its rejection?' Further he considered that the nation could not afford 'to allow such a potent moral influence as that of women to lie fallow.' He noted the change from the dominance of an agricultural economy and considered that 'With our vast cities and ever-increasing complication of interests and industries, combination of influence and co-operation in good works have become absolutely necessary unless the feminine element is to be entirely eliminated.'[30] Dilke was typical of those who faced the problem of women's rights in honest confusion, convinced of considerable differences between the sexes and equally convinced of women's right to a political voice.

But many who felt that women should be denied a political voice did so not on the grounds that women lacked intelligence but because of the innate character of the sex. The Countess of Galloway,writing three years earlier than Mr Dilke, affirmed that it was not because 'women are more ill educated or ignorant than men'. 'Both in the upper and the lower classes,' she went on, 'this is distinctly not the case.' However she considered that 'the higher the education of women, in its true sense, the greater will be her capacity to understand and appreciate distinctions, and to understand exactly the extent of her powers without usurping those of men, or claiming an impossible equality.'[31] In 1890 Katie, Countess Cowper wrote forthrightly, 'As far as public life is concerned, I confess I should infinitely prefer that women's assistance, however useful, should be forever dispensed with, sooner than that by their admission to share what has hitherto belonged exclusively to men our women should lose one jot or fraction of the nobility of their sex, or should become one jot less mindful of those womanly virtues which are the glory of a civilized country.'[32] Again, Mrs Sutherland-Orr; 'Where, in the final results of female emancipation shall we find that highest differentiation of the two sexes which creates the varying forms of love? Where, amidst creatures trained to the same mental exercise, the same nervous discipline, the same habits, the same associations, shall we find that presentment of an untried world of feeling and experience which causes one sex to gravitate towards the other in the blind instinct of self-completion or creates for the more self-conscious soul

Infinite passion, and the pain
of finite hearts that yearn?'[33]

There is a great temptation to wonder whether the last speaker had any idea of physical attraction as a human attribute, any concept of emotion outside 'sex-in-the-head'.

There was a great deal more to arguments about women's suffrage than a clash between those who considered it a natural development of political democracy and those who believed that the entry of women into politics meant the debasement of their femininity and 'a lowering of the ideal of womanhood amongst men'.[34] The status and position of women throughout the community was brought into question by the argument over their rights to full participation in the political structures of late nineteenth-century Europe. Arguments were started by questioning masculine rule, which had permitted the existence of working conditions for both men and women that were condemned even by those who considered this world no more than a resting place before a better dispensation. Arguments sprang from the legitimacy of authority exercised over those who were refused participation in the formation of government. But above all arguments were raised over the exact nature of the differences between men and women, and the extent to which government should be involved in reinforcing these differences. Underlying all these arguments, inescapably if rarely openly acknowledged, ran the question of human sexuality, its needs, its proper conduct, and its influence upon society. As the nineteenth century drew to a close, the debate began about all these matters, a debate that shows no signs whatever of ending, even though its present clash of ideas is something far removed from the positions advanced in 1900.

During the last three decades of the nineteenth century Europeans entered into an overwhelming bout of introspection and self-analysis. They compared their achievements to those in other parts of the globe. They considered their customs in the light of new information about peoples elsewhere. They examined their conduct in the framework of what sort of community they hoped to bring about, and they considered the problems that faced them in the context of what they considered it was practical to do. Their most enduring bequests were a belief in an organizing principle for human conduct, whether that principle be based upon an estimation of a human being as an animal with a soul, or merely, as the American anthropologist Kroeber once wrote, 'a unique interaction of quantitative variables', and an equal belief in the usefulness of statistics, case studies, numbers that could be compared and analysed. The twentieth century was born with a thrust to look for a demonstrable norm, a practical numerical foundation for future policies, and a belief that the historical process was progress towards a desired end. Such was part of the mental equipment of both men and women of the west as they confronted the events of the new century.

NOTES

[1] W. H. McNeill, *The Rise of the West: A History of the Human Community* (University of Chicago Press, 1963), p. 729.

[2] Lord Macauley, *The History of England from the Accession of James the Second* (Longmans, Green, 1880), vol. 10, pp. 453, 441, 442.

[3] Available in English in pamphlet form from the Catholic Truth Society, London.

[4] Sidney and Beatrice Webb, *Socialism in England* (Baltimore, 1889), pp. 116-17.

[5] Zola to Eduard Rod, 16 March 1884. Quoted in E. Grant, *Zola's Germinal: A Critical and Historical Study* (Leicester University Press, 1970), p. 9.

[6] *Ibid.*, p. 19.

[7] E. Zola, *Germinal* (Scribner), p. 511, trans. N. E. S. Griffiths.

[8] Lord Brabazon, 'The Early Closing Movement', printed in M. Goodwin, *Nineteenth Century Opinion: An Anthology of Extracts from the first fifty volumes of The Nineteenth Century 1877-1901* (Penguin, 1951), p. 27.

[9] *Ibid.*, pp. 19-26.

[10] Glen Petrie: *A singular Iniquity: The Campaigns of Josephine Butler* (Viking Press, 1971).

[11] Quoted in S. Chodorow and P. N. Stearns, eds., *The Other Side of Western Civilization*, (Harcourt, Brace, 1973), vol. II, p. 159.

[12] J. E. Butler to Albert Rutson, 7 May 1868, in Petrie, *op. cit.*, p. 67.

[13] J. E. Butler to F. Harrison, 9 May 1868, *loc. cit.*

[14] M. Ryan, *Philosophy of Marriage* (1837), quoted in R. Pearsall, *The Worm in the Bud: The World of Victorian Sexuality* (Pelican, 1969), p. 293.

[15] Lombroso and Ferrerio, *La Donna Delinquente* (1893), quoted in Pearsall, *op. cit.*, p. 298.

[16] Petrie, *op. cit.*, p. 140.

[17] *Report of the Royal Commission on the Contagious Diseases Act*, 1871, quoted in Petrie, *op. cit.*, p. 117.

[18] Petrie, *op. cit.*, p. 167.

[19] *Ibid.*, p. 95.

[20] *Ibid.*, p. 96.

[21] *Ibid.*, p. 15. Josephine Butler testified that she herself had seen hardened prostitutes having to be removed unconscious from the surgical couch after examination. *Ibid.*, p. 107.

[22] *Ibid.*, p. 141.

[23] J. E. Butler to the Liverpool Association, 18 March 1872, in Petrie, *op. cit.*, pp. 122-3.

[24] Petrie, *op. cit.*, p. 111.

[25] *Ibid.*, p. 25.

[26] *Ibid.*, pp. 20-1.

[27] Benjamin Jewett to Florence Nightingale, December 1869, *ibid.*, p. 40.

[28] Joseph Edmonson to J. E. Butler, 7 February, *ibid.*, p. 175.

[29] Goodwin, *op. cit.*, pp. 84-5.

[30] *Ibid.*, pp. 110-11.

[31] *Ibid.*, p. 105.

[32] *Ibid.*, p. 102.

[33] *Ibid.*, pp. 95-6.

[34] L. Creighton, 'Appeal Against Female Suffrage', August 1889, in Goodwin, *op. cit.*, p. 104.

Eight

Canadian Identities

The arrival of the twentieth century found Canadians as enthusiastic about examining the bounds of their lives as their contemporaries in Europe. Just over thirty years earlier, Confederation had brought together the maritime colonies of Nova Scotia and New Brunswick, whose life was bound by the vagaries of the seas as much as by the forests, and Lower and Upper Canada, settlements characterized as much by the St Lawrence and Ottawa rivers as by the siren call of undeveloped land. Historical process, the weaving of people, event, and ambition, had ensured that the basic natural differences between the colonies would be underlined by social and political traditions, linguistic and religious differences. The organization of Manitoba into a province in 1870, the addition of British Columbia in 1871, and the incorporation of Prince Edward Island into the Dominion in 1873 added to the richness of the ingredients for future development. As Blair Neatby has written in his essay in *The Canadians, 1867-1967*, by the turn of the century 'National pride was there and a new found assurance that Canada would survive and prosper, but there was as yet no way of knowing what Canadian society would be like or what kind of nation-state Canada would become. Canadians were still searching for a sense of national identity.'[1] The search was confined within certain limits: the strength of identities within the provinces and the vision of a confederation rather than a union meant that not all imaginable solutions were a possibility, only those that respected what had already been achieved. And whatever doubts one province might have about the structure of society that another had achieved, none had doubts about the essential validity of its own ways of life. Any Canadian identity that would catch up the hearts of people from sea to sea must openly value the different natures of the component parts.

Since there were these different components in Canada, the discussion of any Canadian attitude must always start twice over. Whether the choice is to begin with the provinces or with the federal scene, the alternative has always to be presented. Even those areas that have been placed squarely within the jurisdiction of one or other authority demand this dual treatment, since each province does not react to the federal government in the same manner. Such diversity, however, is not the only characteristic of the Canadian people, otherwise the experiment attempted in 1867 would soon have come to an abrupt end. The opportunities of Confederation were not merely the chosen solution of separate colonies to the problems of the late nineteenth century, they were also a chosen asset in working out the ambitions of the separate colonies. While considerable differences in needs and in beliefs, in population make-up and in environment gave, and give, each part of Canada distinctive traits, the organization of Confederation helped to emphasize those similarities of outlook that did exist and to encourage the growth of new attitudes in common.

The pattern of settlement differed from province to province, but all had, as well as villages and towns that had existed for a considerable time, land where none had yet established permanent dwellings. Further, while the urban population was growing, farming, fishing, trapping, logging, mining, and quarrying were the major occupations. In 1901 just over 40 per cent of the population was still engaged in agricultural pursuits.[2] In the United States the percentage had already dropped to 38 per cent, in Germany it was 35 per cent, and in the United Kingdom, 9 per cent.[3] At the same time those in Canada who did live in towns— 1,867,260 in 1901—most often lived in small towns.[4] Toronto and Montreal accounted for just under half a million, some 343,266 people lived in towns of between 30,000 and 100,000, another half million in towns of between 5,000 and 30,000, and the last half million, 545,037 in towns of less than five thousand.[5] Not only was rural life more pervasive in Canada than elsewhere, but it remained a dream that was also a practical possibility for people of all provinces. It was always possible, and still is to some extent, to go back to farming or to living in the country in Canada. The myth of rural life has remained strong, as is shown in its literature. These roots in rural life were a common factor in the experience of all Canadians at the opening of the twentieth century.

The lives of many Canadian women were close to that described by the novelist Ralph Connor in his autobiography, *Postscript to Adventure*. Connor had been born in Glengarry in 1860. He admitted that in 1882, 'when I personally voted for the extension of university privileges to women, I was conscious of a secret feeling of which I was somewhat ashamed, that something of the lofty splendor of university life had departed with the advent of women.' But he was a solid supporter of votes for women and he considered that 'It is one of the great tragedies of literature that historians fill their pages with the doings of men and leave unsung the lives of the heroines . . . ' For, he went on, 'The loneliness, the dangers, the hardships of fathers and sons in the remote lumber camps or in rafts down the river are as nothing to the appalling loneliness, the dangers, the hardships that mothers and daughters have to meet and endure in the little log houses in the clearing, with children to clothe and care for in health and sickness, and to keep regularly at school, to train and discipline, with beasts to water and feed, with fires to keep alight when snowdrifts pile round the little house to the eaves, shutting them off for days and nights from their neighbours . . . ' Connor had been a shrewd observer of the life surrounding him as a child, and he recalled details about everyday concerns, noting that 'Everything we wore, except our boots and moccasins, was home-made . . . I cannot halt', he went on, 'to speak of the cleaning, the carding, the dyeing, the spinning, the weaving of the wool necessary to produce blankets, sheets, quilts for beds, or dresses for girls. But think, will you, of the hours at the spinning wheel, the sitting little wheel and the walking big wheel, the dyeing, the weary banging and shuttling of the looms necessary for these glorious results.' And he concluded: 'We cannot give space to the other multitudinous tasks of the women, such as the milking, the butter and cheese making, the pickling and transforming of various wild fruits into delicious jams and preserves, the curing of pork and beef, the drying of herbs. Then, outside, there was the care of hens, ducks and geese and of their wayward and wandering offspring, the safe delivery of spring calves and lambs and pigs. And always the baby to nurse or attend to, or Jimmie to keep from the fire or from falling into the well, or Maggie from the jam-jar or the milk pan.[6]

The particular details brought together in this description might not be the lot of all women in rural Canada at the close of the nineteenth century, but its essence was common property. Whether it was life in the fishing ports of Nova Scotia, in the farm villages of Quebec, in the forests of Ontario, in Manitoba's wheat lands, or among the migrant Indian and Eskimo people, the contribution of women was still a vital element to survival. It was not that without them no new generation would replenish the earth, but that without their active participation the present generation would barely maintain an existence. This could perhaps be said in some measure of those who lived in cities, but in rural Canada the contribution of women was an obvious and visible necessity.

The difference in emphasis becomes clear when the two major organizations for women are compared. The National Council of Women of Canada, whose founding spirit was Lady Aberdeen, the wife of the governor-general, was organized in 1893. It was, as Ramsay Cook has remarked, for the most part middle-class and urban in membership, and its first aim was the support of woman as home-maker. Speaking about it to a Montreal audience Lady Aberdeen said: 'in attempting this work we are most anxious to have it remembered that we do not desire to overlook the fact that woman's first duty and mission is to her home.... People sometimes speak as if ... woman's first mission in itself prevented her from taking part in public work. They forget that a woman to do her duty, if she is to do her duty truly to her sons and daughters, must keep in touch with the world, its thoughts, its activities, its temptations.'[7] In 1900 this organization ensured that a volume entitled *Women in Canada* was made available by the Canadian government at that year's Exposition in Paris. One of the articles included in the work listed the attainments of the National Council, such as the appointment of Women Factory Inspectors,[8] the appointment of women on the Boards of School Trustees in New Brunswick, changes in the conditions of women in prisons, the establishment not only of several hospitals but of the Victorian Order of Nurses, and the inauguration of the National Home Reading Union. Basically the National Council was the Canadian counterpart of the American and European organizations for women's suffrage, and by 1913 it had become such without question. In that year Sonia Leathes spoke to a meeting of the Council and pointed out what political power meant in the twentieth century: 'We shall not rest until we have secured the power vested in the ballot: to give or to withhold our consent, to encourage or to forbid any policy or course of actions which concerns the people—our children, everyone.'[9]

The movement started by Mrs Adelaide Hoodless in February 1897 at Stoney Creek, Ontario was a very different matter. This was the founding of the Women's Institutes, dedicated to 'the broadening and enriching of rural life.' At this first meeting Mrs Hoodless stressed the essentially practical nature of her idea, and the constitution that was presented at that time stated that 'the object of this Institute shall be to promote that knowledge of household science which shall lead to improvement in household architecture with special attention to home sanitation, to a better understanding of economics and hygienic value of foods and fuels, and to a more scientific care of children with a view to raising the general standard of the health of our people.' While the sphere of women's activities envisaged at this stage was narrow, as the Institutes spread so did their programs. By 1902 there were twenty-four Institutes; by 1904, 149; by 1907, 500.[10] Within twenty years of that first meeting the idea had spread to England, Wales, Scotland, Belgium, and France. At the same time the activities undertaken by the branches multiplied. As Ruth Hawes has commented:

They began with child care and home management. Government teachers gave condensed courses in cooking, dressmaking, and home nursing, and government bulletins on such subjects were distributed. The work soon spread into many channels. Much energy was devoted to improving rural schools, providing playground equipment, introducing hot lunches, dental clinics and medical inspection. Institutes helped set up local libraries, cottage hospitals, rest rooms for country women in towns, to introduce music teaching, handicrafts such as rug and glove making, recreation facilities such as playgrounds and swimming pools. They encouraged amateur dramatics, choral singing, labour-saving devices, and improvements in homes, did war work, helped the Red Cross and the Navy League.[11]

The two organizations—the National Council of Women of Canada and the Women's Institutes—were complementary. They gave to the country a forum where women exchanged opinions and ideas, where knowledge and beliefs were transmitted and could be made into a significant political force. During the years immediately preceding the First World War the growing pressure for women's suffrage came from women's organizations, and was augmented by support from elsewhere in the community. The Honourable John Dryden, then Ontario's Minister of Agriculture, wrote in 1893 of the theological reasons why woman's place was 'in submission to man'. Barely two years later, in 1895, Dr Hughe, at that time the superintendent of education in Toronto, 'put forth a pamphlet in which he blasted the forty-two stock objections to enfranchisement . . . and presented . . . a staggering weight of testimony supporting the equality of sex from both the old and the New Testaments, as well as written endorsements (in favour of women's suffrage) from leading churchmen of Toronto.'[12] And as Catherine Cleverdon has pointed out, 'It was not only women's organizations which allied themselves with the movement. The women of the Prairie Provinces found their staunchest backers in the vigorous farmers' associations of Manitoba, Saskatchewan and Alberta, all three of which openly endorsed suffrage in 1911 and 1912. These farmers did more than pay lipservice to the movement; they joined their women in petitions and delegations, and carried the idea of equality into their own organizations by admitting women to full membership.'[13] It is interesting that in his excellent short work, *Suffragettes International*, published in 1971, Trevor Lloyd could write that 'the suffrage movement had not been strong in Canada before the (1914) war.'[14] While there was not the violence that characterized women's fight for the vote in both England and the United States, the Canadian suffrage movement before 1914 was strong, co-ordinated, and in no wise lacked opponents.

The appreciation of the worth of women in rural life, the acceptance of women as voters in a number of elections for School Board Trustees and in some municipal elections, the admittance of women to university education, if not to the full sweep of the curriculum in all institutions, did not mean that both prejudice and discrimination against women were absent from Canada. Even Mrs Hoodless, whose life was dedicated to the good of home, marriage, and family, ran into bitter criticism in her organization of the Women's Institutes. Her son recalls that she was 'derided in the press and from the platform as one of the "despised" new women.'[15]

All the arguments used in Europe against the right of women to professional careers and an active participation in political life were, to some degree, reproduced in Canada and answered by both men and women with equal vigour. For example there was Dr Emily Howard Stowe, Canada's first woman medical doctor, who had graduated from the Women's New York Medical School in 1868, and practised in Toronto until her death in 1903. It was largely owing to her efforts that the University of Toronto opened its doors to women in 1886, and her work in the field of family medicine and health care for women was both the stimulus and the support for her work for the political enfranchisement of women.[16] She worked with a group of women who formed the Toronto Women's Literary Club, which not only set about educating the general public to the need for women's suffrage but also acted as an important pressure group on the provincial legislature. By 1882 their efforts had succeeded in obtaining the vote for unmarried women with property qualifications on questions of municipal bylaws.[17] As in England, the movement for political rights for women found considerable backing among women who were already part of the privileged sections of society. But the movement quickly mobilized, both in the countryside and in the towns, considerable support from those of less privileged circumstances.

In many ways the cause was popularized because of the vigorous personalities of its leaders. In women like Emily Murphy, who in 1916 was the first woman to be appointed a police magistrate in the British Empire, and Mrs Nellie McClung, Canada had people who could battle with as much wit as fervour, as much humour as determination. Emily Murphy's writing has perhaps a somewhat laboured air about it to a late twentieth-century taste, but in her book of travel sketches, *Janey Canuck in the West*, first published in 1901, she could paint the possibilities of a life in the west where women would be relatively free of silly conventions.[18] Nellie McClung has a much more modern ring to her words, commenting tartly at one point that she did not consider womanhood a disease. Heckled in a public meeting in 1916 with the statement that 'The Prime Minister would quit politics if a woman were ever elected', she replied 'This proves what a purifying effect women would have on politics.'[19] She was born in 1873 in Grey County, Ontario, and died in Victoria, British Columbia in 1951. It was in 1880 that she went with her family to Manitoba.

Her entry into public life came in 1912 when she helped organize the Winnipeg Political Equality League. She was as concerned with social justice as with political equality, and when Manitoba's Premier Roblin told her that 'nice women' did not want the franchise, she replied: "By nice women . . . you probably mean selfish women who have no more thought for the underprivileged, overworked women than a pussycat in a sunny window for the starving kitten in the street. Now in that sense I am not a nice woman for I do care.'[20] Her quick answers were not only apposite but shrewd. Those who argued that giving women the vote meant domestic discord were answered: 'If a husband and wife are going to quarrel they will find a cause for dispute easily enough and will not be compelled to wait for election day.'[21] Her sparkle of humour gave the struggle for votes for women a resilience that it would otherwise have lacked. At the same time her ability to organize, to speak and write with energy about the issue, kept the public well aware of the arguments for the extension of the franchise.

The work for women's suffrage was less dramatically flamboyant in Canada than it was elsewhere, but it was work that had begun well before the nineteenth century ended. By 1914 the struggle was well on the way to victory and the course of the holocaust that erupted that year brought success at most levels of Canadian government, as it did in the majority of European countries and the United States. The contribution of women to the war was undeniable and by 1916 Manitoba, Alberta, and Saskatchewan gave the vote in provincial elections, British Columbia and Ontario ceding the right in 1917. That same year the Wartime Election Act gave the vote in federal elections to those women whose husbands or other close relatives were fighting in the forces. But it was an act that took away the vote from those who were considered to be of enemy alien birth, or who habitually spoke a foreign tongue, and who had not become British subjects until after March 1902.[22] Cleverdon has computed that during its passage through the House of Commons, less than a third of the debate on the Act was actually about women's suffrage, the rest being argument over the disenfranchisement clauses.[23] In 1918 a further Act was passed that granted female suffrage at the federal level without exception, and in 1919 yet another piece of legislation conceded that ' . . . any British subject, male or female, who is fully of age twenty-one years may be a candidate at a Dominion election.'[24] The final political right accorded women at the federal level was the right to become members of the Senate. This struggle was eventful and lengthy, ending in victory in 1929 when the Judicial Committee of the Privy Council in London, England allowed that women were persons and as such 'are eligible to be summoned and become members of the Senate of Canada.'[25]

The right to vote in provincial elections in the Maritimes and Quebec was accorded after campaigns that reflected the differences in those provinces. Cleverdon considered that the suffrage movement in Nova Scotia was basically the result of the activities of the Women's Christian Temperance Movement. Nova Scotia accorded women the right to vote and to sit in the provincial legislature in 1918. One of the women who fought for these results remarked to Cleverdon in 1943 that: 'At the end it came without a struggle in recognition of women's services during the war. Things often work out that way I find. You struggle and struggle to no direct effect, and suddenly in a lull the whole thing snaps into place.'[26] The campaign in New Brunswick produced more widespread public action; there was a greater volume of petitions and more frequent delegations to the government at Fredericton.[27] The province gave women the right to vote in 1919 but managed to avoid granting them the right to hold office until 1934.

Prince Edward Island holds the distinction of never having had any form of suffrage organization.[28] The local Councils of Women displayed a complete lack of interest in the question and even the temperance groups barely raised the issue. Enfranchisement came about through the actions of male legislators who moved in 1918 that 'Whereas the women of Prince Edward Island as well as women in other parts of the Empire have taken a very active part in the various industries and War Charities and by the good and useful work performed by them are materially assisting in winning the War; And whereas in England, the U.S.A., in several provinces of Canada, the franchise has been extended to women and a Bill has now been introduced in the Canadian House of Commons to the same effect; Therefore Resolved that in the opinion of this House An Act of the Legislature should be passed extending the franchise to the women of Prince Edward Island.'[29] While no one opposed this resolution, the actual Act to enfranchise was not passed until 1922. Newfoundland, during these years not part of Confederation, was slightly more enthusiastic about the matter than Prince Edward Island. Local activists formed organizations to press for the right and received 'quantities of suffrage literature' from the Continent. In 1925 the vote was accorded, but whereas the age of enfranchisement for men was 21, that for women was set at 25.

Quebec was the last Canadian province to accord women the right to vote in provincial elections. Yet at the opening of the nineteenth century, when voting in elections depended on property qualifications, certain women had exercised the vote. Cleverdon quotes the example of the vote cast for Joseph Papineau in the Montreal election of 1809. The vote was given orally and the widowed Papineau was thus able to vote: 'For my son, M. Joseph Papineau, for I believe that he is a good and faithful subject.'[30] This right was lost in the vicissitudes of the next decades. By the end of the nineteenth century there was considerable articulate opinion against the political rights of women in Quebec. During the debates in the federal parliament French-Canadian members fought bitterly and eloquently against the extension of the franchise. One Quebec member, Fournier, asserted that 'A country cannot, without paying the full price, act contrarily to the laws of God and nature. There is an essential distinction between man and woman. . . . And to keep up the birth-rate of Canada we must keep our women within their sphere; we must attract them towards the accomplishments of the duties of their sex, duties specified by the unchangeable laws of nature. . . . It [woman suffrage] is the antithesis of that highest and sweetest mystery, conviction by submission, conquest by sacrifice . . . '[31] Another French Canadian, Jean Joseph Denis, considered that 'the Holy Scriptures, theology, ancient philosophy, Christian philosophy, history, anatomy, political economy, and feminine psychology, all seem to indicate that the place of women in this world is not amid the strife of the political arena, but in her home.'[32] Over the next twenty-two years such attitudes confronted men and women in Quebec whenever they pressed for an extension of the franchise. The battle was finally won in 1940.

Perhaps the most striking characteristic of the Canadian movement for women's suffrage was the tremendous emphasis placed on ideas rather than upon rights. The question of extending the ballot to women is more complicated in the United States than in Canada, because it cannot be separated from the question of extending it to the negro,[33] but the attitude of American women was dominated by the stand taken at the Seneca Falls Conference in 1848, which declared: 'We hold these truths to be self-evident: that men and women are created equal.' An advertisement in the New York *Tribune*, placed in support of votes for women, emphasized the need 'to apply the principles of the Declaration of Independence to women; Governments derive their just powers from the consent of the governed.'[34] Neither the American nor the Canadian movement concentrated solely upon one set of arguments for votes for women, but suffragist literature produced in the United States emphasized questions of equal pay for equal work and the right of the governed to elect their government. Canadians on the other hand tended to emphasize the influence that women would provide in political life, the question of a new order of morality based upon the addition of the feminine viewpoint to the rough-and-tumble of public questions.

There was, of course, concern about conditions of employment for women in the early stages of the movement for women's suffrage in Canada. In 1890 Minnie Phelps commented that 'in the factories of our province [Ontario] there are 7,594 women, 247 girls between the ages of 12 and 14; 1,588 between the ages of 14 and 18 years. These women, working side by side with the male laborers, battling the same physical struggles, full of the same high aspirations, the value of the world's market of exchange being equal, find they receive from one third to one half less wages, doing the same work with as much skill as their brother workers.'[35] She was convinced that the vote was the sole path to remedy such an injustice. But while Toronto and Montreal were industrial cities, and while the urban-rural equation was changing rapidly, Canada was not a manufacturing state. Consequently the emphasis of those who fought for votes for women was very often based upon a vision of the work of women on the farms, in the forests, and in the fishing villages. Canadians frequently took the argument that women, being the more delicate part of humanity, should confine their activities to the home, and turned it into an argument that would allow the values of the home to civilize the rest of life. The strong connection between the Women's Christian Temperance Union and the suffragettes further strengthened the belief in the moral influence that women would bring to political life once granted the vote. As well as moving society towards a teetotal age, Nellie McClung hoped that women in politics might bring a society without war.[36]

Whether it was fought for as a matter of justice or a question of morality, whether it was granted as a matter of expediency or the reward for women's contribution to the war effort, by the middle of the 1920s female suffrage was accorded for the majority of the electoral processes of Canada. The enfranchisement was the removal of an obvious political injustice and the necessary recognition of women as people with political characters. It remained to be seen what women would do with the responsibilities and the privileges of enfranchisement. Any assessment of this question, however, has to begin with the realization that the society that gave women the vote was a very different society from the one that had seen the struggle begin. Canada before the First World War had had a number of testing experiences such as the Riel Rebellion, but the events of 1914-18 were an ordeal of a new magnitude. During these years 61,326 Canadians were killed and 172,950 wounded; and there had been a bitter controversy over the conscription of men to serve in Canada's forces overseas. Further, the organization of the country on the basis of a wartime economy led to greatly increased government regulations. One way and another, the First World War presented Canada with a surge of internal problems and external demands, and the methods that were evolved to cope with them made Canadian society much more regulated at the end of these years than it had seemed at the outset.

During the 1920s the newly acquired rights did not produce a flood of women entering political careers, major legislation to deal with legal discrimination against women in the matter of property acts, nor an outstanding reform program to prevent the exploitation of women in sweated labour. To a certain extent this was a predictable result. The majority of both men and women considered political affairs an esoteric occupation, and while men had had the right to vote for a considerable time, those who entered politics were relatively few in number. Further, while the possession of the vote had often been represented as the possession of a magic talisman for the betterment of society, the accepted role of government was prevention and cure, and legislation was seen very much as something that regulated conditions and forbade certain practices, rather than a process to initiate a new structure of life. Factory acts regulated working hours and conditions of employment but did not propose the organization of the best possible life for the worker. Acts against prostitution did not include training programs for alternative occupations. Even legislation dealing with education and medical care was concerned with the provision of the inescapable minimum rather than the exploration of the most fruitful paths for humanity. Those who had struggled for votes for women had often seen women as bringing a concern for the quality of human life into the political arena. While it is true than there was a beginning of the idea of government responsibility for planning life rather than merely organizing life planned elsewhere, this development was slow indeed. The first woman federal M.P., Agnes Macphail, was one of those who fought for increased government intervention, but her efforts, along with men and women of like mind, were completely derouted by the Great Depression.

There were few factors common to the lives of all the women of Canada on the eve of the Dirty Thirties. The status and position of any woman was as much the result of her hereditary and immediate environment as it was of the traditions and institutions of the wider Canadian society. But there were some common experiences for all Canadian women. Most basic, of course, were those related to being a lover, mother of a child, and a wife. These experiences, whether in Medicine Hat or in Come by Chance, were the foundation of that bonding between women that Kipling knew: 'For the Colonel's Lady and Judy O'Grady are sisters under their skins.' A few women might experience none of these things; some women might rejoice in being all three at once. But women knew that the importance of these experiences was a central concern of much of their existence.

Further, most women discovered that their lives were affected by the way in which Canadian society recognized the importance of family life and laid down rules for the conduct of marriage. Such rules limited the lives of men as well as women, of course, and the experiences of being lover, husband, and father were central to the existence of most men. But Canadian society limited the choice of women more narrowly than that of men, and exacted a more brutal fine from those who ignored its dictates.

Jean Burton in her story 'Phyllus', published in the *Canadian Forum* in 1927, vividly described the teeth of one particular trap that caught women. She depicts the world of the beauty-parlour and the hairdresser in Vancouver, and the people who above all want approval from their milieu, who try desperately to mould their actions to obtain this evanescent support. Phyllus, young, in love, unmarried, and pregnant, moves to suicide as the only solution. 'There is always a certain joy in doing the right thing at the right time, which is the basis of all convention and civilization;' wrote Jean Burton, 'and Phyllus, at this moment, savoured the zest of undeniable correctness.'[37] Without suggesting that this was the usual path for the unwed pregnant woman to take, the story, and the reaction to it in letters to the editor after its publication, illustrate a facet of women's experience in Canada on the eve of the Depression—the social importance attached to sexual conduct.

In other words, the demands of family were seen as one of the paramount responsibilities of women, and many men and women considered that neglect or carelessness in this area warranted savage punishment. This should not suggest a society that was nothing more than a male dictatorship—the society was more intricate than that. A novel such as Martha Ostenso's *Wild Geese*, published in 1925, shows the complex pattern of human life, the flow of tensions between dominating male and a woman of vibrant independence. Set in the northern lakes of Manitoba, the book tells of love of men and women for each other, for their children, for those they know. It is about Caleb, 'holding taut the reins of power, alert, jealous of every gesture in the life which he moved and governed', and about Amelia who, at the end of the book, stood firm against his will. It is the story of men who care for their brothers, of women who suffer so that other women might have wider horizons. And it is the story of the land, with its dogwood trees and sky as 'clear and blue as a harebell'. *Wild Geese* gives no one liberty from the constraints of human life, the necessity of work, the need for love, the solitude of the heart. For many Canadian women this book reflected reality, the limited choice of possibilities, though not necessarily more limited than those of the men of the community.

Perhaps it is best to look upon this type of common experience as reality everywhere, the common life of all people. What is perhaps distinctive in Canadian interpretations of this experience is the solid belief in the value of love between husband and wife, between siblings, between neighbours, that is a constant of so much Canadian writing at this time. The bitterness of 'Phyllus' can only exist if people consider that there is an alternative reality to the loveless structure of her life. What novels such as *Wild Geese* emphasized was the probability of this other dispensation. At the same time this faith in the possibility of human affection was accompanied by a celebration of woman as the right companion for man. This particular identification would remain part of Canadian literature over the next quarter century: it is central to the development of the characters in a novel published by Frederick Niven in 1935, *The Flying Years*, and the theme is celebrated in Thomas Raddall's *The Nymph and the Lamp*, first published in 1950. While it is true that European literature in these years produced important works about women's experience, there is little comparable to the optimistic tone of these Canadian works and much that denigrates this aspect of human communities. Margaret Atwood has seen in Canadian literature an absence of women as human, that instead the models are women as Nature, Ice Virgins, and gnarled old matriarchs.[38] The other tradition does exist. It is not the sole tradition, admittedly, but in the 1920s the picture of woman as partner was strong in Canadian writing.

This is not to say that women were not sometimes exploited or crushed by rural life. Nor is it to suggest that there were not patriarchal traditions in many families that were merely thin disguises for tyranny. Nor is it to ignore the conventions, especially in French Canada, that women should not actively seek to organize their lives but merely work with what was given to them. But it is to assert that one of the commonly accepted identities available to Canadian women was that of helpmate, most necessary complement to the male. The long tradition of encouraging women to emigrate to those areas of Canada overpopulated with unmarried men was not wholly based upon a malicious, intentional capitalist plot to keep workers happy in order that they might be the better exploited. There was the very definite belief that the growth of Canada depended upon the establishment of families in the underpopulated provinces, and families cannot be made up of one sex alone. There is no denying that the life offered was hard, but it was not necessarily more burdensome than that of the man. The prejudice against women in rural

Canada was rarely more than that, a prejudice expressed by some people rather than an organized attitude in the community reinforced by a conscious application of social institutions and conventions.

But by 1931 Canada was a land of railways where more than fifty per cent of the population lived in towns,[39] twenty-five per cent in large towns, and where people could not avoid being affected by the conventions of the society. And it is in the social organization of the community that the status and position of women becomes not just the organization of life between two people, not just the arrangements between the sexes of humanity, but the result of a pattern built up and established by traditions and regulations; prejudice becomes an articulated position, reinforced by everyday practice and by legislation that may allow it to flourish or may even actively encourage it. Women become a group apart from the community like other minority groups. It matters little whether the judgement is based on race, religion, language, or sex: what is at work here is the decision that a group can be singled out, can be seen to have certain characteristics that stamp all people in the group adversely, and that it should therefore be excluded from at least part of the process of organizing the community into a society.

Obviously prejudice existed against both men and women for being Indian, for being black, for being newly arrived immigrants, for being any one of a number of different combinations of characteristics. Prejudice against women merely added a further burden to those who found that in Canadian society particular characteristics were valued more than others. But quite obviously such prejudices did not apply uniformly across the country in all situations: they were, and are, merely common hazards, depending on circumstances, and experience of them would, and does, vary enormously from one person to the next. In the 1920s Canadian women, depending on the attitude of family unit, neighbourhood, village, town, or city, met both prejudice and the struggle against prejudice.

During the debate on women's suffrage there was a deep and continuing argument about the political role of women, about the justification of careers for women, and inevitably about the innate capacities of women. However women in minute numbers were entering work that had previously been the preserve of the male.

Nor were such preserves merely the professions—lawyers and doctors. In 1901 the number of women earning their living by fishing and trapping was 24, in 1931 it was 496; women construction workers had climbed slowly during the same period from 65 to 96.[40] In other words, in the 1920s women were becoming a significant factor in the labour force, but tradition still emphasized the importance of the home, the duty of women to be full-time wives and mothers. By 1931 46 per cent of Canadian women between the ages of 20 and 24 were in the labour force, a figure that fell abruptly for those aged 25-34 to 27.5 per cent.[41] The social reinforcements for this tradition were many and various, but to a certain extent the community provided such obvious examples of women having ordinary human capabilities that certain of the worst excesses of anti-feminism had to be imported from Europe or the United States.

This is not to say that Canada did not have enough home-grown discrimination against women, enough legal barriers to the independence of women, enough social dislike of the female. The difficulties facing women who did not wish to marry included not only the difficulties of the world of work where wages for her work would be the smallest possible and certainly not equal to those of a man, but also the difficulties to be found in a society that considered single women to have failed in their mission in life. This convention—that marriage was the sole, most important function for women—was one of the strongest barriers to the development of a society without discrimination against women. It made marriage the summation of women, and insisted that no real woman would choose not to marry, with the exception perhaps of the dedicated missionary or the Catholic nun. Unwed women were not merely undesirable as wives and partners, but obviously were not fully fledged human beings. The spinster was accorded a contempt rarely extended to the bachelor.

While both discrimination and prejudice against women were more obvious and more brutal in the environment of the cities, nevertheless opposition to them was more conspicuous there. It was in the towns that the suffrage movement gathered strength, that the impact of the first professional career women—doctors and lawyers—was most frequently noticeable. It was the cities, in the nascent industries, that the organization of women for better working conditions took place, and that reading circles supportive of women could most easily be formed. The work of Agnes Macphail and many other women was manifest to many sectors of the urban population of Canada. If social conventions could be enforced more rigidly in the cities, they could also be more rigorously and more continuously challenged there. Canadian urban history is being explored at present by a number of historians, and the flavour of Canadian urban life at the opening of the twentieth century is just now being distilled. Without prejudging the work in progress it is possible to see that there was no blanket exploitation of women on a scale and of a type not experienced by men. The attitude towards prostitution was as savage as anything Josephine Butler discovered in Europe, but Canada too had vigorous personalities to confront society with the rights of the outcast.

In sum, on the eve of the Great Depression the status and position of women in Canada was a mixture of two traditions: the stifling mutilation of human potential brought about by belief in male supremacy, and the exhilarating freedom of a vision of woman as equal partner. While the definition of woman as something less than human, as a being limited by the role of wife and mother, was current within Canada, at the same time much of Canadian life forced upon significant groups within the community an appreciation of woman as a human being. Sexism existed in Canada, but there was a considerable force within the community to counteract this trend. The social implementation of the belief in women as people was cut short by the economic crisis that wounded so much else within the community. Hard times came, and an experiment in equality was cut down before it started; the dreams of those who had worked so hard for the enfranchisement of women were postponed, one way and another, for thirty years.

NOTES

[1] B. Neatby in J.M.S. Careless and R. C. Brown, eds., *The Canadians 1867-1967* (Macmillan, 1968), p. 139.

[2] M.C. Urquhart and K.A.H. Buckley, *Historical Statistics of Canada* (Macmillan, 1965), p. 59.

[3] C. Cipolla, *Economic History of World Population* (Penguin, 1962), p. 27.

[4] Urquhart and Buckley, *op. cit.*, p. 15.

[5] Toronto, 248,040; Montreal, 267,730: other statistics from Urquhart and Buckley, *op. cit.*, p. 15.

[6] Charles Gordon, *Postscript to Adventure: The Autobiography of Ralph Connor* (Heritage Books, 1975), pp. 29, 14-16.

[7] Quoted in R. Cook, 'Introduction', in C. Cleverdon, *The Woman Suffrage Movement in Canada* (University of Toronto Press, 1975), p. xiii.

[8] Quoted in M. Anderson, *Mother was not a Person* (Black Rose Books, 1972), pp. 8-10 passim.

[9] Quoted in Cook, *op. cit.*, p. xiii.

[10] R. Hawes, 'Adelaide Hoodless', in Mary Q. Innis, ed., *The Clear Spirit* (University of Toronto Press, 1966), p. 45.

[11] *Ibid.*, pp. 115-16.

[12] Cleverdon, *op. cit.*, p. 8.

[13] *Ibid.*, p. 13.

[14] T. Lloyd, *Suffragettes International* (BPC, 1971), p. 99.

[15] Quoted in Hawes, *op cit.*, p. 111.

[16] Cleverdon, *op cit.*, p. 19.

[17] *Ibid.*, p. 21.

[18] A new edition with an introduction by Isabel Bassett has just been published (McClelland and Stewart, 1975).

[19] J.R. Colombo, ed., *Colombo's Canadian Quotations* (Hurtig, 1974), p. 370.

[20] Quoted in V. Strong-Boag, 'Introduction', in N. McClung, *In Times Like These* (University of Toronto Press, 1972), p. x.

[21] Quoted in Cleverdon, *op cit.*, p. 9.

[22] House of Commons *Debates*, 1917, VI, 5854-5.

[23] Cleverdon, *op. cit.*, p. 127.

[24] Statutes of Canada, 191, ch. 48.

[25] Montreal *Gazette,* 19 Oct. 1929.

[26] Quoted in Cleverdon, *op cit.*, p. 176.

[27] *Ibid.*, p. 177.

[28] *Ibid.*, pp. 198-9.

[29] Prince Edward Island: *Journals,* 1918, p. 8081.

[30] Cleverdon, *op. cit.*, p. 215.

[31] House of Commons *Debates*, 1918, I, 637-8.

[32] *Ibid.*, 644.

[33] On this question see particularly A. S. Rossi, ed., *The Feminist Papers from Adams to de Beauvoir* (Bantam, 1974), pp. 239-438 and M. B. Chesnut, *Diary from Dixie* (Peter Smith, 1961).

[34] New York *Tribune,* 1 Oct. 1867.

[35] Quoted in Cook, *op. cit.*, p. x.

[36] N. McClung, *In Times Like These* (University of Toronto Press, 1972), pp. 34, 88.

[37] J. Burton, 'Phyllus', in *Canadian Forum*, Oct. 1927.

[38] M. Atwood, *Survival* (Anansi, 1972), pp. 197-211.

[39] Urquhart and Buckley, *op. cit.*, pp. 14-15.

[40] *Ibid.*, p. 59.

[41] *Ibid.*, p. 63.

Nellie McClung.
Courtesy Public Archives Canada.

Adelaide Hunter Hoodless.
Courtesy Public Archives Canada.

Antonine Maillet, French-Canadian author.
Courtesy CP Picture Service.

Senator Muriel Fergusson, first woman speaker of the Senate.
Courtesy CP Picture Service.

Sylvia Ostry, Head of Statistics Canada.   *Courtesy CP Picture Service.*

Margaret Atwood, Canadian poetess
and novelist. *Courtesy William E. Toye.*

Florence Bird, Chairman of the
Royal Commission on the Status
of Women. *Courtesy CP Picture Service.*

Pauline McGibbon, first woman Lieutenant-
Governor of Ontario. *Courtesy Toronto Star.*

Nine

Women and the Webs of Society

The success of the campaign for women's suffrage, which had brought women the vote in most parts of the western world by the 1930s, meant neither the end of political action for women's rights nor an end to discussion about woman's nature and proper attributes. In concluding her work on the women's suffrage movement in Canada, Cleverdon wrote about the slow of pace of change in the country after enfranchisement. The number of women who became members of the legislature was miniscule and there was no action comparable to that taken by the Japanese women when the latter were allowed to vote in the first post-war election of that country in 1946. There, in a culture known for its subjection of women, one tenth of the members of the new Diet, 39, were female. Further these 'new feminine members showed a surprising degree of political astuteness when they promptly formed a club and agreed to vote as a bloc, regardless of parties, on such basic issues as food control, which they felt women were more capable of solving than men.'[1] In Canada, however, even by 1949 only five women had become members of the federal House of Commons and only two women had ever been appointed to the Senate.

Part of the explanation can be found in the timing of the success of the Canadian struggle for votes for women. Barely had this been achieved that the country encountered, along with the rest of the world, the great Depression, its inescapable arrival being marked by the Wall Street Crash of 1929. For many historians and politicians only the arrival of the Second World War brought the end of the misery, replacing unemployment with army life, offering the possibility of quick death in battle to slow life-in-death in poverty.

In such circumstances the possibilities of new advancement for women, the implementation of legislation setting up better working conditions, the organization of educational opportunities for women were measures that, like similar legislation for men, would have to wait until the hard times were over. Even such provisions as did exist were often inadequate to prevent exploitation of people. Barry Broadfoot's outstanding collection of the memories of Canadians who survived the Depression, *Ten Lost Years*, records example after example of people who had to choose between a job of work at any price, or no job. As one witness said:

> Women. They employed women. Those who might have come in off the farms, towns, northern Quebec and Ontario. The Province had set a minimum wage law for women at $12.50 a week. Now remember that's a week. What's a week? How long is a piece of string? That week could be 48 to 70 hours, whatever these people figured they could get away with. They knew all the loop-holes.[2]

In fact the general level of unemployment was so great that not only were there no new entries of women into particular jobs but, notwithstanding unequal pay for equal work, there was an actual decline in the rate of participation of women aged 20-35 in the labour force.[3] Young girls could not get work, no matter what conditions they were willing to accept. There was nothing equivalent to the farsighted measures brought forward in Sweden, where a determination to ensure that women would not undercut men led to the passage of well-policed legislation giving equal pay for equal work.

But the economic conditions of the thirties are only part of the explanation of why that decade saw little alteration in the position and status of women in Canada. The fight for the vote had, after all, been precisely that: a fight. Opponents did not fade away merely because the battle was lost. There was still, in Canada and elsewhere in the western world, a very strong belief in the inferiority of women. It pervaded social structure and convention as a prevailing wind of negation, something that could stunt, warp, and diminish even though, in most countries, it was not the sole determinant of social belief. The great Canadian painter, Emily Carr, experienced it and wrote in her diary on Christmas day,

> . . . two would-be art critics came to the studio. They were

'pose-y' waved their paws describing sweeps and motions in my pictures, screwed their eyes, made monocles of their fists, discoursed on aesthetics, asked prices, and expounded on technique. One paints a little and teaches a lot, the other 'aesthetics' with I do not quite know what aim. Both think women and their works beneath contempt but ask to come to the studio on every occasion. Why?[4]

For her and for many other women artists there was a distinct pressure of anti-feminism that had to be fought. She wrote about this quite explicitly in 1937 when commenting on a Toronto review of her work:

I am also glad that I am showing these men that women can hold up their end. The men resent a woman getting honour in what they consider is essentially their field. Men painters mostly despise women painters.[5]

One of the strongest statements of the pressure that anti-feminism could exert upon women is in Dorothy Richardson's semi-autobiography, *Pilgrimage* She was born in 1873, died in 1957, and was one of the many women in the life of British writer H. G. Wells. Her thirteen-volume work took her twenty years to write and she had great difficulty in persuading anyone to publish it. Not only did she feel the pressure of social disapproval because she was a woman who had achieved something, but she was greatly exercised about the possibility that twentieth-century science would confirm the place of women as the 'second sex'. The heroine of her work, Miriam, is confronted not only with the tremendous achievements of men, lauded and discussed by the heaped books around her, but also with the possible truth of a view of woman as 'nothing but gynaecology'.[6]

And the modern men were the worst—'we can now, with all the facts in our hands, sit down and examine her at our leisure'. There was no getting away from the scientific facts—*inferior*; mentally, morally, intellectually, and physically—her development arrested in the interest of her special functions—reverting later towards the male type—old women with deep voices and hair on their faces—leaving off where boys of eighteen began. If that is true everything is as clear as daylight. 'Woman is not undeveloped man but diverse' falls to pieces. Woman is undeveloped man—if one could die of the loathsome visions—I *must* die. I can't go on living in it—the whole world full of *creatures*; half human. And I am one of the half-human ones, or shall be, if I don't stop now.[7]

Richardson's fear that science would define women as a kind of container for male reproduction, important solely for the birth of men, is a very real fear for many women in the twentieth century. It is a fear that has produced, and is producing, much of the anger felt by people in Women's Liberation. It is a fear that is fuelled by writings of scientists such as E. W. Overstreet, a contemporary gynaecologist. In 1963 he concluded an article on the physiological basis of menstruation and reproduction with the words: 'When you come right down to it, perhaps women just live too long. Maybe when they get through having babies they have outlived their usefulness—especially now that they outlive men by so many years.'[8] One wonders what Overstreet sees as a solution for this problem: some kind of execution of all women without children over the age of thirty or so and of those women whose children are over eighteen? It is possible, if not probable that he thought he was merely being 'practical', or 'funny'. But to women the crudity of that statement seems enormously threatening. It is not merely that it betrays the belief that women are objects, interchangeable baby-making machines, but it underlines the belief of many women that real power lies with the male, and that those who have power see women solely as a collection of convenient spaces.

It is important to emphasize that while women are bitter about the implications of child-bearing they are not necessarily hostile to motherhood. But for many women Freud's statement 'anatomy is destiny' is so often encountered as a bludgeon that their reaction is the same as that of the Canadian poet, Mary Melfi:

a big hole,
   sits in my body
     soon ready
to become me, entirely.[9]

So much has been written about this fear over the last thirty or forty years that it perhaps needs no further emphasis. Yet unless it is understood as a basic reality behind the ideas of many women, there is unlikely to be much progress in a discussion of whether sexual characteristics are a final determinant, an inescapable control of individual achievement. Women are not reacting against their fate as child-bearers but against the conclusion that motherhood means that all women are intellectually inferior to all men, all women are destined to become mothers if they are not to be human failures, all women are weak because they are dominated by their sexuality.

Further, women are not rejecting the social heritage that suggests that women have a particular capacity for expressing tenderness and concern for others, for valuing the reality of emotions, for delighting in the beautiful, for finding satisfaction in creating joy for others. The bitterness comes from being made aware that it is too often assumed that men should not display these characteristics, that all the compassion humanity needs can be found in one sex alone. And the bitterness is augmented by the assumption that not only should women alone preserve these qualities but that, since these qualities are the business of women, they are of lesser importance than those usually accorded men. Finally the ultimate cause of women's anger is to be told that the important virtues that they alone can cherish, but that are obviously not quite of major value for day-to-day life, are virtues that bar them from acquiring characteristics seen as the heritage of the male: logical thinking, ambition for honest achievement, judgement about human priorities, to name only a few.

The 1930s was a decade that saw such assumptions adopted by the Nazi party as their official attitude towards women. Richard Grunberger in *The 12-year Reich: A Social History of Nazi Germany, 1933-1945* has commented that the 'kernel of Nazi thinking on the women's question was a dogma of inequality between the sexes as immutable as that between the races.'[10] The anti-feminism of the Nazi party was something that caught up in one useful emotional outlet a wide variety of feelings: 'paterfamilias authoritarianism, anti-permissiveness, Philistine outrage at sophistication, white collar workers' job insecurity, virility fears and just plain misogyny.'[11] Whatever the reason, the attitude to women in Nazi Germany was one of cynical exploitation. Hitler himself considered any form of the emancipation of women a sign of degeneracy. Frick, the Minister of the Interior, considered that women should be graded according to their child-bearing capacities.[12]

On the one hand there is the picture of women as sitting, in the words of one Nazi writer 'with her beloved husband in her cosy home' listening 'inwardly to the loom of time weaving the weft and warp of motherhood.'[13] On the other hand during the thirties skilled women in Germany earned '66 per cent of men's wages, unskilled ones 70 per cent, which explains why during the Depression nearly one man in three (29 per cent) was dismissed but only one woman in every ten (11 per cent)'. As Grunberger points out, woman's place might be in the home but in '1933 women formed 37 per cent of the total employed labour force in Germany', and 'Every second agricultural worker was female.'[14]

The Nazi program was not merely one of exploiting women in the work force, skilled women being paid less than untrained men, while paying lipservice to their presence in a comfortable home. It was one of ensuring that women would be removed from positions of power and influence. To quote again from Grunberger:

> Married women doctors and civil servants were dismissed immediately after the seizure of power. The number of women teachers at girls' secondary schools had decreased by 15 per cent in 1935. In the following academic year the entry of girls to training departments for university teachers was completely suspended. By this time the number of women academics had declined from fifty-nine to thirty-seven (out of a total academic teaching body of over 7000).... From June 1936 onwards women could no longer act as judges or public prosecutors ... (and) were declared ineligible for jury service on the grounds that 'they cannot think logically or reason objectively, since they are ruled only by emotion.'[15]

At one and the same time women were barred from the professions, fully exploited in the more menial tasks of the labour force, and told that their rightful place was, in the words of Goebbels, Minister of Propaganda, 'out of the miasma of parliamentary democracy.'[16]

Protests within Germany against this attitude of the Nazi régime took two major forms. In the first place there were complaints from people within the party who, having accepted the vision of the rightful sphere for women being Kinder, Kirche, Küche (children, church, and kitchen) found that the reality of the

Third Reich did not, in fact, establish this vision. The organization of the young men in barracks, their separation from women for significant periods of time during their early manhood, did not help communication between the sexes nor make marriage a matter of importance for the male. As one work presented to Hitler in 1934 commented: 'Today, man is being educated not for but against marriage. Men are grouped together in *Vereine* (clubs) and *Kameradschaftsheime* (hostels).'[17] The rosy picture of woman, queen of a domain peopled by husband and children was, in reality, far more often the bleakness of a house with an absentee husband and father, and sons who looked upon their mothers as a kind of superior servant. Any idea of the woman having a moral authority springing from her closer association with the dictates of religion was vitiated by the emphasis upon her intellectual inability to understand anything of value. German women quickly understood that the separation of home from the business of life meant a terrible isolation and loneliness. Instead of spending their lives in creating a sanctuary of human values, women found their work denigrated and themselves despised.

The second argument against the relegation of women to the domestic scene was based on the logical consequences of the belief that sexual difference is more important in life than common humanity. If this was indeed so, then trained women should be produced to cope with the special needs of women. On 3 December 1938, for example, the *Danziger Vorposten* argued that perhaps 'Women doctors could give aid and comfort to fatigued mothers. . . . Women teachers would be most suited to instruct adolescent girls in such delicate subjects as biology. . . . Women jurists would be most qualified for dealing with cases involving children. . . . Women scientists and economists could be employed in the planning of consumption and domestic matters.'

With the arrival of the Second World War, some notice was taken of this argument, and whereas in 1938-9 there were some 9,000 women in German universities, in the academic year 1943-4 the number had reached 25,000.[18] The war, in fact, meant that the idea of women in the home had to be placed in abeyance. In 1939 women in Germany had constituted one third of the employed labour force, comprising nearly 7 million workers. On 27 January 1943, the Reich attempted to bring into being a total mobilization of female workers, and by 1944 there were some

14½ million women in the work force.[19] No amount of propaganda would obscure the fact that while Nazi rhetoric spoke of woman's place as being in the home, caring for husband and children, German women made up three-fifths of Germany's wartime labour force.[20]

This utilization of women in the labour force during the Second World War was common to all countries engaged in that struggle. In Canada the national war effort meant the mobilization of women as well as men into factory work, farm work, and the armed forces themselves. Broadfoot remarks that 'at the time of peak production, half of the 1,100,000 Canadians fighting Hitler at home' were women.[21] In other words the demands made upon the west by the Second World War brought, in all countries—France, England, Belgium, Holland, Canada, Germany, and the United States—a much greater number of women into the work force, at a very much faster pace, than could have been envisaged during the years of the Depression. The actual statistics for Canada show that during the years of the Depression the number of women in the workforce increased from 790,000 in 1931 to 959,000 in 1939: a net addition of some 169,000 women. But between 1939 and 1945, some six years, the number rose from 959,000 to 1,418,000: an addition of some 459,000.[22]

At the end of the war the attitude to the status and position of women within western society was ambiguous. On the one hand their participation in the war effort had meant that their abilities and talents had received a public recognition that would act as a constant repudiation of any idea of feminine incapacity. As one woman remembers it:

> Husbands and boyfriends came back from the war and found their wives and girlfriends just weren't prepared to start washing dishes again. It must have been quite a shock. But some women had ferried air force bombers to Britain, and others drove ambulances and worked in canteens serving the troops, or in war plants handling very expensive tools, working on equipment, planes, instrument panels and things and companies found they could do better than men. . . . You could almost say that women fought a war the same as their men, the war against them just being women, household machines.[23]

But while the world war was a time when more women entered

wider spheres of action, it was at the same time a cataclysm of tragedy. Canada did not suffer defeat or occupation as did many other countries. But even in Canada, as Colonel Stacey has pointed out, the war meant personal grief and anguish, 'The sorrow and deprivation resulting from the prolonged absence overseas of hundred of thousands of sons and husbands, the constant fear for their safety, the all-too-frequent telegrams bringing news of death or wounds suffered in action against the enemy by land or sea or air. And many a home was broken by the long separation, leaving tragic social consequences which are felt to this day.'[24] The aftermath of this experience for western civilization as a whole was a tremendous questioning of how such events came about, and what path must be taken to avoid a repetition: how could the western world have come to concentration camps and atomic weapons? Answers were sought in conflicting political ideologies, in philosophy, and theology. But one of the strongest currents in the western world, if one of the least remarked, was the force that emphasized the rights and needs of individuals, that set up civil-liberties groups, that appealed for a decent life for ordinary people. And it was this force that, during the 1950s, once more pictured family life as a sanctuary and woman's place in the home.

This is the force behind the trend documented in 1963 by Betty Friedan in *The Feminine Mystique*. In the second chapter, 'The Happy Housewife Heroine', Frieden analysed the ideas behind the stories published in the American mass-circulation journals for women during the late 1950s and the early 1960s—*McCall's*, *Ladies Home Journal*, *Redbook*. Her conclusion was:

> The feminine mystique says that the highest value and the only commitment for women is the fulfillment of their femininity. It says that the great mistake of Western culture, through most of its history, has been the under-valuation of this femininity. It says that this femininity is so mysterious and intuitive and close to the creation and origin of life that man-made science may never be able to understand it. But however special and different, it is in no way inferior to the nature of man; it may even in certain respects be superior. The mistake, says the mystique, the root of women's trouble in the past is that women envied men, women tried to be like men, instead of accepting their own nature, which can find fulfillment only in

sexual passivity, male domination, and nurturing maternal love.[25]

But, as Betty Frieden went on to show, however soothing such a vision might be, it was a vision that implied femininity without intellect, emotion without intelligence. She cited story after story where the heroine was a model of passive dependence, a kind of pure warmth, protected, cared for, paid for by her husband. Motherhood was presented as so great a gift and such a total fulfillment that no preparation was needed for it and no other activity could be compared to it. In October 1956 *Look*, one of the most popular of the American weekly journals, could represent the status of American women in the following light:

> The American woman is winning the battle of the sexes. Like a teenager, she is growing up and confounding her critics. . . . No longer a psychological immigrant to man's world, she works, rather casually, as a third of the U. S. labour force, less towards a 'big career' than as a way of filling a hope chest or buying a new home freezer. She gracefully concedes the top jobs to men. This wondrous creature also marries younger than ever, bears more babies and looks and acts far more feminine than the 'emancipated' girl of the 1920s or even the '30's. Steelworker's wife and Junior Leaguer alike do their own housework. . . . Today, if she makes an old-fashioned choice and lovingly tends a garden and a bumper crop of children, she rates louder hosannas than ever before.[26]

A great deal lies behind this description. If women made up a third of the labour force, the importance of their contribution to the economy must be considerable. How many years did women work? If the steelworker's wife and Junior Leaguer alike did their own housework, which one of them also went into the labour force? The article subtly suggested that only young women ever worked, and only by choice, and only for luxuries rather than necessities. It is the woman's choice that she takes no responsibility, for her mind is set on higher matters, a neat explanation for the absence of women in positions of power. The vision of women = home = sanctuary and man = work = the tough world meant in reality something very different. This vision has little relevance to the urban or rural poor, to those whose circumstances still demanded two wages for the survival of the family unit. It had no relevance at all to women bringing up children without the support of a man, to men or women caring for sick relatives single-handedly, to the old living on welfare, or the single, men and women, living alone. How did you lovingly tend a garden in an urban slum? Was it choice or circumstance that gave you a 'bumper crop of children' if you were poor, Catholic, or subject to other pressures?

But even for what might be called 'middle America' this vision was a poisoned apple, giving the two sexes mutually exclusive roles. The woman was supposed to create a home that cherished the essential human values that could be felt and understood and never analysed. The man was to provide the economic base for this life, to protect the woman, to save her from any contact with the harsh realities he dealt with, and his reward was to experience what he could never create. Even before the 1950s there had been an awareness of the dangers for both sexes of this ideal. Philip Wylie, an American novelist writing in 1942, had attacked what he called 'momworship'. As H. R. Hayes remarked, Wylie was commenting upon 'the Victorian cult of the virgin, (which) was grafted onto the frontier situation in America in which men were popularly supposed to be so concerned with taming the continent and building industry that ethical and cultural values were left to the woman.' The result was, according to Wylie, that 'the gals (taught) their men that dowry went the other way, that it was a weekly contribution [from the male] and that any male worthy of a Cinderella would have to work like a piston after getting one so as to be worthy, also, of all the other moms in the world.'[27] Relationships between the sexes became based upon a material exchange, 'unless you keep me as you know you should, you are a weakling and a barbarian.'

Already in the 1930s Rebecca West, British journalist and philosopher, had commented upon the development in Europe of this attempt to put men and women into watertight compartments of home and the rest of the world, and suggested that it would provoke a form of madness in each. Those who concentrated upon the personal, upon the life of the emotions, not seeing the power held over the individual by the society, became idiots, while those who refused to admit the necessity of an emotional life, of personal relationships, of the demand of loved ones, concentrating only on the business of the society, became lunatics.[28] West wrote 'the word idiot comes from a Greek root meaning private person. Idiocy is the female defect; intent on their private lives, women follow their fate through a darkness deep as that cast by malformed cells in the brain. It is no worse than the male defect, which is lunacy; they are so obsessed by public affairs that they see the world as by moonlight, which shows the outline of every object but not the details indicative of their nature.'

In so many ways the reaction against the attempt to define women in terms of family and home is a rejection of a simplistic dream by both men and women. It is the realization that a human 'utopia' of love and caring cannot be brought about by one sex alone. Because the dream warped the development of women and barred them from exploiting their potential, the reaction against it has been most often seen as 'Women's Liberation'. It is, in reality, a demand for the liberation of both men and women. It does not mean so much a rejection of ideas of masculinity and femininity as an attempt to discover how closely these ideas are linked to the biology of sex. The findings of twentieth-century anthropologists, showing that different cultures in the world have very different ideas of what society should emphasize as correct behaviour for men and women, has been an added spur. Margaret Mead, one of the early American women anthropologists, found traditions of male love for children as well as traditions of female aggression and hostility in the tribes in New Guinea. Other anthropologists working in Brazil have discovered tribes where there is 'a complete lack of emphasis on temperamental differences between the sexes.'[29] Information from Africa and from the south-western Pacific underlined the same point: cultural emphasis could produce very different behaviour patterns in men and women than those usually associated with masculinity and femininity in western civilization.

Paradoxically enough, by the time women themselves had been aroused to argue for changes in society's conventions, institutions, and legal structures, western civilization as a whole was considering how to set about the construction of a 'just society', and in this quest was about to consider the implications of human sexuality. While the anger and vision of western women has led to the organization of Women's Liberation as a force in western society over the last three decades, this movement is really only part of a much wider movement to bring about a better dispensation in human affairs. The development of the social sciences has meant a questioning about the right ordering of human life that has, inevitably, also meant questions about the best ordering of human sexuality. But, as Simone de Beauvoir remarked in *The Second Sex*, little progress will be made in finding answers to these questions 'as long as men and women fail to recognize each other as peers.'[30] Here is the real and fundamental issue: unless men and women can start their work by considering both sexes equally important, the results will be research tailored to support a hierarchical relationship between men and women.

Recognition of men and women as each others' peers does not demand that they should be considered as patterned replicas of each other. It does mean that ideas of innate capacities be considered most carefully, with the constant realization that overall statistical variation between the sexes should lead, not to prohibition but to examination. In other words, should it be proved that the ability to analyse spatial concepts is found more readily among men than among women, something that present research indicates is probable, the reaction should be tests to help select the most capable among those women who wish to enter the fields where such a skill is needed, not the exclusion of all women *a priori* from such fields. After all, the ability to distinguish colours is an important ability for pilots, but even though more men than women are colour blind no one has suggested that women should monopolize careers in flying; instead a screening for this defect is built into the procedure for selecting pilots. Nor does recognition of sexual equality mean that humanity ought to strive for a society where there is no emphasis upon gender differentiation. There has been such a tremendous emphasis in western civilization upon gender roles that their values ought to be investigated with great care before they are summarily jettisoned. But this investigation can only be fruitful if there is a fundamental acceptance of the real contribution of both concepts, the masculine and the feminine, to human society.

Again the present discontent has emphasized the damage done to women by the contempt in which feminine values have so often been held. It is salutary to remember that misogyny has a feminine counterpart. During the Second World War Vera Brittain, a leading British writer, published a pamphlet condemning the indiscriminate bombing of civilian populations, in particular the horror of 'killing women and children'. George Orwell, then a British journalist, commented: 'Why is it worse to kill a woman than a man? The argument usually advanced is that in killing women you are killing breeders, whereas men can be more easily spared. But this is a fallacy based on the notion that human beings can be bred like animals.... Human beings, however, are not cattle. When the slaughter caused by a war leaves a surplus of women, the enormous majority of those women bear no children....'[31]

Men and women are not cattle; they are not interchangeable groups of abilities, to be organized efficiently for the ease of those who have managed to construct a hierarchical society to benefit themselves. They are neither bees responding to hive orders nor wolves kept in rank by fear alone. In considering the structure of human lives the reality of human emotions must be granted, something far too frequently overlooked by both parties.

Esther Vilar, born of German parents in Argentina in 1935, a medical doctor and now living in Germany, wrote in *The Manipulated Man* that 'Women let men work for them, think for them, take on their responsibilities—in fact they exploit them',[32] and that this is the exploitation of the strong by the weak. In one chapter entitled 'A Dictionary' she writes of the real motives that inspire women by comparing what she calls coded phrases with their real meanings. Here are a few examples from her list:[33]

CODED	DECODED
A man must be able to protect me.	A man must be able to spare me from all forms of discomfort. (What else could he protect her from? Robbers? An atom bomb?)
I need a man to make me feel secure.	Above all, he must keep his money worries to himself.
I must be able to look up to a man.	To be a possible candidate as a husband, he must be more intelligent, responsible, courageous, industrious, and stronger than I am. Otherwise, what purpose would he serve?

Of course I would give up my career if my husband asked me.	Once he is earning enough money, I am never going to work again.
I don't believe in Women's Liberation.	I'm not such a fool. I'd rather let a man do the work for me.
After all, we are living in an age of equality.	If he thinks he can order me about just because he earns money for me, he is sorely mistaken.

The picture of woman presented here is of a calculating being motivated by psychological cunning and the profit motive. Vilar's final chapter is called 'What is Love?' and she writes: 'To a woman love means power, to a man enslavement. Love provides woman with an excuse for financial exploitation, man with an emotionally charged excuse. "For the sake of love" woman will do things that are of advantage only to herself, while man does only those things that harm him. . . . When a man marries, he will have to work for two "for the sake of love".'[34] Nowhere is there any discussion of love outside the parameters of sexuality. That it is a human emotion of an intricate vastness, stuff not only of poets and theologians but of politics and psychologists, is never considered in these pages. But then her people are really only cardboard cutouts, linked to humanity by but the slightest thread. What could they know of the emotion behind the discovery, after the Guatemalan earthquake, of a baby balanced on the hands of her mother, resting just above the earth that swallowed her mother's body?

Shulamith Firestone wrote *The Dialectic of Sex*, subtitled 'The Case for Feminist Revolution' in 1971. She was born in Ottawa in 1945 but has spent the majority of her life in the United States. Her book is a much more substantial and complex entity than *The Manipulated Man*, but it is equally didactic. What she has called 'sex class' she sees as all pervasive and all important, for 'sexism presents problems far worse than the black militant's new awareness of racism: feminists have to question, not just all of *western* culture, but the organization of culture itself. . . . '[35] For her, too, the question of love is vital; she, too, sees it as a political matter and she too, devotes a chapter to it. She writes: 'For love, perhaps even more than child-bearing, is the pivot of women's oppression today.'[36] She firmly believes that 'women live for love and men for work' and that '[male] culture was built on the love of women and at their expense . . . ' She, too, finds herself capable of a short summary of her beliefs, drawing three conclusions:

(1) That men can't love. (Women traditionally expect and accept an emotional invalidism in men that they would find intolerable in a woman.)

(2) That women's 'clinging' behaviour is necessitated by their objective social situation.

(3) That this situation has never changed significantly.

Here men are automatons controlled by appetite and women powerless servants. Again love is primarily a sexual commodity, a tool for enslavement. Belief in selflessness is obviously self-delusion. One wonders whether she has ever met a male factory worker, or a male garbage man, or any of that sex who mine coal or asbestos or work at something that is a paying occupation rather than a chosen profession or career. One wonders, too, how she has managed to avoid meeting any woman who has a burning dedication to nursing, teaching, writing. But the world of *The Dialectic of Sex* is really as unreal as the men and women who people it, the events and problems with which it is concerned so much less complex than reality.

Western civilization has seen society after society attempt to organize people as self-creating robots but it has seen the opposite view constantly and passionately argued. It is the challenge of the twentieth century that visions of freedom and equality are now being considered in the context of sexual relationships as well as in the sphere of political matters. The extraordinary difficulties provided by such a challenge can be seen clearly enough by an investigation of Canada's efforts in this area, in particular the Royal Commission on the Status of Women.

NOTES

[1] C. L. Cleverdon, *The Woman Suffrage Movement in Canada* (University of Toronto Press, 1974), p. 270.

[2] B. Broadfoot, *Ten Lost Years, 1929-1939: Memories of Canadians who Survived the Depression* (Paperjacks, 1973), p. 126.

[3] M. C. Urquhart and K. A. H. Buckley, *Historical Statistics of Canada* (Macmillan, 1965), p. 63.

[4] Quoted in M. J. Moffat and C. Painter, *Revelations: Diaries of Women* (Random House, 1974), p. 387.

[5]*Ibid.*, p. 388.

[6]Quoted in J. Goulianos, *By a Woman Writt: Literatue from Six Centuries by and about Women* (Penguin, 1974), p. 270.

[7]*Ibid.*

[8]E. W. Overstreet, 'The Biological Make-up of Women', quoted in A. Oakley, *Sex, Gender and Society* (Harper, 1972), p. 190.

[9]In Margret Andersen, comp., *Mother Was Not a Person* (Montreal, 1972), p. 127.

[10]R. Grunberger, *The 12-year Reich: A Social History of Nazi Germany, 1933-1945* (Ballantine, 1972), p. 277.

[11]*Ibid.*

[12]Quoted in Grunberger, *op. cit.*, p. 278, from *Dokumente der Deutschen Politik*,vol. I., p. 17.

[13]Kurt Rosten, *Das ABC des Nationalsozialismus* (Berlin, 1933), p. 198, quoted in Grunberger, *op. cit.*, p. 278.

[14]Grunberger, *op. cit.*, pp. 278-9.

[15]*Ibid.*, p. 285.

[16]Joseph Goebbels, 'Das Frauentum', in *Signale der Neuen Zeit* (Berlin, 1934), p. 118, quoted in Grunberger, *op. cit.*, p. 277.

[17]Quoted in Grunberger, *op. cit.*, p. 284.

[18]*Ibid.*, p. 286.

[19]*Ibid.*, p. 279.

[20]*Ibid.*, p. 282.

[21]Broadfoot, *op. cit.*, p. 353.

[22]Urquhart and Buckley, *op. cit.*, p. 63.

[23]Broadfoot, *op. cit.*, p. 353.

[24]C. P. Stacey, 'Through the Second World War', in J.M.S. Careless and R. C. Brown, eds., *The Canadians, 1867-1967* (Macmillan, 1968), p., 184

[25]B. Friedan, *The Feminine Mystique* (Dell, 1970), p. 37.

[26]Quoted in *ibid.*, pp. 52-3.

[27]Quoted in H. R. Hayes, *The Dangerous Sex: The Myth of Feminine Evil* (Pocket Books, 1966), p. 257.

[28]R. West, *Black Lamb and Grey Falcon* (Viking Press, 1941), p. 3.

[29]Quoted in A. Oakley, *Sex Gender and Society* (Harper Colophon, 1972), p. 55.

[30]*Ibid.*, p. 725.

[31]'As I Please', *Tribune*, 14 July 1944; in G. Orwell, *The Collected Essays, Journalism and Letters of George Orwell* (Penguin, 1970), vol. 3, p. 214.

[32]E. Vilar, *The Manipulated Man* (New York, 1972), p. 5.

[33]*Ibid.*, pp. 66-8.

[34]*Ibid.*, pp. 182-3.

[35]S. Firestone, *The Dialectic of Sex* (Bantam, 1971), p. 12.

[36]*Ibid.*, p. 121.

Ten

The Royal Commission

The Canadian Royal Commission on the Status of Women was established by a minute of the Privy Council on 16 February 1967. Mrs Florence Bird, news commentator and journalist, was appointed its chairman. In her work she used the pen name Anne Francis and published her autobiography using that name as its title. The autobiography includes a great deal on the organization and work of the Royal Commission. From the moment when an announcement was made in the House of Commons that such a Commission would be established, some two weeks before the Privy Council minute, there was considerable public reaction. The press was sceptical, the TV and radio commentators were less than enthusiastic, and the general consensus seemed to Florence Bird herself to be that it was 'a political gimmick to allow women to let off steam', and that the final report 'would be pigeon-holed and forgotten'.[1] There were six other commissioners appointed, one of whom, the political science professor Donald Gordon, resigned after eight months. He was replaced and the permanent members were:

Mrs Florence Bird, born Philadelphia, 1908, writer and broadcaster;

Mr Jacques Henripin, born Lachine, Quebec, 1929, a demographer, then head of the Department of Demography at the University of McGill;

Mr John Humphrey, born Hampton, New Brunswick, 1905; he replaced Donald Gordon; Humphrey had been both a professor of law and the former secretary-general of the Human Rights Commission of the United Nations from 1946-1966;

Mrs Lola Mary Lange, born in Edmonton, Alberta, 1922; she had had considerable experience with the Alberta Farm Women's Union;

Miss Jeanne Lapointe, born in 1915 at Chicoutimi; a professor of French literature at Laval University; she had been a member of the Quebec Parent Commission on education;

Elizabeth Muriel Gregory MacGill, born in Vancouver in 1905; the first woman in Canada to become an aeronautical engineer;

Mrs Robert Ogilvie, born in Halifax, Nova Scotia in 1919; she was admitted to the New Brunswick Branch of the Canadian Bar Association in 1964, and was appointed Deputy Judge of the Juvenile Court in 1965.

The task of the Royal Commission was set out bluntly enough in the Privy Council minute. It was to 'inquire and report upon the status of women in Canada, and to recommend what steps might be taken by the Federal Government to ensure for women equal opportunities with men in all aspects of Canadian society. . . . In particular the Commissioners were directed to 'inquire into and report on:

1. Laws and practices under federal jurisdiction concerning the political rights of women;

2. The present and potential role of women in the Canadian labour force, including the special problems of married women in employment. . . . ;

3. Measures that might be taken under federal jurisdiction to permit the better use of the skills and education of women . . . ;

4. Federal labour laws and regulations in their application to women;

5. Laws, practices, and policies concerning the employment and promotion of women in the Federal civil service . . . ;

6. Federal taxation pertaining to women;

7. Marriage and divorce;

8. The position of women under the Criminal Law;

9. Immigration and citizenship laws, policies and practice with respect to women;

and

such other matters in relation to the status of women in Canada as may appear to the Commissioners to be relevant.[2]

As the Commissioners themselves later complained, the subjects covered in these directives 'were so extensive and diverse that they could have been the subject matter for separate Royal Commissions.'[3]

The opening months of the Commission were ones of some difficulty as a secretariat had to be assembled and working quarters had to be found. By the beginning of 1969, however, these problems had been overcome and a momentum achieved. The Commission proceeded to work by organizing research programs on a variety of topics, by meeting themselves 178 times over a period of nearly four years, by requesting and receiving briefs from individuals and organizations, and by setting up thirty-seven days of public hearings. They received 468 briefs and about 2000 letters of opinion. The whole Commission went to some fourteen cities in the ten provinces. The Chairman and one other Commissioner also held hearings in Whitehorse and Yellowknife, and in all some 880 witnesses appeared before the Commission. Finally in 1970 their *Report* was released: a majority of six members presented it and the minority report of John Humphrey was appended to it. There were 167 recommendations.

Undeniably one of the most important results of the Commission was the education of both public and government about the status of women. A comparison of editorials in one newspaper, the Ottawa *Journal*, is a graphic demonstration of this. On 4 February 1967 this paper greeted the establishment of the Commission with an editorial that read, in part, as follows:

The reaction of Canadian men to news that a royal commission on women's rights has been appointed is what one would expect of a tough, hard-working, straight-talking male: fear. Everyone knows what commissions are like at their worst. Everyone knows what women are like at their worst. Put the two of them together—well we could end up with the longest established permanent royal commission in history. Somebody once said that individually women are something, but together they're something else. . . .

What makes these girls think any Canadian man in his right mind would sit on such a commission . . . ?

By all means let the girls gather facts and opinions about women's rights in Canada and see how they can be strengthened where they need it. Bosh! But we suggest to them, for their own good, of course, that they do it in the same way that they have advanced their cause in recent years—quietly, sneakily, and with such charming effectiveness as to make men wonder why they feel they need a royal commission. . . .

The same newspaper commented four years later, on 8 December 1970, on the *Report* itself in the following editorial:

There is much to approve in the content, in the calm, deliberate tone and lucid exposition of facts and opinion in the Report of the Royal Commission on the Status of Women. The report is a masterpiece of condensation, so crammed with information and so sweeping in scope that the length of time required to bring it forth is now almost understandable. Moreover, women's Lib and all, it has not been overtaken by events: the report is almost agonizingly relevant.

The Commission's work should be approached with some humility, especially by males. The report is too complex to be either uncritically praised or damned. . . .

The systematic and thorough searching out of inequities experienced by women in the work force, in education, under the law and, yes, in the family, is the most useful part of the commission's work. The documentation of discrimination is irrefutable, whether deliberate or an unthinking perpetuation of male prejudices. . . .

It would be false to give the impression that the Commission made its impact without help of work done in previous years by both federal and provincial bureaus working for women. Nor, of course, was it the sole voice speaking about women between 1967 and 1970. But its work, especially the public hearings, helped to focus and unite much diffuse opinion on the subject into a coherent whole. In the words of Florence Bird:

Sometimes the Commission hearings took place in the auditorium of a shopping centre or in a gymnasium, sometimes in hotels, so that we could reach people living in different parts of a city. Usually there was an audience of from two to five hundred people, most of them women. On a number of occasions women travelled as far as three hundred miles by automobile from small towns which we could not visit in order to bring us their opinions. . . .

There was a significant sameness about the kind of people who came to the hearings day by day, in city after city. Most of them were women in their forties and fifties. Many spoke from harsh experience, having come up against discrimination and prejudice at work, where they found that equal pay legislation did not give them the same pay as men even when they did work of comparative value and responsibility. Many were housewives who found themselves bored, dissatisfied and depressed, sitting in mechanized homes, no longer needed by their children, with thirty-five years of potentially active and useful life ahead of them.[4]

The coverage of Canada by the Commission was, of course, nothing in comparison with that of the Royal Commission on Bilingualism and Biculturalism. But it was, nevertheless, a Commission that was visible throughout the land and that slowly changed the attitudes of both press and public towards the questions for which answers were being sought.

It was perhaps in the provision of information that the *Report* of the Commission scored its real triumph. The statistical material that it contained had, for the most part, been available but scattered through the multitudinous documents of such bodies as the Women's Bureau of the Federal Department of Labour and the Public Service Commission of Canada. But now in 1970 it was brought together, pointed out, and commented upon. For Florence Bird herself, some of the highlights brought out were:

1. Although a million women entered the labour force in the ten-year period between 1961 and 1971, the percentage of women in management only rose from 3.7 to 3.9 per cent.
2. In 1973 there were only five women in a House of Commons of 264 seats. . . .
3. A recent survey made by the Department of Labour in four cities showed that in each of ten occupations, women's average weekly salary rates were less than those of men for similarly described work. . . . in Halifax, the average weekly salary rate for women material record clerks was $71 compared with $106 for men. In Toronto it was $86 compared with $120 for men.
4. This inequality in pay rates goes right on up to the top. . . . The Commission found that women professors receive an average of $2,226 a year less than men with the same or lower academic degrees.[5]

This sort of material is an invaluable public resource. It is the best counter to myth, and its worth was immediately recognized by those working for women's rights. In fact the Women's Bureau of the Federal Department of Labour issued in 1974 a book entitled

Women in the Labour Force, which contains some seventy-seven tables and a multitude of charts showing the present status of women in the Canadian work world. Those who continue to argue that women's place is in the home have now to consider the fact that in 1972 there are 2,953,000 women in a Canadian labour force of 8,891,000. Those who considered absenteeism the woman's disease now have to recognize that in 1972, 1.76 per cent of women in the full-time force were absent from work for the whole of a particular week; the percentage of men who were absent for the same cause and for the same length of time was 1.95 per cent. The provision of material such as this makes arguments about the needs of women infinitely easier to pursue. The continuing problem of equal pay becomes that much more obvious when one can turn to data backed by the prestige of Statistics Canada, which shows that in occupation after occupation women doing the same work as men are paid less. The 1973 edition of *Women in the Labour Force* provides endless examples, summarized at one point as follows:

> The average annual earnings of women employees who worked 50 to 52 weeks were $4,785 in 1971, compared with $8,646 for men. The earnings of men exceeded women by 80.7%.[6]

If the Royal Commission had achieved nothing else, the inauguration of serious discussion about women in the Canadian labour force and the compilation of reliable data about their contribution would have been enough to justify its existence.

It did, of course, much more. In May 1973 the federal government set up an Advisory Council on the Status of Women, which reports to the Minister of Labour, and is at present responsible for seeing that the recommendations of the Royal Commission on the Status of Women are implemented. In 1974 the Council published a report entitled *What's Been Done?*, a survey of what recommendations had actually been put into effect. In a brief summary at the end the following statistics are given:

No. of recommendations within the federal
jurisdiction: .... 122.
No. implemented .... :   42 34.4%
No. partially implemented .... :   37 30.3%
No. not implemented .... :   43 35.3%[7]

The positive results were achieved by action at the level of the federal government. In the final chapter of her book Florence Bird discussed what has been done and what remains to be done. Her emphasis is also on action at the federal level. The Public Service has created an Equal Employment Opportunities Office to recruit and train women. There have been amendments to the Fair Wages and Hours of Labour Regulations and the Fair Wages Policy Order to add, age, sex, and marital status to the prohibited reasons for denying employment by a contractor on federal government work. The Adult Occupational Training Act has been changed and, as a result, the last six months of December 1972 saw an increase over the same period in 1971 of 35 per cent in the number of women taking courses under this provision. Questions of maternity leave have been considered at both the federal and the provincial level, and pregnancy can no longer be cited as cause for dismissal.

Advances such as these, brought about by legislation, have been parallelled by the advancement of women to positions of importance within the structure of government. Senator Muriel Fergusson has become the first woman Speaker of the Senate, Pauline McGibbon the first Lieutenant-Governor of Ontario. Five women judges have been appointed, and Sylvia Ostry has been made head of Statistics Canada with the rank of deputy minister. Even though these appointments appear to be a very small advance numerically, their impact if gradual is nevertheless real. It is this kind of impact that the philosophy behind the *Report* was hoping to obtain. In describing the way in which the final *Report* was written, Florence Bird states that after a considerable discussion, one result of which was that John Humphrey decided to present a minority report, a number of general principles were evolved.[8] The most important of these were presented in 'Criteria and Principles', two pages that form a preface to the *Report* itself. The criteria themselves were stated with almost as much breathtaking simplicity as had been the original directives to the Commissioners. The issue of what rights ought, in a moral sense, to be ascribed to women was answered with reference to Canada's support of the United Nations' resolution, passed in the General Assembly on 10 December 1948: 'All human beings are born free and equal in dignity and rights.' The *Report* went on to affirm that by its adoption of this resolution 'Canada is, therefore committed to a principle that permits no distinction in rights and freedoms between men and women.' And what this principle meant, the Commissioners decided, was that 'equality of opportunity for everyone should be the goal of Canadian society.' To achieve this it was above all necessary that 'women should be free to choose whether or not to take employment outside their homes; ... that the care of children (is acknowledged) as a responsibility to be shared by the mother, the father and society; ... that society has a responsibility for women because of pregnancy and child-birth; ... that in certain areas women will for an interim period require special treatment to overcome the adverse effects of discriminatory practices.'

The result of this stand was that the Commission set out less to challenge the life style of the Canadian people than to consider the extent to which women were able to participate in that life style. And in accepting that their main task was to recommend ways in which more women could participate within the contemporary organization of the Canadian community, the Commissioners seem automatically and perhaps inevitably to have accepted a particular vision of that community as a polity of 'Law, order and good government' already in being. In some ways the *Report* gained a great deal from this approach, above all considerable support from those already in positions of power in Canada, and a great deal of pressure has been mobilized to change those elements most obviously and flagrantly unjust to women. After all, there *is* considerable health in the political and social life of this country. Many structures within the community and institutions of the polity are, if inevitably imperfect from the standpoint of the ideal, nevertheless serviceable for the present, capable of permitting growth and enduring change without a resort to violence.

But this belief that the basic organization of Canadian society is both just and logical, if it gave the final *Report* instant credibility in some quarters, also made it a much less powerful document than it might have been. Although he is listed among the consultants of the Commission, John Porter's *The Vertical Mosaic* is not referred to once among the footnotes of the *Report*. Nor is there any trace of the impact upon it of his striking analysis of the prejudices—of religion, language, economic status, and heritage—that control the status of people. Canada, for the Commission, is seen as an established 'meritocracy'. The Commissioners seem to have been convinced that in all areas objective tests for abilities existed and were applied, that the importance of family connections and articulate adherence to particular beliefs were negligible. Ostensibly the Commission believed that patronage was nonexistent in Canada and that 'paper qualifications' alone obtained advancement: no man ever was promoted except for merit; language, ethnic origin, the necessity for provincial representation at federal levels, all these ideas were set aside and equality of talents reigned supreme. The *Report* held that positions of power within the community that demand high educational qualifications for their holders were, are, and should be the preserve of those who hold such qualifications. They therefore argued that the absence of women in positions of power was solely because of the lack of a sufficiently qualified number of women. The *Report* presented the following résumé:

> Women make up one half of the total population but only one third of the university college and university graduate enrolment. . . . At the graduate level, although there has been a gradual increase in female enrolment since 1955, the percentage of graduate students who are female has not yet reached the 1921 figures . . . women earn about 20% of the master's degrees and about 8% of the doctorates. . . . The largest groups of women are concentrated in the faculties of Arts and Education, with a significant increase in the numbers in the faculty of Education. Of all women enrolling in undergraduate courses, the proportion enrolling in law and medicine are decreasing.[9]

No real analysis followed this passage. There was no investigation of why there had been a percentage decline in the number of women in certain fields since the 1920s. The Commissioners merely went on to say that the present reason for the absence of women in higher education was lack of community support, without any analysis of what had changed community support between 1920 and 1970. The point of view of the brief presented by the Federation of Medical Women of Canada and other Canadian physicians was endorsed without any further examination. It had stated that 'lack of encouragement is the main reason for the low percentage of women medical students compared to men', and explained it by the early sex-role typing of children and the general expectations of what it had earlier labelled the 'cultural mould' of Canadian society. It was noted that 'inevitably a nurse's outfit is given to the girl and a doctor's case to the boy.'[10] If women did not venture into the higher and more specialized areas of human activities, a major reason was their recognition of society's perception of their proper place. It was pointed out that even at the elementary-school level, although the curriculum is similar for both sexes, a certain segregation is practised with 'boys in shop and girls in home economics courses.'[11]

It is true that a person is affected by community pressures and that many community pressures in Canada today work to restrict the choice of occupation for women, but this needs much more discussion. The way in which social pressures are formed, how they work to affect someone, and the way in which a person responds to particular pressures are matters that are not yet fully understood. The *Report* is written as if they were. One wonders how the Commissioners were able to cut from their mind knowledge of the events in Europe from 1940 to 1950. The average age of the Committee members was fifty-two, the youngest being thirty-eight. The towering volumes on human behaviour in the concentration camps, the endless studies of how to brainwash, the aching testaments of individual spirit, all this testimony might have given the Committee some inkling that the question of social pressure on individual action was not a simple one. Every German who died rather than submit to the domination of the Nazi party is an argument against the final control of social pressure over the life of the individual. Solzhenitsyn is a witness to the ability of people not to succumb to the bullying of the powerful. The fact that over and over again communities have been established to bring about a way of life that would be lived unaltered from generation to generation, and have failed to achieve this vision no matter how strongly control has been exerted on their members, ought to have persuaded the Committee to look at the question in broader terms.

But the general theme of the *Report* is that once society recognizes the rights of women, once it fully supports women's demands for free choice of life style, the question will be solved. Women will be psychologically enabled to develop fully and will find no barriers to their fulfilment. One cannot blame the Committee for not writing a new philosophy for twentieth-century society. Yet one can criticize them for not admitting the complexities of the situation. An open statement of the wider issues involved in their work would have added, not detracted, from the decision to limit the area of investigation.

There is no denying that social approval of the full participation of women in all aspects of Canadian life would be a significant and valuable achievement. At the same time, even at this level one finds a number of questions that still demand an answer. Two of them spring from the vision of the *Report* itself. Addressing the question of equal pay for women, the Commission recognized the power of the unions in the matter, and quoted the report of the Quebec Federation of Labour:

> We believe we are in a position to state, however, that unionized women enjoy with one exception, the same working conditions as men: working hours, paid holidays, job security, private social security schemes and so on.... It has unfortunately been impossible we must admit, to secure real implementation of the principle of equal pay for equal work in certain sectors.[12]

The recommendations that followed were basically that the existing legislation should be more carefully applied. There was no discussion of why this legislation had not worked in the past and no discussion of why it would work now. This inability to see the need for greater analysis, and this blind faith in the good intentions of the present Canadian institutions is in stark contrast to the path taken by Sylvia Gelber, Director, Women's Bureau, Canada Department of Labour, in her speech to the directors of Canada's trade unions on Labour Day, September 1973, in Toronto. She made three points:

1. equal pay for equal work had not been fully accepted as a principle because of male attitudes;

2. the possibility of women founding their own unions to look after this matter was now a probability;

3. should this probability become an actuality the parent unions would be dangerously weakened to the extent of one third of the Canadian labour force, its votes and its dues.

This speech analysed and presented a view of the equal-pay problem on a very basic level, but it is a level that inspires more confidence for action than the assumption of the Commission that legislation that has not worked in the past will, without radical alteration, be made to work in the future.

The second query is also linked to the economic sphere. This is the decision of the *Report* to demand equal rights for women on the grounds of economic necessity. The emphasis here is the same as that of the Swedish *Report to the United Nations on the Status of Women* in 1968. The Canadian *Report* talks about 'the full use of human resources (being) in the national interest'.[13] In the Swedish *Report* it is noted that

> ... increased *efficiency* and more rapid economic progress are dependent on abandonment of scales of evaluation based on physical characteristics such as sex and race instead of individual aptitude and ability. A Swedish economist and labour market researcher has calculated that the Swedish national income could be increased by some 25% if the unused potential of women were to be fully utilised and by some 50% if sex discrimination and other barriers were to be totally abolished.[14]

What both reports share is a fundamentally materialistic approach to humanity and its problems. Justice for women is to be promoted because it will be profitable, not because the ideals of society are outraged by the present situation.

It is true that since the concentration camps and the atom bomb appeals to the innate idealism of humanity have become suspect. It is also true that Royal Commissions are above all creatures of the political system, rooted in time and place, here and now. But however tentatively it has to be done, however sceptically it has to be presented, there are some questions that must have reference to the beliefs and ideals of the human spirit in their discussion. By placing all its arguments within a materialistic context the *Report* dismisses without discussion a major cultural tenet of Canadian life—the concept that biological male and female should be accorded some recognition by the social order. Paragraph after paragraph reads as if the Commissioners were convinced that the bisexuality of humanity was not a matter of importance, and that except for the process of birth, men and women can function interchangeably if necessary. To a quite remarkable extent the phrase 'a human being' can be sensibly substituted for the noun 'woman', its synonyms and derivatives, as has been done in the following passage:

A 'human being' suffers when not recognized as having an individual identity as a person with 'individual' aspirations, strengths and weaknesses, tastes and ideas that are not necessarily those of all 'others' whether married or unmarried.[15]

To a certain extent, of course, this emphasis upon the essential humanity of women—that they are human beings before and above being women—is both valid and important. But the refusal to accept that in Canada there is a debate about how the biological differences between the sexes should be translated into cultural roles is deplorable. Marriage comes to be considered almost solely in material terms—how much should the activities of the housewife earn her? To say that there is more to the institution of marriage is not to deny the need to talk about the economics of the institution. It is to ask for the consideration that there can be, and often is, more to marriage than a convenient arrangement, a temporal exchange of services and money. To gloss over the emotional realities of human life is to falsify it quite as much as when such concerns are overemphasized.

In the area of philosophical considerations the *Report* is disastrous. It is interesting to note that the *Poverty Report*, which was being written by a Committee of the Canadian Senate at approximately the same period of time that the Royal Commission on Women was active, had a much greater regard for an honest statement of complexities. The Senate Committee did not minimize the immensity of the task before it, nor did it overlook the variety of opinion among its members about attitudes to the poor, but decided to reveal to the public the change in opinion that occurred during its meetings. In its foreword it admitted that the attempt to come to grips with ideas about poverty had meant a continual debate over moral judgements and philosophical beliefs as well as questions of economic necessity. In contrast, the Royal Commission in its eighteen opening pages on 'Canadian Women and Society' managed to avoid any argument about the basic biology of the human species, any discussion as to why all cultures reinforce biological gender with social conventions, and any real debate over why sexual identity is as much a matter of emotion and belief as it is physical urge.

In essence the Commissioners, in deciding to provide a philosophical framework for what is basically a study in social attitudes and political necessities, tried to present such a framework as briefly as possible. The result is a number of slick, superficial, inadequate, and shoddy generalizations about humanity. Proposition 34 reads:

> The three principal influences which have shaped Western society—Greek philosophy, Roman law and Judeo-Christian theology—have held, almost axiomatically, that woman is inferior and subordinate to man and requires his domination. This attitude still persists today; for example, in most religions, a woman cannot be ordained or authorized to be a spiritual leader.[16]

One wonders how the Commissioners would defend their decision to make the Athenians represent all Greek traditions, rather than the Spartans, whose women had tremendous prestige within their society. One wonders why Roman law was chosen as more important in western civilization than ideas derived from Germanic traditions. The status of women amongst the German tribes who toppled the Roman Empire granted authority to the queen, Bertha, who ruled in southern France towards the end of the fifth century. She dealt with dissidents to her rule by inviting them to supper and having them split down the middle with an axe. There was no question of the serious nature of rape in this tradition: its penalty was castration.

Above all, one wonders how Judeo-Christian theology can be summed up and tossed aside in two sentences. Here is the most superficial reading of the Old Testament, with not even a recognition of the women of Proverbs, in charge of the family property, buying and selling the fields of the estate, trading with the merchants who come from distant lands, commenting upon theology, and whose 'price is above rubies'. If women had always been dominated, how explain the power held by women in the Song of Songs? What has happened to the saints of the Middle Ages: Catherine of Sienna counselling the Pope; Elizabeth of Spain bringing peace between warring families? Or those of later centuries: St. Teresa, the great sixteenth-century Spanish mystic, recognized as a Doctor of the Catholic Church, as one capable of interpreting doctrine? Where do these women stand? Their contributions need consideration, their actions some judgement, their achievement some recognition. The *Report* made a gratuitous assault upon the ideas and beliefs of many by attempting to oversimplify the complexities of western civilization. What was required as an introduction for its work was less a hurried survey of human achievement than a careful analysis of what sorts of status were to be the subject matter of the investigation undertaken, and on what grounds, here, now and today, judgements about human liberties were to be made.

The *Report* would thus have been able to pose a number of problems on the status of women in Canada that are barely raised within its pages. In particular, do Canadian women want more status in the sort of society Canada has today? Or would they prefer to work towards a society that accorded status on a different basis? Do women want full-time employment, or do they want the work world rearranged to allow part-time employment for both men and women, with both husband and wife being considered equally responsible for the economic health of the family unit? But above all, a decision to admit the complexity of the issue would have permitted the Commission to begin its work with an authoritative review of what is known about human sexuality, instead of tossing the question aside in proposition 38:

> What then are the innate differences between men and women and what are the ones imposed by education and culture? Aside from physical differences there has been no scientific proof of differences, either psychological or intellectual in the genetic inheritance of men and women.[17]

Analysed with any attention, this proposition is meaningless. Genetic endowment has been found to be related to chromosome structure, and this structure is not the same for male and female. In fact it has been argued that the female pattern of XX chromosomes can, in some ways, give a considerable advantage. Should there be any genetic defect of one chromosome, there is no loss of a particular ingredient. But the male chromosomes are XY, and damage to either may mean the cancellation of certain characteristics. As Marmor has written:

> That the anatomical differences between the sexes must inevitably be reflected in some personality differences, regardless of variations in cultural patterns, would seem to be almost axiomatic. Differences in body image, in the experience of menstruation, in the subsequent monthly cyclical variations of endocrine functions, and in the experiences of sexual inter-

course, pregnancy, child-birth and menopause are all aspects of bodily sensation and function that are uniquely different for the woman as compared to the man; and in the biological environmental interaction that leads to personality formation, these *must* result in significant personality variances between the sexes. To deny this, and to argue, as some strongly oriented feminists have done, that personality differences between the sexes have *nothing* to do with biological differences but are *totally* a reflection of cultural factors is to miss the mark no less than do those who have overemphasized the importance of the biological factor. The fact is that only by taking into consideration *both* the biological differences between the sexes *and* the variations in cultural reactions to these differences—that is the *field situation*—can the personality similarities and dissimilarities between men and women, at any given time and place, be fully understood.[18]

Even bearing such factors in mind, the Commission might still have found it possible to state the principle that the existence of such differences should not affect the political rights or economic opportunities of women, and that the social role chosen by a woman ought to be as much her individual decision as is the social role chosen by a man.

Had the *Report* attempted to sum up present knowledge about the structure of humanity it would neither have finished its work before 2000 A.D. nor confined its pages to one readable volume. However it would have been quite possible for the *Report* to have opened with a clear statement of the contemporary controversies over the relative importance of physical, psychological, and social elements in the development of human beings. That catch-all phrase that concluded the nine directives presented to the Commission, to investigate 'all matters relevant to the status of women in Canada as may appear to the Committee to be relevant' permitted such a survey, which would have linked the *Report* to one of the most important and vigorous debates in contemporary intellectual life. There is a growing realization that biological factors as well as matters that are considered the proper study of the social sciences affect the nature of our present civilization. Questions are now being asked about the precise relationship of humanity as animal species and humanity as a species with that spark of fire, born of intelligence and imagination.

The debate itself has been summed up by the zoologist Tinbergen. In his view the ability to pass experiences on from one generation to the next has allowed humanity to change the environment out of all recognition. The world of 10,000 B.C., cityless, to our eyes semi-populated, where wind, water, and animal power controlled the technology, is vastly different from the world of 1976 A.D. Genetically, Tinbergen writes, 'We have not evolved very strikingly—but culturally we have changed beyond recognition and are changing at an ever-increasing rate.' For Tinbergen this means danger, for he believes that 'there are good grounds for the conclusion that man's limited behavioural adjustability has been out-paced by the culturally determined changes in his social environment, and that is why man is now a mis-fit in his own society.'[19]

The Royal Commission on the Status of Women has made certain that the question of the status of women is discussed seriously in Canada. It has done an enormous amount to bring to the attention of the Canadian people some of the political questions involved in this discussion. But it did not manage to confront the broader questions that are the real ground of the present debate about women. The Commissioners were able to accept without question the position advanced by Esther Greenglass in the interview quoted in the first chapter: 'Everyone will be a human being first and a man or a woman second.' There is no doubt that the work of the Commission has brought Canada into the mainstream of present-day debate about women, even if, as is inevitable, one can always wish a sufficiency had been a feast.

NOTES

[1] F. Bird, *Anne Francis: An Autobiography* (Clarke Irwin, 1974), p. 8.

[2] *Report of the Royal Commission on the Status of Women in Canada* (hereinafter called the *Report*) (Information Canada, 1970), pp. vii-viii.

[3] *Report*, p. ix.

[4] Bird, *op. cit.*, p. 274.

[5] *Ibid.*, p. 289.

[6] *Women in the Labour Force* (Information Canada, 1974), p. 84.

[7] Advisory Council on the Status of Women, *What's Been Done?* (Information Canada, 1974), p. 30.

[8] Bird, *op. cit.*, p. 287.

[9] *Report*, pp. 170-71.

[10] *Ibid.*, p. 173.

[11] *Ibid.*, p. 174.

[12] *Ibid.*, p. 73.

[13] *Ibid.*, p. 3.

[14] *Report to the United Nations on the Status of Women* (1968), p. 11.

[15] *Report*, p. 3.

[16] *Ibid.*, pp. 10-11.

[17] *Ibid.*, p. 11.

[18] J. Marmor, 'Changing Patterns of Femininity', in J. B. Miller, ed., *Psychoanalysis and Women* (Pelican, 1973), pp. 228-9.

[19] N. Tinbergen, 'On War and Peace in Animals and Man', in H. Friedrich, *Man and Animal* (Paladin, 1971), p. 131.

Eleven

Women Without Boundaries

Thinking about the status and position of women involves two questions: what the nature of human beings is, and what the institutions and conventions of the state ought to be. Arguments about both questions will be fierce, for the questioning involves something fundamental to human beings and of immense emotional importance. Not only does the human community assign a sexual identity to every person, but each person is the product of both sexes. And in each person's childhood images of sexuality, self, and the other are taught and enforced. People very quickly establish a vision of the right and proper conduct of the two sexes that incorporates their own beliefs and actions, so that criticism of their ideas in this area very quickly becomes criticism of themselves. So while dispassionate argument about the position of women is not perhaps impossible, it is highly improbable. In these circumstances perhaps the best one can hope for is some consensus that the issue is important, complex, and controversial.

It is important because social expectations of how women should behave are, for good or ill, an enormous force in the lives of women. The translation of these pressures into individual patterns of action means that everybody within the human community is affected to some degree by the generally accepted view of what it is to be feminine. So important has the cultural translation of gender become that the basic biological determination of the sexual characteristics of each person is often ignored. Except for the very rare person whose hormone structure has been scrambled, the biological sex is written into the chromosome pattern. The sexual differentiation of human beings is so fundamental that not only is it imprinted in their cell structure, but it can be determined through the analysis of one hair root. (This method of determining the sex of competitors in events for one sex only has been urged on the authorities of the Olympic games.) But the charge that someone is not 'feminine' or is less than a 'proper man' has nothing to do with the fundamental physiological nature of a person; it is a charge based on cultural definitions of male and female. This distinction between the given physiology of a human being and the behaviour pattern demanded by culture has ramifications that are often left unexplored because the extent to which measurable physiological sex characteristics imply particular psychological and social behaviour patterns is not known.

Because of the importance that western culture attaches to sexual distinctions between human beings, there is little acceptance of the idea that the answer to the debate on whether the behaviour of human beings is determined by hereditary or environment may be: 'it all depends on physiological and cultural variables'. The possibility that the sex drive is, like other human characteristics from a tolerance for alcohol to an ability to reason, an indiviual variable is an argument still struggling for acceptance. Although there is a general belief that there is a norm of sexual appetite rather than a wide variation between human beings, there are two interesting exceptions to an insistence on this norm. Those with more than the supposedly average appetite are often accepted with what amounts to amazed and envious wonder, witness the reaction to Babe Ruth's reputation, or the idea implicit in Mae West's 'Come up and see me some time.' But those people who deny having sexual appetite or claim to have only a mild interest in sexual matters are often the butt of unbelieving criticism and are regarded as warped, repressed, inhibited, perhaps all three. The sex drive is looked upon, and indeed is a most powerful human drive. But society has stressed and stressed again its searing force in order to justify the restraints put on its expression, and so the very possibility of wide individual variation, while often conceded intellectually, is rarely believed emotionally.

The pressure to do more than concede the possibility for individual variation is mounting. This comes in part from the general trend in twentieth-century western life to emphasize, in the cant term, 'doing your own thing.' However 'doing your own thing' in sexual matters is coming to suffer the same fate as 'doing your own thing' in any other sphere. In Saul Bellow's *Mr. Sammler's Planet* Sammler says:

I was saying that this liberation into individuality has not been a great success. For a historian of great interest, but for one aware of the suffering it is appalling. Hearts that get no real wage, souls that find no nourishment. Falsehoods, unlimited. Desire, unlimited. Possibility, unlimited. Impossible demands upon complex realities, unlimited. Revival in childish and vulgar forms of ancient religious ideas, mysteries, utterly unconscious, of course—astonishing. Orphism, Mithraism, Manichaeanism, Gnosticism. . . . But one notices a most peculiar play-acting, an elaborate and sometimes quite artistic manner of presenting oneself as an individual and a strange desire for originality, distinction, *interest*—yes *interest*. A dramatic derivation from models, together with the repudiation of models. Antiquity accepted models, the Middle Ages—I don't want to turn into a history book before your eyes—but modern man, perhaps because of collectivization, has a fever of originality. The idea of the uniqueness of the soul. An excellent idea. A true idea. But in these forms? In these poor forms? Dear God! With hair, with clothes, with drugs and cosmetics, with genitalia, with round trips through evil, monstrosity, and orgy, with even God approached through obscenities? . . . the idea no longer is blasphemy, but hygiene, pleasure which is hygiene too, and a charmed and *interesting* life. An *interesting* life is the supreme concept of dullards.[1]

Here conformity in the name of freedom is being called in question. The paradox of twentieth-century thought is the difficulty of knowing why conformity exists, what amount of it is necessary, and how much the structure of modern life can admit of personal freedom while achieving 'the greatest good for the greatest number'. Given the fundamental connection between the family and the survival of the community, given the sexual nature of humanity, and given the obvious tension between forms of sexual behaviour and the organization of society, which demands conformity, it is not surprising that a movement such as Women's Liberation should rouse such passion.

It ought to rouse passion. Society, as Janeway has pointed out, teaches sex roles 'with more sternness than goes into most present-day education.' Of itself this may not be wrong. What matters is how close such sex-role teaching is to human reality. The work begun by Eleanor Maccoby and Carol Jacklin needs to be carried much further. These researchers have tried to find out what is myth and what is reality in sex differences. Their work has shown that girls and boys are equally social and concerned with people; that both sexes are equally suggestible; that girls have just as much self-esteem as boys, and just as much motivation to achieve; that both boys and girls are capable of rote-learning and of reasoning, and that boys are no better than girls at analysis; that neither sex is more vulnerable to environment, to harmful agents in their surroundings before and after birth; and finally, that both girls and boys respond in the same way to stimulation by sight and sound. In these areas sexual differences are very much social myth, despite the general belief to the contrary.

Their work has also shown some observable differences. Males are more aggressive than females: 'They engage in mock-fighting and aggressive fantasies as well as direct forms of aggression more frequently than girls,' and according to this study, 'The sex difference manifests itself as soon as social play begins, at age two or two and a half.'² Females do have a greater verbal ability than males, something that does *not show before eleven* but is measurable during and after high school. Males do have excellent visual-spatial ability and acquire quantitative concepts at a faster rate than girls. One might argue that these measureable differences could be the result of cultural expectations.

There has been a tremendous amount of work done by psychologists during the last twenty years showing the extent to which very young children respond to the way parents approach them during the first six months of life. If men and women tend to expect little boys to stand up to rougher caresses than little girls, to hold to a less rigid feeding time-table, to be picked up more frequently when they fret, then this treatment may produce certain characteristics in later life. The whole question of such influences in determining sex differences needs much more clear work than has at present been done. Further, the question needs to be faced whether, if these differences are a social heritage, they should be encouraged. Human beings are more than animals, they shape their institutions to shape themselves, and a trait that is developed as a result of social institutions is not necessarily to be despised on those grounds alone.

Finally Maccoby and Jacklin pose a number of questions that they feel have not been answered in any way. The possibility of a difference in tactile sensitivity has not been investigated, nor has any research been done on whether women are more prone to anxiety. The question of differences in activity and vigorous play has not been looked at, and the work done on competitiveness has been shown to be the victim both of its own definitions of competitiveness and of social expectations. The work of Professor Meredith Kimball has revealed the whole complexity of this issue. Her studies showed that the ability of women to mask their ambition makes nonsense of most of the research work already done on differences in competitiveness. The same problems would apply to ideas of dominance, compliance, nurturance, and passivity. Gunnar Myrdal in his massive *Asian Drama: An Inquiry into the Poverty of Nations*, examines the need for social scientists to be aware of themselves and their own motivations. While he is specifically concerned with the judgements made by developed countries about the needs and the potential abilities of the Third World, his remarks can be applied to those concerned with describing the behaviour patterns of either men or women. What does dominance mean? The desire to lead? A determination to have positive action taken? What does compliance mean? The decision to agree because to differ would mean hard work? A decision to agree because the other person first voiced the ideas that the listener had already conceived? What is nurturance? The war correspondents from Vietnam took enough photographs of men in agony over the fate of their children to substantiate male caring patterns. The 'battered baby syndrome' shows women can cause intense physical suffering to their offspring. Maccoby and Jacklin's work is an admitted and important first step: the journey still lies ahead.

That journey is the search for a reorganization of priorities in western civilization. A new status and position for women is only part of the journey, but once this is granted the social organization of the community will have been changed beyond imagining. In her work *Earth and High Heaven*, a Canadian novel written in 1944, Gwethalyn Graham says once and for all what women want in terms of simple recognition. The book is about antisemitism in Canada during the Second World War, and the people are two lovers and their families. Marc, in love with Erica, considers that they cannot marry because she, a Gentile, must not be exposed to the prejudice that Jews have to suffer. At the end of the book Marc renounces Erica, against her will.

He wanted to think about Erica.... Only a few days before, when she had been trying all over again to tell him what mattered most to her, she had said, 'I wish you'd believe me,' and when he had protested that he did believe her, she had answered hopelessly, 'No, not quite.' ... Like her father, he had always assumed that Erica did not know what she would be letting herself in for, and ... he had considered himself to be in some mysterious way better qualified to decide what would be best for her in the long run than Erica herself.[3]

This demand to be listened to and to decide for oneself, the demand that a person be recognized as a human being first, is the eternal cry of those who suffer prejudice. Shylock's speech can be written for all:

Hath not a Woman eyes? hath not a Woman hands, organs, dimensions, senses, affections, passions? fed with the same food, hurt with the same weapons, subject to the same diseases, healed by the same means, warmed and cooled by the same winter and summer as a Man is? If you prick us, do we not bleed? if you tickle us, do we not laugh? if you poison us do we not die?

If this demand for recognition were all there were to the question, there would never have been an International Women's Year. But John Stuart Mill pointed to the difference between prejudice against women and other forms of human oppression. 'They are so far in a position different from all other subject classes,' he wrote, 'that their masters require something more from them than actual service. Men do not solely want the obedience of women, they want their sentiments. All men, except the most brutish, desire to have, in the woman most nearly connected to them, not a forced slave but a willing one, not a slave merely but a favourite.'[4]

The second volume of Solzhenitsyn's work, *The Gulag Archipelago*, presents evidence to substantiate this view of Mill's. Solzhenitsyn describes the experiences of women in the destructive-labour camps: in circumstances where forced congress was easy to impose upon women, most men set out to bribe those they wished to possess.[5] Intercourse with the illusion of consent was infinitely preferable to intercourse with a hating slave. Here, in the most powerless of circumstances, women's consent was still considered a status symbol. While women have been, and are often treated merely as hygienic conveniences in western civilization, nevertheless the weight of opinion has been against this practice. To begin with, the idea of equality is embedded in western civilization even if it is followed infrequently in practice. Secondly the western idea of love is a belief in mutual love. Western literature might contain a Don Juan, but even this retarded adolescent has to woo. It is only recently that the perversity of rape as an admirable form of 'normal' sexual intercourse has been lauded, and even here it depends on a belief that a woman 'enjoys' rape, a self-contradictory assertion. The fundamental complexity of the question about prejudice and discrimination against women comes from the knotting together of three elements: ideas concerning the proper social personality of women; ideas about the extent to which people are considered crippled if their conduct does not embody such ideas; and beliefs about the extent to which such ideas limit the capacity of the sex as a whole for particular tasks.

A member of the Philosophy Department at Concordia University, Christine Garside Allen, has been considering the spectrum of images of women in western civilization. Her analysis has led her to distinguish woman as 'evil temptress' (the woman = sex, woman = evil syllogism referred to earlier), the collectivity of women defined by Eve, by witches, by prostitutes, and by the femme fatale. This archetype she sees as balanced in some measure by woman as 'Virgin Goddess', as represented by Mary, Mother of God, as Athena, or in the ideas of courtly love in the Middle Ages. Then she has distinguished the image of woman as 'Earth Mother', the traditionn of regarding her as fertility symbol, as the great matriarch who cares and soothes. In contrast to this image is woman as 'passive object', the obedient helper in another's projects, the follower of another's plans. 'Woman as Genius' is her next category, the personnification of woman as muse and as the seat of intuition. Finally she considers women as political activists —Boadicea and the great hereditary rulers who have been women, the women who organized the suffrage movement, and women in the feminist movement today.[6]

Professor Allen's work is exciting because the images of women in western civilization are not all of incompetent, inefficient, unintelligent, downtrodden puppets. The positive images of women are recognized as an important part of the traditions of western civilization. It is interesting that none of the positive images imply a hierarchical relationship between male and female. The force of woman as Mary, Mother of God has the power of a male God. Athena is balanced by Zeus. The Earth Mother needs the male to carry out her work. The idea of woman as genius requires man as craftsman, and women as political activists work within the community containing both sexes. When woman is portrayed as temptress, however, she becomes a threat that the male may not have the strength to resist. When woman is portrayed as passive object the male becomes a fragile ego unable to work with peers and capable only of a relationship based upon the crudest elements of strength rather than upon an exchange of powers.

The way in which these images of women become the dominant concepts in particular societies is a story that is yet untold. *Penelope's Web* has offered some evidence that women since the seventeenth century have been acting in day-to-day life in accordance with the positive images of their sex as well as with the negative aspects. The theme that has been emphasized is the way in which ideas of standardized behaviour patterns for women came to be accepted by important sectors of society. As I worked on this book I was surprised to discover not only that this development was challenged by those who fought for philosophical equality among human beings, but the extent to which it was challenged by those who fought in particular against the belittlement of one sex. The idea that a person comes into the world to fulfil the expectations of others, that a pattern existed to which all must conform has been seen by John Wren Lewis as the great neurosis of western civilization, and he has proposed that the essential message of Christianity is one of the strongest weapons against this neurosis, since its force comes from the injunctions 'Judge not, lest ye be judged;' 'Condemn not those that condemn you'.[7]

For if society adopts an image of femininity for its women, it similarly forces men to conform to an archetype. If there are images of male as God, there are images of male as weak Adam. The warrior image, while it may be a positive construction of force and power, far too often denies to men the reality of love, the validity of emotion. The social education of both sexes into rigid moulds is an aberration, and it is possible to see this particular aberration as a movement in western civilization that started in the seventeenth century, gained strength in the eighteenth century, became a powerful control in the nineteenth century, but is now being successfully questioned.

If Women's Liberation is a discussion of feminism in the context of the human condition and an argument for women's rights based on the assumption that human beings come in two sexes of equal importance for the race as a whole, then it is a significant issue. It is hoped that Women's Liberation will assert that questions about the roles of either sex must be discussed within this framework, and the great benefit from placing the discussion in this framework is the sense of freedom it gives. As Margrit Eichler has pointed out, it does not really matter what roles have been laid down for the sexes in other societies, nor does it really matter what our own civilization has done in the past. What is absolutely essential is a decision on what we want our society today to be, and to what extent we can use past traditions to build that society.[8]

In order to determine what our society should be, all viewpoints are grist to the mill, because each reveals assumptions about human relationships derived from different experiences. For example, the point of view of leading radical feminists such as Shulamith Firestone, however unacceptable as a possible rule for all, can nevertheless be looked at as information about what some women believe. Firestone's hope—that the development of children in laboratory conditions will soon be brought about, completely relieving the woman from the necessity of physical pregnancy—can be considered as the response of some women to the biological possibilities of the twentieth century.[9] It is feminine. As feminine as the point of view put forward by Kate Millet—that deep human relationships ought to flower into sexual relationships whether the friendship is heterosexual or between two members of the same sex.[10] As feminine as Betty Friedan's remark to Simone de Beauvoir about motherhood, that it 'is neither necessarily good, nor necessarily desirable, to renounce all the values of motherhood as long as one has a choice and as long as girls are not conditioned to think they must, or should spend their whole lives in that role.'[11]

It may not be more feminine to bear and bring up children than to remain without offspring, but the life of a woman who of free choice wishes to be a housewife and mother and build a family around her can be admired as a life of value and of enrichment for the society as a whole. It may not be more feminine to forego career advancement in favour of a balanced personal life, but it is no less feminine than the path chosen by women working eighteen hours a day in administrative jobs. The final goal must be a sense of personal freedom that need not in any way conflict with the establishment of an orderly society, so that society becomes once more the servant of the community, not its tyrant. And if the distance between the goal and the actuality is still great, there is an encouraging advance. The exclusion of women from certain activities on grounds of sexual characteristics rather than on tested ability has become much less acceptable. The statement made at Yale University—that women were intellectually so inferior to men that no women could be appointed to their faculty—has been condemned as thoroughly as if the statement had referred to Jews or blacks.

But perhaps more important than changes in the rules and regulations of institutions is the gradual assertion of the true worth of those characteristics hitherto seen as the particular preserve of women. Gentleness, kindness, tenderness, love of beauty, care of detail, sensitivity to emotional wants are once more considered valuable for all human beings, both men and women, and the possibility for a less rigid society becomes much greater. If a wide variation in the characteristics of individual women can be accepted while also admitting the validity of what has been formerly considered 'women's business' for all people, then the struggle for a better dispensation may win considerable victories. The revolution, the real revolution and not merely the exchange of labels, may yet take place. In the meantime, however, the work remains to be done. The eradication of obvious injustices in the work force needs to be carried out. The question of the abortion laws needs to be settled. The matter of equal access to positions of influence within institutions has to be regulated, if necessary by making direct appointments. After all, the method is one used often enough in Canada, but the appointments must not be mere tokenism—the important distinction between tokenism and patronage is that a token appointment can sit preening, knowing that it is sufficient just to be, while an appointee *must* be capable. Those chosen, all other things being equal, because they are women must be adequate to the position filled.

In sum, the outlook is perhaps much like the old Chinese curse, 'may you live in interesting times'. It is uncomfortable because justification is being demanded before rigid social values will be accepted; because, as in all movements, extremists seek confrontation and bedevil a reasonable cause with irrational demands; and because the righting of any wrong demands the acceptance of guilt, the restitution of the stolen. But it is interesting because it is a movement that is optimistic about the possibility of changing society for the better; because it is linked with the basic trend of twentieth-century society, the desire to provide not merely the greatest happiness for the greatest number but the most acceptable life for the greatest number; and because it emphasizes traditions of thought in western civilization that have been too long ignored.

As stated in the preface, *Penelope's Web* was written not as a scholarly work but in an attempt to understand the present status and position of women. It grew from a belief in the complexity of human existence, a suspicion of sweeping judgements about whole groups of human beings, and a limited personal knowledge of exceptions to what apparently was being cited as the general rule of women's lot in past centuries. As I conclude it I find my ambition for the status of women much as it was four years ago. I would like to see prejudice against women accorded the same attention, the same concern, as prejudice against other groups of human beings; I would like to see discrimination against women—society's acceptance that women are treated lesss advantageously than men—abolished; I would like to see a person's sexuality regarded merely as part of a person's makeup, something neither more nor less important than their intellectual or emotional makeup; and I would like to see ideas about femininity and masculinity discussed with some poetry, some vision, some feeling for human beings.

For unless this last condition is fulfilled I think the debate about the status of women will be 'full of sound and fury, signifying nothing'. Somehow that dangerous reality love has to be given a weight, even if it is only marked as 'ingredient x', volatile, inexplicable, uncontrollable. For, after all, it is an ingredient of the relationship between mother and child, between father and child, an element in the comradeship between men, and part of the feeling that led Ruth to follow her mother-in-law, Naomi, through 'fields of alien corn'. And love between man and woman is not a one-way street, where one person offers comfortable reassurance of excellence in return for social status and economic security. Love is that patient angel that chooses to hew to the best in the other, that seeks the reality of the other, and rejoices in being likewise regarded. In some way the debate over woman's rights, over human liberation, has to take into account this characteristic of humanity: the need, the capacity, and the reality of human love. Penelope spun her web out of a desperation to guard for herself the importance of her love. Perhaps the social pressures making a new web for western society will make it one that also serves the ends of human love.

NOTES

[1] Saul Bellow, *Mr. Sammler's Planet* (Fawcett Crest, 1970), p. 208.

[2] E. Maccoby and C. Jacklin, *The Psychology of Sex Differences* (Standford, 1974).

[3] G. Graham, *Earth and High Heaven* (New Canadian Library, 1966), pp. 247, 245.

[4] J. S. Mill, 'The Subjection of Women', quoted in A. Rossi, ed., *The Feminist Papers*, p. 201.

[5] A. I. Solzhenitsyn, *The Gulag Archipelago* (Harrper and Row, 1975), pp. 227-50.

[6] Professor Allen's work will be published in the C.A.U.T. monograph series in 1977. Articles giving some of her ideas are in print, cf. especially 'Methodology for Women's Studies', *C.A.U.T. Bulletin*, (September 1975), vol. 24, 1, where the outline of her ideas is presented.

[7] J. W. Lewis, 'Love's coming of Age', in C. Rycroft, ed., *Psychoanalysis Observed*, (Penguin, 1968), p. 101.

[8] Toronto Conference on University Reactions to Feminism, 1974: to be published in C.A.U.T. monograph series, 1976.

[9] Juliet Mitchell, *Psychoanalysis and Feminism* (1975) has a magnificent critical analysis of the leading feminists from the viewpoint of psychology, including Firestone, pp. 346-50.

[10] This is my reading of Millet's standpoint from her recent autobiography, *Flying*.

[11] 'Sex, Society and the Female Dilemma', a dialogue between Simone de Beauvoir and Betty Friedan, *Saturday Review*, 14 June 1975, p. 56.

Select
Bibliography

A great deal of very good material about the status and position of women in western civilization is available now, in 1975. Some of the most stimulating works are those that bring together excerpts from a number of sources and therefore inevitably lead the reader on to consult the originals from which the material has been drawn. In this category I found three works extremely valuable: *By a Women Writt: Literature from Six Centuries by and about Women*, edited by Joan Goulianos (Penguin, 1974) who has gathered together a wide variety of opinions and statements about women's experience seen through literature; *Not in God's Image: Women in History from the Greeks to the Victorians*, edited by Julia O'Faolain and Lauro Martines (Harper, 1973) is a magnificent compendium of documents about women starting from the time of the Greeks and ending with material about nineteenth-century French prostitutes. The third work, *The Feminist Papers from Adams to de Beauvoir*, edited with an introduction by Alice S. Rossi (Bantam, 1974), is a most intelligent selection of writings concerned with feminist thought and action and spanning two centuries.

The above titles provide some basic documentary evidence about women. There are also a large number of works that provide theoretical explanations of the present state of women in western civilization. Most of these have gained considerable fame in their own right. However it is interesting to read what the authors actually wrote, as opposed to what a critic has said about the work in question. Simone de Beauvoir's *The Second Sex* (Knopf, 1953) remains one of the most logically argued works to put forward the view that women have always been suppressed by the ways of civilization. Betty Friedan's *The Feminine Mystique* (Dell, 1963) also holds its own as a stimulating discussion of the problems of American suburban women in the mid-twentieth century. A much less well known work by H. R. Hayes called *The Dangerous Sex: The Myth of Feminine Evil* (Pocket Books, 1972) is an interesting account of traditions of misogyny in western civilization, and it underlines the dislike of sex that can be found in certain western customs and beliefs. The works of Germaine Greer and Kate Millett, published within months of each other, scarcely need recommending. The two books are very different. Germaine Greer's *The Female*

Eunuch (Paladin, 1971) is a sweeping political work that illumines all the ways and means whereby women and feminine concerns have been scorned in western civilization. Kate Millett's *Sexual Politics* (Equinox, 1970) is a much more staid cry of pain over the image of women in popular literature of western countries since the nineteenth century. To both of these works Norman Mailer's *Prisoner of Sex* (New American Library, 1971) acts as a kind of counterpoint, not precisely either an argument or a rebuttal so much as a further commentary on the relationship of men and women in the twentieth-century western world.

Two works that look at the problem with a cool appraisal, very different from the works mentioned above, are Elizabeth Janeway's *Man's World, Woman's Place: A study in Social Mythology* (Delta, 1971), an attempt to analyse the many ways in which present-day western society pressures people to conform to sex-role typing. Her work is methodical, literate, and immensely stimulating since she writes with concern for both men and women. Similarly Juliet Mitchell's *Psychoanalysis and Feminism* (Allen Lane, 1974) is a clear account of the ways in which psychology has considered the experience of women. It contains a hundred-page critique of the viewpoints of other feminist writers including de Beauvoir, Friedan, Eva Figes, Shulamith Firestone, and Millett.

In the more general field of writings about sexuality, a number of Pelicans provide good introductions to the more complex works of other writers. Georgene H. Seward's *Sex and the Social Order* was first published in 1946 and became a Pelican in 1953. It introduces the reader to anthropological ways of thinking about the consequences of the sexual characteristics of human beings. The book by Kenneth Walker and Peter Fletcher, *Sex and Society* (1955), has a very solid analysis of the accepted code of sexual behaviour in the western world in the middle of the twentieth century, the standards of action that the 'Establishment' would consider proper. Alex Comfort's *Sex in Society* (1963) is a much less conventional work and not only considers what people think should be the moral standards of society but also how people actually live. C. O. Carter's *Human Heredity* (1962) discusses what makes up an individual human person, the traits determined by genes and chromosomes. *Psychoanalysis and Women*, edited by Jean Baker Miller and published as a Pelican in 1973, is a collection of essays that tries to work out that thin boundary between the biological givens of sexual characteristics and the psychological organization of masculine and feminine gender roles. The work of Ann Oakley, *Sex, Gender and Society* (Harper Colophon, 1972) is a good companion to this work, since it presents considerable anthroplogical knowledge of human sexuality. In terms of general works that give a background to an understanding of human psychology, male and female, there are three books of great insight: J.A.C. Brown's *The Social Psychology of Industry*, published as a Pelican in 1954, which looks at the expectations that industrial society has about the 'norms' of human behaviour; George A. Miller, *The Psychology of Communication*, published as a Pelican in 1968, which examines in seven essays the problems of various systems of communications between human beings; and Gordon R. Lowe's *The Growth of Personality from Infancy to Old Age*, published as a Pelican in 1973, which deals with the whole human life span.

There are a number of books dealing specifically with women and history that are very worthwhile. The pioneer work in this area is *Woman as force in History* by Mary R. Beard (Collier, 1962). Beard deals with the impact of the emerging state system in eighteenth-century Europe. Two hardcover works, unfortunately not, to my knowledge, available in paperback editions are those by Ivy Pinchbeck and Doris Mary Stenton. Ivy Pinchbeck wrote *Women Workers and the Industrial Revolution, 1750-1850* in 1930; it was republished as a new edition (Cass, 1969). It remains an outstanding report of the impact that the change in technology made on women in western civilization. Doris Mary Stenton's *The English Woman in History* (George Allen and Unwin, 1957) is both broader in scope and more specialized. She has documented the achievements of English women from the middle ages to the nineteenth century, her work asserting clearly the sorts and types of power women in England achieved during this period. Not quite in the same category as the above works, but nevertheless very good value and also, unfortunately, available only in hardcover is the work of G.E. and K.R. Russell, *The English Countrywoman: A Farmhouse Social History 1500-1900* (Melrose, 1953). This provides a very clear account of country life in England and has some excellent information about what woman's role actually was in the small villages.

Two books on England in the nineteenth century are worthwhile reading because they provide material about the accepted moral standards of that country at a time when it had enormous influence in western civilization. Ronald Pearsall, *The Worm in the Bud: The World of Victorian Sexuality* (Pelican, 1969) is a fascinating study of the sex life of all ranks of Victorian society. He shows not only the existence of the 'double-standard' during that age but also the false image that the present age has of those times. The beliefs and practices of the Victorian middle class have been taken as the beliefs of people of all conditions of life and Pearsall shows how false this is. Kellow Chesney in *The Victorian Underworld* (Pelican, 1970) provides more detail about the dregs of society and how the rest of the people looked at the life of those considered criminal. The question of prostitution is fully examined in this work.

This is a 'select bibliography' and the choice of books has been based upon their availability and upon the extent to which their own bibliographies carry the reader forward to new sources of information. With these criteria in mind, the next four works rate excellent. Heinz Friedrich, ed.,

Man and Animal: Studies in Behaviour (Paladin, 1971) is a collection of essays about ethnology, the comparative study of animal behaviour, with an emphasis upon what such studies imply for understanding humanity. Teodor Shanin, ed., *Peasants and Peasant Societies* (Penguin, 1971) is a collection of essays about agricultural life and the sorts of traditions found in agricultural societies. Nigel Harris's short work, *Beliefs in Society: The Problems of Ideology* (Penguin, 1971) is a clear account of how a social consciousness is formed, how it is both the creature and the master of the individual. Finally Peter L. Berger and Thomas Luckmann's *The Social Construction of Reality: A treatise in the Sociology of Knowledge* (Penguin, 1973) is a clear exposition of theories about the way in which individuals construct pictures of reality.

In conclusion there are the books that relate particularly to Canadian experience. The *Report of the Royal Commission on the Status of Women in Canada* (Queen's Printer, 1970), having had a chapter to itself needs no further comment. But one other government publication might sometimes be overlooked. This is the work of the Women's Bureau, Federal Department of Labour on *Women in the Labour Force*, a work that is published at intervals and that gives the statistical picture of women in the labour force in Canada. Three recent works present ideas about the position and status of women in Canada. Margaret Andersen compiled *Mother was Not a Person* (Content Publishing and Black Rose, 1972), a fascinating collection of essays and personal statements about the present-day feminist movement in Canada. The section of the book devoted to the *Report of the Royal Commission on the Status of Women* contains four good critical commentaries, and other sections contain intelligent discussion of what the women's movement means to women in different social circumstances. Marylee Stephenson edited *Women in Canada* (New Press, 1973), a work devoted to ideas about the immediate situation in Canada, but at the same time containing both a guide to historical literature pertaining to Canadian women by Veronica Strong-Boag, and a bibliography of materials about Canadian women published between 1950 and 1972, put together by Margrit Eichler and Lynne Primrose. The third work is by Myrna Kostash, Melinda McCracken, Valerie Miner, Erna Paris, and Heather Robertson, entitled *Her Own Woman: Profile of Ten Canadian Women* (Macmillan, 1975). This is a very uneven book, but it brings together biographical sketches of people as different as Madeleine Parent, Abby Hoffman, and Barbara Frum.

Books relating particularly to the experience of women in Quebec and easily available are: C. Carisse and J. Dumazedier, *Les femmes innovatrices, problèmes post-industriels d'une Amérique francophone: le Quebec* (éditions du Seuil, 1975), a very detailed analysis of present-day Quebec society from the point of view of women; Marcelle Dolment and Marcel Barthe, *La Femme au Quebec* (Les Presses Libres, 1973), a much slighter book, presenting a point of view of two people about the actual work to be done to improve the position of women in Quebec.

Two books make an attempt to look at the position of women in a Canadian context. Catherine Cleverdon's *The Woman Suffrage Movement in Canada*, recently reissued with an introduction by Ramsay Cook (University of Toronto Press, 1975) is a scholarly account of the process by which Canadian women gained the vote. Marvin A. Zuker and June Callwood, *Canadian Women and the Law* (Copp Clark, 1971) is an attempt to sum up what particular laws apply to women exclusively or in a different way than they apply to men. Both these works are useful, the Cleverdon book in particular being an invaluable guide to the fight for the franchise in different provinces.

Throughout *Penelope's Web* the publications of the *New Canadian Library* series have been used. Their list of novels, poetry, and memoirs by Canadians is an invaluable collection of Canadian literature and a magnificent field for discovering the experiences of Canadian women in the circumstances of their real worlds.

Index

Aberdeen, Lady, 172
Acadians, 69ff., 124, 126, 128
Adams, Abigail, 96ff., 164
Adams, John, 96ff., 111
Advisory Council on the Status of
    Women, 214
Age of Absolutism, The, 53
Age of Reason, The, 53
Agricultural revolution, 61, 62
Albertia, Leon Battista, 108
Allen, Christine Garside, 233
Ancien Régime in Europe, 1648-1789, The,
    54
Ancien Régime, The, 53
Ashley, Lord, 113
Ashton, T. S., 57, 114
*Asian Drama: An Inquiry into the Poverty
    of Nations,* 231
Atwood, Margaret, 24, 183
Austen, Jane, 120
Ayorama, 36

Babin, Jean, 73
Backwoods of Canada, 1836, The, 130, 132,
    135
Baie St Marie, 126
Balzac, H., 107
Beard, Mary, 81, 82
Behrens, C. B., 53
Bellow, Saul, 228
Beloff, Max, 53
Berger, Peter, 81
Bias of Communications, 41
Bird, Florence, 209, 212, 213, 215
Blais, Marie Claire, 25
Brown, J. A. C., 81
Bowden, W., 57

Boyle, Alice, 37
Boyle, Sarah, 37
Brabazon, Lord, 154
Braudel, F., 34, 35, 62, 69
Brittain, Vera, 204
Broadfoot, Barry, 193, 199
Buchenwald, 94
Burton, Jean, 182
Butler, Josephine, 156ff., 186

Callwood, June, 16
Canadian Forum, 182
Canadian Settler's Guide, The, 132, 138
Canadians, 1867-1967, The, 169
Capitalism and Material Life, 1400-1800,
    34
Carr, Emily, 193
Cassedy, James, 42
Castiglione, Baldassare, 104
Cavendish, Margaret, 90, 92f.
Champlain, Samuel de, 36
Charles II, 36
Chatelaine, 15f.
Chesterfield, Lord, 89, 90, 92, 93
Cipolla, Carlo, 56
Class, 68, 103, 134, 135, 142, 143, 157
Cleverdon, Catherine, 174, 176, 177,
    178, 192
Cobbett, William, 112
Cogswell, Fred, 10
Comfort, Alex, 22
Communications, 68, 77, 105, 115, 127,
    145
Comus, 86
Confederation, 102, 127, 145, 170
Connor, Ralph, 171
Contagious Diseases Acts, 160

Cook, Ramsay, 172
Cork, Earl of, 37
Councils of Women, 177
Courtly love, 44, 104, 233
Cowper, Countess, 166
Crawford, Isabella Valency, 141
Cross, Michael, 128
Culture, 103ff., 110, 120, 127, 163
Culture and Society, 1780-1950, 77

Dance of the Happy Shades, 24
Darwin, Charles, 148
Davies, Robertson, 23
de Beauvoir, Simone, 204, 235
de Coccola, R., 36
d'Egmont, Countess, 83
d'Harcourt, Princesse, 40
de la Rochefoucauld, Duc, 40
de la Tour, Madame, 45, 46
de l'Enclos, Ninon, 90
de l'Incarnation, Marie, 46
de Medici, Marie, 45
de Navarre, Philippe, 86, 89
d'Orléans, Duchesse, 40
de Pompadour, Madame, 54, 83, 84
Depression, 181, 182, 186, 192, 197, 199
de Sévigné, Madame, 88
de Stael, Madame, 110
Dialectic of Sex, The, 206f.
Dilke, M., 165
Discrimination against women, 28, 50,
    81, 85, 86, 89, 96, 99, 107, 109, 120,
    121, 125, 142, 145, 156, 174, 180, 185,
    233, 237; see also Prejudice against
    women.
Dorchester, Lord, 52
Double standard, 113, 158
Dow, Almira, 129
Dryden, John, 174

Earth and High Heaven, 231
Economic History of Europe since 1750, An,
    57
Edible Woman, The, 24
Education, 61, 93, 103, 108, 109, 110,
    144, 165, 181, 229, 234
Eichler, Margrit, 235
Elizabeth I, 33

Employment, 107, 114, 116f., 119, 131,
    179, 181, 223
Enclosures, 59, 62
Enlightenment, 32, 53
Equal Employment Opportunities
    Office, 215
Erikson, Eric, 23
Essay on Population, 58
Europe of the Ancien Régime, 1715-1783, 54

Fanshawe, Ann, 45
Farmer's Magazine, 60
Fawcett, Millicent Garrett, 164
Female Eunuch, The, 23
Feminine Mystique, The, 200
Fénelon, F., 50, 61, 108
Fergusson, Muriel, 215
Fichte, J., 112
Fiennes, Celia, 46
Firestone, Shulamith, 206, 235
First Blast of the Trumpet Against the
    Monstrous Regiment of Women, The, 50
First World War, 32, 174, 180
Firth, Edith, 142
Flaubert, G., 151
Flying Years, The, 183
Franchise, 144
Francis, Anne, 209; see also Bird,
    Florence.
French Revolution, 32, 75, 76, 102, 121
Freud, S., 19, 20, 21, 88, 95, 111, 195
Friedan, Betty, 200, 201, 235
From the World's Olio, 92
Fry, Elizabeth, 161

Galloway, Countess of, 165
Gelber, Sylvia, 219
George IV, 106
Germinal, 151ff.
Gin Acts, 58
Globe and Mail, 16, 17
Gordon, Donald, 209
Goubert, P., 33, 102
Graham, Gwethalyn, 231
Granby, Lady, 85
Greenglass, Esther, 17, 18, 225
Greer, Germaine, 23
Grunberger, Richard, 196, 197

Gueguen, Joseph, 125
Gulag Archipelago, The, 232
Gypsies, 140

Hammond, Barbara, 62
Hammond, John, 62
Hawes, Ruth, 173
Hayes, H. R., 86, 89, 202
Hébert, Anne, 25
Hegel, G., 112, 119
Henri IV, 32, 33
Henripin, Jacques, 209
History of England, 149
Hitler, Adolf, 196, 198
Hogg, Edith, 154
Homemaker's Digest, 17
Hoodless, Mrs Adelaide, 173, 174
Hufton, Olwen, 56, 60
Hughe, Dr, 174
Huizinga, J., 36, 37
Humphrey, John, 209, 211, 215
Hutchinson, Anne, 46

Ibsen, Henrik, 110
Industrial Revolution, 62, 63, 77, 114
Innis, Harold, 41, 42, 77
International Women's Year, 13, 232
Inuit, 36

Jacklin, Carol, 229, 230, 231
Janeway, Elizabeth, 23, 229
Janey Canuck in the West, 175
Johnson, Leo, 139, 141
Johnson, Samuel, 57

Kant, Immanuel, 111
Karpovich, M., 57
Kimball, Meredith, 231
King, P., 36
Kipling, Rudyard, 181
Knox, John, 50
Kostash, Myrna, 15

Labarge, M. W., 45
Lace Ghetto, The, 26
Ladies Home Journal, 200
Lange, Lola Mary, 209
Langton, Anne, 132, 133, 134

Lapointe, Jeanne, 210
La Sagouine, 24, 25
Laslett, Peter, 39, 40, 41, 43
Laurence, Margaret, 24
Lavelle Case, 16
Leathes, Sonia, 172
Leblanc, Sylvain, 71
Lenin, 150
LePrince, Anne, 69ff., 76, 77, 124
Lequeux, Barbe, 45
Letters to a Young Man About Town, 107
Lewis, John Wren, 234
Lewis, W. H., 40
Life of Jesus, 148
Lives of Girls and Women, 24
Lloyd, Trevor, 174
Locke, John, 10, 53
Look, 201
Louis XIII, 37, 41
Louis XIV, 32ff., 37, 40ff., 47, 48, 54, 68, 76, 105, 108, 127
Louis XV, 54
Louis XVI, 69, 76
Lower, A. R. M., 11, 133, 141

Macauley, T. B., 149
McCall's Magazine, 200
McClung, Nellie, 175, 180
Maccoby, Eleanor, 229, 230, 231
McGibbon, Pauline, 215
MacGill, Elizabeth Muriel Gregory, 210
McLuhan, Marshall, 41
McNeill, W. H., 102, 148
Macphail, Agnes, 181, 186
Madame Bovary, 151
Maillet, Antonine, 24
Maisonnat, Marie Magdalen, 71
Malthus, R. T., 58
Manipulated Man, The, 205, 206
Man's World, Woman's Place, 23
Manticore, The, 23
Mantoux, P., 114
Marie-Thérèse of Austria, 54
Marmor, J., 223
Martineau, Harriet, 120
Mascarene, Governor, 72
Mead, Margaret, 203
Melbourne, Lady, 68

Melfi, Mary, 195
Menninger, Karl, 19
Meredith, G., 21
Mill, John Stuart, 120, 232
Millet, Kate, 235
Milton, John, 44, 86, 88, 90, 112
Mitchell, Juliet, 13, 14, 26
Montague, Lady Mary Wortley, 91, 92
Moodie, Susanna, 132, 135, 139ff.
More, Hannah, 61
Morgan, Edmund S., 44
Mother Was Not a Person, 28
Mr. Sammler's Planet, 228
Munro, Alice, 24
Murdoch, Irene, 16, 17
Murphy, Emily, 175
Myrdal, Gunnar, 231

Namier, Sir Lewis, 10
National Council of Women of Canada, 172, 173
National Home Reading Union, 172
Nazis, 196ff., 218
Neatby, Blair, 169
Need, Thomas, 140
New France, 50, 72
Nicolson, Harold, 53
Nightingale, Florence, 161, 162
Nineteenth Century, 164, 165
Niven, Frederick, 183
Not In God's Image, 111
Nunes, Maxine, 26
Nymph and the Lamp, The, 183

O'Brien, Mary, 132, 133
Ogg, David, 54
Ogilvie, Mrs Robert, 210
Ontario Department of Education, 14
Origin of the Species, The, 148
Orwell, George, 205
Ostenso, Martha, 182
Ostry, Sylvia, 215
Overstreet, E. W., 195

Paradise Lost, 44, 87
Pearsall, Ronald, 103, 120, 158
Penelope, 8
Petrie, Glen, 161

Phelps, Minnie, 179
Pilgrimage, 194
Pinchbeck, Ivy, 60, 61, 63, 115, 117, 118
Poor in Eighteenth Century France, The, 56
Pope Leo XIII, 150
Population, 58, 118, 128, 170
Porter, John, 216
Portrait of an Age, 163
Postscript to Adventure, 171
Powell, Mrs W. D., 143
Prejudice against women, 28, 29, 49, 50, 80, 81, 85, 87, 92, 95, 96, 99, 111, 145, 174, 183, 184, 232, 233, 237; see also Discrimination against women.
Pride and Prejudice, 120
Prostitutes, 91, 156, 159, 160, 161
Prostitution, 159, 162, 164, 181, 186
Proust, M., 151
Public Service Commission of Canada, 213

Quebec Federation of Labour, 219.

Raddall, Thomas, 183
Rainborowe, Thomas, 43
Redbook, 200
Renaissance, 44, 48, 104
Renan, E., 148
Rerum Novarum, 150
Richardson, Dorothy, 194, 195
Richelieu, Cardinal, 41, 75
Rise of the West, The, 102
Robertson, Rev. F. W., 107
Rouge et Le Noir, Le, 151
Roughing it in the Bush, 132, 139
Rousseau, J.-J., 53, 93, 94, 111
Rowbotham, Sheila, 49, 121
Roy, Gabrielle, 25
Royal Commission on the Status of Women in Canada, 26, 45, 207, 209ff.
Russell, G. E., 61, 62
Russell, K. R., 61, 62
Ruskin, J., 103, 157

St Augustine, 80
Saint-Simon, 40, 90
Salisbury, Marchioness of, 68
Saturday Review, 107

Second Sex, The, 204
Second World War, 24, 35, 192, 198, 199, 204
Senate, 177, 192
Sesame and Lilies, 103
Sex and Society, 22
Sexism, 186, 206
Sexist, 14, 28, 50, 162
Shaftesbury, Anthony, 161
Sigogne, Abbé, 126
Society, 106, 107, 110, 120, 127, 133, 134, 135, 139, 143, 145, 151ff., 162, 181, 182, 184, 202, 203, 205, 218, 228, 229, 234ff.
Solzhenitsyn, A. I., 218, 232
Splendid Century, The, 40
Stacey, C. P., 200
Statistics Canada, 18, 214, 215
Status of Women, 16, 23, 31, 37, 38, 40, 43, 44, 46, 47, 52, 54, 55, 63, 105, 107, 109, 118, 124, 126, 141, 144, 148, 166, 181, 184, 186, 193, 199, 210, 211, 222ff., 227, 231, 237
Stendhal, 107, 151
Stowe, Emily Howard, 175
Suffrage, 166, 172, 174ff., 180, 184, 185, 192, 233
Suffragette, 122, 164, 165
Suffragettes International, 174
Survival, 24
Sutherland-Orr, Mrs, 166
Swedish *Report to the United Nations on the Status of Women*, 220

Talbot, Colonel, 141
Ten Lost Years, 193
Tennyson, Lord, 103
Thackeray, W., 106, 107, 151
Thirty Years War, 35, 58
Thirty Year's War, The, 35
Thomas, Clara, 138
Thornton, Alice, 84
Three Essays on Sexuality, 21
Tinbergen, N., 225
Tolpuddle martyrs, 140
Toronto Women's Literary Club, 175
Traill, Catherine Parr, 132, 135, 138
Trollope, A., 151

12-year Reich: A Social History of Nazi Germany, 1933-1945, The, 195
Tyndal, Margaret, 44

United Nations, 57
United States Department of Health, Education and Welfare, 14
University of London, 120, 149
University of Toronto, 175
Upper Canada, 131, 134, 135, 140, 143
Usher, D., 57

Vanity Fair, 151
Vertical Mosaic, The, 216
Victorian Order of Nurses, 172
Vilar, Esther, 205, 206
Village Labourer, The, 62
Vindication of the Rights of Women, A, 109, 110, 124
Vital Balance, The, 19
Votes for women, 162, 164, 171, 176, 179, 181, 192

Wallace, C. N., 142
Webb, Beatrice and Sydney, 150, 162
Wedgewood, C. V., 35
West Rebecca, 202
White, Deanna, 26
White Man Listen, 46
Wild Geese, 182, 183
Williams, E. N., 54, 56
Williams, Raymond, 77, 103ff.
Winnipeg Political Equality League, 176
Winthrop, John, 37, 44ff.
Wise, S. F., 35, 124, 127, 133
Wollstonecraft, Mary, 11, 109, 110, 124
Women as Force in History, 81
Women in Canada, 27, 172
Women in the Labour Force, 25, 214
Women's Bureau of the Canadian Federal Department of Labour, 25, 213
Women's Christian Temperance Movement, 177, 179
Women's Estate, 13
Women's Institutes, 173, 174
Women's Liberation, 13, 15ff., 23, 26, 28, 29, 195, 203, 229, 235

Women's rights, 14, 75, 76, 164, 165,
175, 218, 220, 235
*Women Workers and the Industrial
Revolution, 1750-1850*, 60
Working conditions, 113, 154, 156, 164,
166
World We Have Lost, The, 39

*Worm in the Bud: The World of Victorian
Sexuality, The*, 158
Wright, Richard, 46
Wylie, Philip, 202

Young, G. M., 163

Zola, Émile, 151, 152, 153